Contemporary Issues in Marketing and Consumer Behaviour

Second edition

Elizabeth Parsons, Pauline Maclaran and Andreas Chatzidakis

Routledge
Taylor & Francis Group

LONDON AND NEW YORK

Second edition published 2018
by Routledge
2 Park Square, Milton Park, Abingdon, Oxon OX14 4RN

and by Routledge
711 Third Avenue, New York, NY 10017

Routledge is an imprint of the Taylor & Francis Group, an informa business

First edition published by Elsevier 2009

Visit the companion website: www.routledge.com/cw/parsons

British Library Cataloguing in Publication Data
A catalogue record for this book is available from the British Library

Library of Congress Cataloging in Publication Data
Names: Parsons, Elizabeth, author. | Maclaran, Pauline, author. |
Chatzidakis, Andreas, author.
Title: Contemporary issues in marketing and consumer behaviour /
Elizabeth Parsons, Pauline Maclaran and Andreas Chatzidakis.
Description: Abingdon, Oxon ; New York, NY : Routledge, 2017. | Earlier
edition: 2009. | Includes bibliographical references and index.
Identifiers: LCCN 2017002758 (print) | LCCN 2017020207 (ebook) |
ISBN 9780203526040 (eBook) | ISBN 9780415826907 (hardback : alk.
paper) | ISBN 9780415826914 (pbk. : alk. paper)
Subjects: LCSH: Marketing. | Consumer behavior.
Classification: LCC HF5415 (ebook) | LCC HF5415 .P2493 2017 (print) |
DDC 658.8--dc23
LC record available at https://lccn.loc.gov/2017002758

ISBN: 978-0-415-82690-7 (hbk)
ISBN: 978-0-415-82691-4 (pbk)
ISBN: 978-0-203-52604-0 (ebk)

Typeset in Times New Roman
by Taylor & Francis Books

Printed and bound by CPI Group (UK) Ltd, Croydon, CR0 4YY

Contents

Illustrations

Figures

Tables

1 Introduction

How has marketing changed?

In the introduction of the 2009 edition of this book we argued that marketing was suffering from a perceived lack of relevance both within organisations and also by consumers themselves. We also observed that this was due to an inadequate conception of what marketing actually is. Over the past eight years we have seen somewhat of a revolution in thinking, not only about what marketing is, but also about consumers and their relationships with marketing. We have also made great strides in thinking through the relationship between marketing and wider society. Therefore we ask the following questions in this introduction: how has our view of marketing changed? How have consumers changed? And how should marketing relate to society?

How has our view of marketing changed?

The content and boundaries of marketing are both blurred and frequently the subject for debate. Marketing is deeply embedded within our society and culture and therefore it must change with the times. Because of this the American Marketing Association (AMA) revisit their definition of marketing on a regular basis. Their most recent agreed definition is as follows:

> Marketing is the activity, set of institutions, and processes for creating, communicating, delivering, and exchanging offerings that have value for customers, clients, partners, and society at large.
>
> (American Marketing Association website, 2013)

One might argue that this definition is now so broad that it fails to really say anything at all other than that marketing isn't only an activity but that it also encompasses a set of institutions and processes; and that it is ultimately directed towards the creation of value. It is perhaps not surprising that many recent developments in the way we think about marketing are focused on deepening our understanding of the institutions and (in particular) processes of markets and marketing on one hand, and on the construction of value on the other. Of course these two rather grand features of marketing intertwine and can't easily be separated. As such they inform discussions of both marketing and consumers below.

Markets as practised

One significant development in recent years has been a welcome focus on markets, what they are and how they are constituted or shaped. Up until quite recently the notion of the market was rather absent from marketing thinking, being seen only as an inert backdrop to the business of marketing activity. One of the problems with this is that marketing therefore implicitly accepts a neoclassical view of the market where markets are thought of merely as exchanges between buyers and sellers (Mele et al., 2015). This view has several challenges built into it. The first is that it focuses squarely on a product-centred view of markets (i.e. what is exchanged) taking the focus away from the concept of consumer value (i.e. what consumers make from these exchanges). Second, the focus on exchange value (i.e. value created at the point of purchase) is at the cost of a focus on use value (i.e. value created during use). On an organisational level this focus on exchange has also been criticised as failing to fully embrace the relational engagement of organisations (Sheth and Uslay, 2007); it also misses out on the idea of interaction as opposed to exchange as facilitating value creation (Gummesson and Mele, 2010). Third, the focus on the two parties of seller and buyer is restrictive because it doesn't take into account the fact that value is most often created by a much larger network of actors. This networked view is particularly pertinent given the increased importance of the internet environment in business transactions.

One particularly interesting recent view on markets is that they are performed or practised into being. This practice approach to markets draws on economic sociology and the sociology of science and technology to examine a series of key questions regarding markets:

> (1) How are market agencies (e.g. buyers and sellers) configured? (2) How do some exchanges become 'economic'? (3) How are objects of exchange shaped and qualified? (4) How do ideas and theories about markets contribute to shape the phenomena they seek to describe?
>
> (Araujo and Kjellberg, 2009: 196)

Clearly this view of markets is very different from the traditional neoclassical view of markets as exchange between two parties. This view asks us to take a step back and question how the various elements within markets are constituted and shaped, but also to reflect on the impact that the theories we use to think about markets has on markets themselves (Araujo et al., 2010). Proponents of this approach argue that it also has significant implications for the way we should think about marketing. Rather than viewing marketing as merely a set of techniques that regulate exchanges it should be viewed as 'something that takes place within a market system and is therefore derivative of the main focus' (Venkatesh and Peñaloza, 2006: 136). This placing of marketing within markets represents a move towards 'market-ing' to explore the various 'practices that help perform markets' of which marketing practices are only one subset (Araujo and Kjellberg, 2009: 197). In this spirit of examining market-ing Zwick and Cayla (2011) ask us to look 'Inside Marketing' to explore how it actually works, they view marketing as: 'an amalgamation of institutional, cultural, economic, and technical processes by which goods and markets – and objects and categories – are determined, contested, and provisionally given stable forms' (2011: 9).

Note the difference between this understanding of marketing and the AMA agreed version above. They contain some of the same elements i.e. the recognition that marketing is about a set of processes which involve a series of different actors, but note that the practice view of marketing opens up questions as to how goods and markets themselves are constituted. This is important for a number of reasons, not least of which it allows us to see with much more clarity how marketing impacts on society, by asking what the mechanisms of marketing are and how they operate.

A service dominant logic of marketing

A second relatively recent approach to understanding both markets and marketing's role within them has been titled Service Dominant Logic. Along with the Markets as Practised view explored above, this school is concerned with examining the logic of value creation. Here scholars argue that the traditional dominant logic underlying marketing comes from economic science, which is based on an economic philosophy which developed during the Industrial Revolution. This traditional dominant logic has been called goods-dominant (G-D) logic (Vargo and Lusch, 2004). 'In short, G-D logic says that the purpose of the firm is to *produce and sell valuable units of output* and, as a corollary, the role of the customer is to purchase and *consume* these units and then buy more' (Vargo and Lusch, 2009: 220, emphasis in original). This approach has also been called a neoclassical view of the market (as discussed above). A service dominant view of markets and marketing involves moving from an output- or (goods)-centred focus to a process (service)-centred focus. Here service is conceptualised as 'the process of doing something for and with another party and is thus always dynamic and collaborative' (2009: 221). It is worth quoting Vargo and Lusch's explanation of S-D logic at length:

> According to S-D logic, economic exchange is about providing service in order to receive reciprocal service – that is, *service is exchanged for service.* Whereas goods are sometimes involved in this process, they are *appliances* for service provision; they are *conveyors of competences.* Regardless of whether service is provided directly or indirectly through a good, it is the knowledge and skills (competences – operant resources) of the providers and beneficiaries that represent the essential source of value creation, not goods.
>
> (2009: 221–2, emphasis in original)

Vargo and Lusch (2004) initially identified eight foundational principles of S-D Logic. Discussions with scholars over the years have resulted in modifications and extensions to these principles. In their most recent paper (2016) they have eleven foundational principles which they have organised into five central axioms (see Table 1.1). The first axiom is at the heart of S-D Logic, that service (as opposed to goods) is the fundamental basis of exchange. Service here is viewed as a process which involves knowledge and skill, not an output as in the traditional use of the term 'services'. Importantly the role of goods in this logic are as a 'distribution mechanism for service provision'. This is therefore a radically different view from the traditional Goods Dominant (G-D) view which places goods at the heart of exchange. The second axiom asserts that value is co-created by multiple actors, always including the beneficiary. This axiom reinforces the idea that value is not contained within goods (as in the traditional G-D view), neither is it folded into goods by the organisation, but rather emerges through relations between actors in the marketplace. The idea of value propositions might perhaps most closely be aligned to the idea of goods in the traditional view – value propositions however include both goods and service provision. The third axiom highlights the issue of resource integration asserting that 'all social and economic actors are resource integrators'. The idea here is that value co-creation is networked as actors integrate resources from a range of public and private sources in the creation of value. The fourth axiom that 'value is always uniquely and phenomenologically determined by the beneficiary' asserts the idea that value is experiential by nature, that value propositions are interpreted,

Table 1.1 The five axioms and eleven associated foundational principles of service-dominant logic

Axiom/FP	Description
Axiom 1/FP1	Service is the fundamental basis of exchange.
FP2	Indirect exchange masks the fundamental basis of exchange.
FP3	Goods are a distribution mechanism for service provision.
FP4	Operant resources are the fundamental source of strategic benefit.
FP5	All economies are service economies.
Axiom 2/FP6	Value is co-created by multiple actors, always including the beneficiary.
FP7	Actors cannot deliver value but can participate in the creation and offering of value propositions.
FP8	A service-centred view is inherently customer oriented and relational.
Axiom 3/FP9	All social and economic actors are resource integrators.
Axiom 4/FP10	Value is always uniquely and phenomenologically determined by the beneficiary.
Axiom 5/FP11	Value co-creation is coordinated through actor-generated institutions and institutional arrangements.

Source: adapted from Vargo and Lusch 2016

perceived and integrated differently by different actors. The fifth axiom that 'value cocreation is coordinated through actor-generated institutions and institutional arrangements' reflects the role of institutions in value co-creation. Institutions here are not seen as organisations but rather 'humanly devised rules, norms, and beliefs that enable and constrain action and make social life predictable and meaningful' (Scott, 2001; see also North, 1990, cited in Vargo and Lusch, 2016: 11).

We have discussed S-D Logic in some depth here because it is one of the key developments in marketing thought in recent years, one which has also had a significant impact on how we think about consumers and consumption. In S-D Logic the role of the organisation shifts from a producer of value to a provider of resources to the consumer in order for them to use the resources in a process of value production. This then begs the question as to how consumers' roles have changed both in relation to the organisation but also in relation to these resources.

How have consumers changed?

Undoubtedly consumers in the developed world have experienced an intensification of marketing activities in their everyday lives from branding and promotional activities to loyalty programmes and increasingly personalised products. At the same time huge strides in computing technology mean that consumers are increasingly informed because they are networked globally. Of course this may well be seen as empowering for consumers, but it also means that their skills and attributes, hearts and minds can be harnessed by and through the marketplace as a form of free labour for the organisation. We explore these twin trends below examining narratives of empowerment and exploitation in the guise of consumer co-creation and consumer work.

Consumer co-creation or consumer work?

Consumer co-creation now seems to be a buzz word in both academic (Neghina et al., 2015; Skålén et al., 2015) and practitioner (Bertini, 2015; Chahal, 2015) circles. Broadly speaking this movement identifies the co-creation of value in markets and places the consumer in a reciprocal relationship with the organisation. As such value is not merely produced by the organisation for consumption by the consumer, but instead value is co-created by the consumer and organisation. This increased involvement of the consumer in the process of value creation results in a blurring of lines traditionally drawn between consumption and production, and between author and audience.

In a seminal paper on co-creation Prahalad and Ramaswamy (2004) observe that it is typically seen as connecting, informing and involving consumers more fully in the marketplace. They argue that these processes empower consumers, not only through the operation of extra knowledge regarding products and services, but also through the ability to connect with like-minded others and share experiences in online brand and consumer communities. New media (such as online communities and mobile technologies) are central to the burgeoning array of interactions and interfaces between consumers and organisations. These online communities are often used by organisations to build their brands and increase customer loyalty. They are also a central facet of moves to create new consumer experiences such as 'experience networks' and 'experience environments' (Prahalad and Ramaswamy, 2004). These experiences are intended to encourage consumers to interact with the brand and thus build brand loyalty.

Practical applications of consumer co-creation cut across all areas of marketing activity to embrace brand management, product design, marketing research, marketing communications and retail environments. Co-creation activities rely heavily on social media networking sites to facilitate ongoing conversations with consumers, increasingly involving them in consumer research and brand building. These sites are then often vital in disseminating and promoting the results of earlier phases of co-creation as co-created products or advertisements are then shared virally. One good example would be Doritos' Crash the Superbowl campaign where consumers were asked to design an advert for the brand. The winning advert was awarded 1 million dollars in prize money and was shown on the big screens at the US Superbowl. The campaign ran annually for ten years from 2006 to 2016; it created a significant amount of online media buzz as the winning and runner-up adverts were shared virally across a range of media platforms. The campaign also received traditional news media coverage.

Consumers are also routinely involved in the process of product design in design workshops or through design competitions. Examples include the online clothing retailer Threadless who invite consumers to design and vote on t-shirt designs, the most popular of which go into production. Made.com encourage consumers to post pictures of their home interiors showing how they have made creative use of Made furniture. Other examples of companies who have used online platforms to encourage consumers to share product use experiences and design ideas include: Burberry's 'Art of the Trench'; Starbucks' 'White Cup Contest' and Coca-Cola's 'Share a Coke'. In an innovative use of co-creation, IKEA sent five employees on a year-long road trip across the US to visit families in need and give their homes a makeover using IKEA products. The makeovers were filmed to make a documentary, 'IKEA Home Tour'.

In general, discussion of the above sorts of initiatives presents the marketplace as a democratic forum which facilitates consumer learning and the exchange of ideas. In these discussions consumers are typically seen as empowered, consulted, knowledgeable and liberated. However, running alongside this positive and celebratory narrative is a recognition that consumers are increasingly engaging in the *work* of the corporation, consumers who: 'today serve as retailers on eBay, media producer-directors on YouTube, authors on Wikipedia, and critical reviewers on Amazon and TripAdvisor; they do all of this and more on Facebook and Myspace' (Hennig-Thurau et al., 2010: 311). In acknowledging networked activity as a form of labour, commentators also observe that this new medium is perhaps not as benign as it first appears (Ritzer and Jurgenson, 2010). Critiques of co-creation see it as a central strand of 'ethical economy' (Arvidsson, 2008) or 'co-creative capitalism' which are 'characterized by a rise of unpaid labor, new forms of control and exploitation, and a shift in the economics of scarcity' (Cova et al., 2011: 235). In this new economy consumers become 'workers' and organisations harness their labour in pursuit of profit. However, whether this work represents exploitation in the traditional sense of the term is open to question. Indeed, consumers don't receive any payment for the knowledge, creative skill and effort they put into co-designing products and services. In addition, they may be paying more for these products produced by the fruits of their labour as co-created and customised products often command higher prices. The key question centres on the genuine freedom of the consumer in the co-creative relationship. From the company point of view their framing and provision of resources for consumer co-creation will always be designed to meet company needs. This then may be seen as a new mode of governing the consumer, as Cova et al. (2011: 232) observe:

> Marketing govern-mentality, then, aims at constructing consumers as partners in mutually beneficial innovation and production processes. Yet, by doing so, companies are not only exploiting consumer labor but are also reducing the risk of consumer behavior evolving in ways other than those desired by the company.

How should marketing relate to society?

The above discussions of new views on marketing and consumers all point towards a deeper understanding of the relations between marketing and society. The move to look inside marketing as a practice in particular has nuanced this understanding. After all marketing is 'a way of knowing and arranging the world that reinforces and alters social structure (class, ethnicity, gender, life course, core/periphery relations) over time' (Sherry, 2011: 343). Given this it may well be time to think much more reflectively about marketing 'as a means of apprehending and recreating the world' (Sherry, 2011: 344). There has recently been a reinvigoration of work in *Macromarketing* and in *Transformative Consumer Research* along these lines.

Much recent work has focused on the issue of sustainability. A double special issue of the journal *Macromarketing* has been devoted to exploring the idea of 'sustainability as megatrend' (McDonagh and Prothero, 2014; Prothero and McDonagh, 2015). This idea suggests that sustainability is 'a trend that is simultaneously economic, political, cultural, philosophic and technological in nature; that is vast in scope; and which reflects the economic, political, cultural, philosophic and technological milieu of its day' (Mittelstaedt et al., 2014: 254). Marketers have worked hard to explore exactly how marketing intersects with this mega-trend. It seems that there are thinkers on two opposing sides of debate. The Developmental School of Macromarketing argues that marketing offers an important set of tools to promote the development and welfare of wider society, whereas the Critical School of Macromarketing sees the structures of markets and marketing as central to the problem of human welfare (Mittelstaedt et al., 2014: 254).

Consumption habits in developed countries and their associated ideologies undoubtedly underpin the sustainable challenges of today. The school of *Transformative Consumer Research* are concerned with addressing this central role of the consumer in order to transform both individual quality of life and that of wider society (see Mick et al., 2012). The current orientation in consumer societies towards consumption as a right and as a means of experiencing the 'good life' means that we are consuming at an increasingly fast pace. The problem is that there is only a limited supply of resource to fuel our consumption appetites. At some point our demands will outstrip supply. While acknowledging that our consumption behaviours do reflect our individual needs, values and beliefs the Critical School argues that on a deeper level these needs are located within a wider consumption ideology. It is almost impossible to escape from this ideology because it contains a set of *collective understandings* and convictions about the role and nature of consumption in which we are profoundly implicated. We are only vaguely aware of these collective understandings and even less aware of the impact they have on our behaviour. Scholars have argued that some elements of a consumption ideology are thoroughly supported by a dominant social paradigm (DSP, Kilbourne et al., 1997). They observe that the DSP has economic, technological and political dimensions and that each dimension has an associated set of beliefs and mechanisms (Kilbourne et al., 1997: 8–16). In the economic dimension these include: individual self-interest, the existence of free markets, the continuous exponential growth of markets and unequal calculations of wealth distribution. The technological dimension includes: science and technology as servants of industry and of perpetual growth and increasing efficiency. The political dimension includes: hierarchical social organisation which is highly centralised and which therefore ultimately undermines participatory democracy. This list of beliefs and mechanisms underscores just how deeply implicated Western and American societies are within a consumption ideology.

Undoubtedly, then, we need to reimagine our relations with consumption. In doing so we need to address the root assumptions of the current consumption ideology and attempt to create a new one. Scholars have made a series of suggestions as to how we should go about doing this: bearing responsibility for the environmental impact of the choices we make; thinking about consumption not as a political right but rather as a responsibility; breaking the link between consumption and carbon emissions; and putting an end to seeing the propensity to consume as the *natural* state of humans (Kilbourne and Mittelstaedt, 2012: 297–8).

Outline of the book

Having broadly considered recent developments in how we think about marketing and consumption the task in this book is to choose some of the key issues to explore in more depth. This is of course a difficult task. This book doesn't attempt to cover every aspect of contemporary marketing but instead focuses on a set of three important and interrelated issues. In the first four chapters we explore the intersections between marketing, consumption and culture more widely. Looking at the big ideas of postmodernism, brand cultures, feminism and psychoanalysis we explore how markets and consumption structure our everyday lives in ways many of us don't even recognise. The next three chapters foreground the ethical and political dimensions of consumption and marketing. We have devoted significant attention to these because (as we discuss above) the structures of markets and marketing are now more than ever before central to the problems of planetary and human welfare. In the closing two chapters we bring together insights from previous chapters on the culture, ethics and politics of marketing to explore how they play out both in the localities of space and place but also on the wider global stage.

Postmodern marketing and beyond (Chapter 2) provides a base from which to appreciate other topics. In this chapter we explore the defining characteristics of the postmodern turn, and the many ways postmodernism has represented a critique of, and challenge to, the underpinnings of conventional marketing wisdom. We also chart developments of the postmodern concept within marketing and explore its links with cultural branding and interpretive consumer research. Despite its own critique of traditional assumptions, postmodernism is itself open to critique, and we consider the various limitations of using a postmodern lens. Significantly, certain current trends indicate that we are now moving beyond postmodernism and we consider the potential impact of this for marketers.

Brands are everywhere in contemporary society. In Chapter 3, *Building brand cultures*, we look at how meaning systems are established around brands, and how these can take on a life of their own as the brand intersects with other cultural phenomena such as, for example, the art world. We explore important synergies between organisational and brand cultures, illustrating the important role of employees in building brand culture and then consider how brand cultures are also co-created with consumers and other external stakeholders. Often communities flourish around consumption of the brand. Thus, the evolution of brand culture is concerned with storytelling, but not, as we might expect, just on the part of marketers. Highly successful brands achieve iconic status through responding insightfully to the wider cultural environment and being aware of the stories circulating about them. Other brands are less watchful, however, and become tainted through negative perceptions that arise and over which marketers sometimes have little control. Whether we like them or not, brands play an increasingly significant role in contemporary lifestyles. They are also increasingly coming under attack from the anti-branding movement, which heavily critiques the role of brands and the impact of brand culture on our lives.

In Chapter 4, *Gender, feminism and consumer behaviour*, we argue that gender inequalities and indeed gendered experiences are inextricably linked with marketplace dynamics. We use a feminist lens to explore some of the ways in which this has come about. The chapter opens by giving a historical overview of the close links between the emergence and development of the feminist movement and the development of marketing and consumer cultures more generally. This history helps us to understand where the received wisdom about gender and feminism has come from. The chapter goes on to explore how gender has been understood and researched in marketing. Discussion then moves on to explore how the key marketing tool of advertising serves to significantly shape both received norms of femininity and masculinity but also the associated roles of men and women in society. Taking this discussion of roles further we explore how the marketplace provides resources (representations through advertising, but also products and services) that shape experiences of motherhood and fatherhood.

Chapter 5, *Psychoanalysis in marketing theory and practice*, introduces psychoanalysis, a discipline that has a long and rather controversial relationship with marketing. More recently, as we explain, psychoanalysis has resurfaced as a gateway to understanding various contemporary marketing and consumption-related phenomena. Accordingly we begin with a brief discussion of the history of psychoanalytic applications in marketing, before introducing three key thinkers: Sigmund Freud, Melanie Klein and Jacques Lacan. We explain how some of their psychoanalytic ideas continue to be applied in three broader domains, namely, marketing research, advertising and consumer culture. The benefits and the potential pitfalls of psychoanalytically inspired approaches to marketing theory and practice are important for marketers to acknowledge in an increasingly complex consumer-driven marketplace.

Chapter 6, *Ethical debates in marketing management*, reviews the debates on marketing ethics, the study of moral principles that guide the conduct of marketers. Here we include discussion of marketing as a profession and also as a wider societal force. The growing diversity of the sociocultural environment in which marketers operate means that they will need to be capable of assessing the ethical implications of their actions across an increasingly broad range of contexts and research questions. Marketers have to take into account three key viewpoints – the company, the industry and society – and it's when these groups have conflicting needs and wants that ethical problems arise (e.g. the tobacco industry).

Ethical consumerism continues to be a growth area. In Chapter 7, *Ethical consumers and the moralised brandscape*, we explore ethical consumption and the increasing tendency of brands more generally – not just those regarded as 'ethical brands' – to associate themselves with moral values. The chapter discusses the growth in ethical consumer behaviours and looks at how marketing thinking must change to bring about a more sustainable future. After profiling the ethical consumer in more detail, we take a closer look at some well-known ethical brands and how they have built their reputations before considering the moralised brandscape more broadly. Certain critical perspectives are useful to help analyse what is happening, in particular ecofeminism, a perspective that examines the relationship between humankind and the natural environment. There are also many trade-offs required by ethical and green consumption whereby being ethically minded over one aspect of a product or service (its fair-trade origins, for example) may mean being less ethically aware over another aspect (the environment damage of long-haul transport).

Chapter 8, *Politicising consumption: Consumerising politics*, moves beyond the ethical dimensions of marketing and consumption to develop a more explicitly political understanding. Acknowledging that the intersection of politics with consumption is inherently contentious and multidimensional, the chapter identifies three key perspectives. Firstly, it looks at the consequences of everyday consumption and how these are addressed politically, through 'individualised collective' choices and actions and through deciding to reduce one's consumption levels altogether. Subsequently, the chapter returns to Marx's notion of 'commodity fetishism', a perspective that has led to distinct politics of consumption centred on ideas of decommodification, including educating consumers and initiating alternative economies that bring consumers and producers together. Finally, we consider the political role of consumption in a broader sense, as a discourse and a set of logics and practices that are favoured under neoliberal regimes. Implications and avenues for more politically progressive consumer-citizen movements are discussed.

Chapter 9, *Marketing spaces and places*, focuses on place as a key marketing concept that stretches way beyond simplistic understandings of it as 'background canvas' to all social activity or as one of marketing's 4 Ps. Place attachments and place-related identities have a powerful effect on consumers and marketers often attempt to influence these. The spectacular nature of many consumption venues has evolved hugely over the last 150 years, transitioning from shopping arcades and department stores to shopping malls and themed shopping environments. Although the social role of third places may be less spectacular in nature, they may be equally implicated in the reproduction of particular consumption logics and practices. We introduce a typology of different (consumption) spaces and a multilevel perspective to analysing the different dimensions of consumption spaces, that is absolute, material and symbolic ones. Altogether, this implies a shift from understanding the consumption *of* place to consumption *in* place.

Chapter 10, *The globalised marketplace*, draws on Ritzer's contrasting narratives of grobalisation and glocalisation to explore the impacts that globalisation is having on consumer culture. The narrative of grobalisation argues that in a drive for growth multinational corporations are extending their power and influence across the globe and stifling local cultures and economies. One of the key vehicles facilitating this process is the rise of the global brand. Narratives of glocalisation on the other hand suggest that rather than being overwhelmed or stifled the interaction of the global and the local produces something creative and new – the glocal. In closing the chapter explores alternatives to these narratives exploring how individuals and communities are organising themselves in the face of globalisation in ways that mean they can stand outside of its effects.

Internet resources

American Marketing Association: www.ama.org/AboutAMA/Pages/Definition-of-Marketing.aspx

References

Araujo, L. and Kjellberg, H. (2009). Shaping exchanges, performing markets: The study of marketing practices. In P. Maclaran, M. Saren, B. Stern and M. Tadajewski (eds), *The SAGE handbook of marketing theory*. London: SAGE, pp. 195–218.

Araujo, L., Finch, J. and Kjellberg, H. (2010). *Reconnecting marketing to markets*. Oxford: Oxford University Press.

Arvidsson, A. (2008). The ethical economy of customer coproduction. *Journal of Macromarketing*, 28(4): 326–338.

Bertini, P. (2015). Co-creation: The missing link between brands and consumers. *Digital Marketing Magazine*, 7 July, http://digitalmarketingmagazine.co.uk/customer-experience/co-creation-the-missing-link-between-brands-and-customers/2202

Chahal, M. (2015). Samsung's Insight Director explains why everyone at the brand wants to use co-creation. *Marketing Week*, 15 June, www.marketingweek.com/2015/06/15/samsungs-insight-director-explains-why-everyone-at-the-brand-wants-to-use-co-creation/

Cova, B., Dalli, D. and Zwick, D. (2011). Critical perspectives on consumers' role as 'producers': Broadening the debate on value co-creation in marketing processes. *Marketing Theory*, 11: 231–241.

Gummesson, E. and Mele, C. (2010). Marketing as value co-creation through network interaction and resource integration. *Journal of Business Market Management*, 4(4): 181–198.

Hennig-Thurau, T., Malthouse, E.C., Friege, C., Gensler, S., Lobschat, L., Rangaswamy, A. and Skiera, B. (2010). The impact of new media on customer relationships. *Journal of Service Research*, 13(3): 311–330.

Kilbourne, W. and Mittelstaedt, J. (2012). From profligacy to sustainability: Can we get there from here? In D.G. Mick, S. Pettigrew, C. Pechmann and J.L. Ozanne (eds), *Transformative consumer research for personal and collective well-being*. New York: Routledge, pp. 283–300.

Kilbourne, W., McDonagh, P. and Prothero, A. (1997). Sustainable consumption and the quality of life: A macromarketing challenge to the dominant social paradigm. *Journal of Macromarketing*, 17(1): 4–24.

McDonagh, P. and Prothero, A. (2014). Special issue on sustainability as megatrend. *Journal of Macromarketing*, 32(4).

Mele, C., Pels, J. and Storbacka, K. (2015). A holistic market conceptualization. *Journal of the Academy of Marketing Science*, 43(1): 100–114.

Mick, D.G., Pettigrew, S., Pechmann, C.C. and Ozanne, J.L. (eds) (2012). *Transformative consumer research for personal and collective well-being*. London: Routledge.

Mittelstaedt, J.D., Shultz, C.J., Kilbourne, W.E. and Peterson, M. (2014). Sustainability as megatrend: Two schools of macromarketing thought. *Journal of Macromarketing*, 34(3): 253–264.

Neghina, C., Caniëls, M.C.J., Bloemer, J.M.M. and van Birgelen, M.J.H. (2015). Value cocreation in service interactions: Dimensions and antecedents. *Marketing Theory*, 15(2): 221–242.

North, D.C. (1990). *Institutions, institutional change, and economic performance*. Cambridge: Cambridge University Press.

Prahalad, C.K. and Ramaswamy, V. (2004). Co-creating unique value with customers. *Strategy and Leadership*, 32(3): 4–9.

Prothero, A. and McDonagh, P. (2015). Special issue on sustainability as megatrend II. *Journal of Macromarketing*, 35(1).

Ritzer, G. and Jurgenson, N. (2010). Production, consumption, prosumption: The nature of capitalism in the age of the digital 'prosumer'. *Journal of Consumer Culture*, 10(1): 13–36.

Scott, W.R. (2001). *Institutions and organizations*. Thousand Oaks, CA: SAGE.

Sherry, J.F., Jr. (2011). The marketing reformation redux. In D. Zwick and J. Cayla (eds), *Inside marketing: Practices, ideologies, devices*. Oxford: Oxford University Press, pp. 343–350.

Sheth, J.N. and Uslay, C. (2007). Implications of the revised definition of marketing: From exchange to value creation. *Journal of Public Policy and Marketing*, 26(2): 302–307.

Skålén, P., Pace, S. and Cova, B. (2015). Firm-brand community value co-creation as alignment of practices. *European Journal of Marketing*, 49(3/4): 596–620.

Vargo, S.L. and Lusch, R.F. (2004). Evolving to a new dominant logic for marketing. *Journal of Marketing*, 68(1): 1–17.

Vargo, S.L. and Lusch, R.F. (2009). A service dominant logic for marketing. In P. Maclaran, M. Saren, B. Stern and M. Tadajewski (eds), *The SAGE handbook of marketing theory*. London: SAGE, pp. 219–234.

Vargo, S.L. and Lusch, R.F. (2016). Institutions and axioms: An extension and update of service-dominant logic. *Journal of the Academy of Marketing Science*, 44(1): 5–23.

Venkatesh, A. and Peñaloza, L. (2006). From marketing to the market. In J.N. Sheth and R.S. Sisodia (eds), *Does marketing need reform? Fresh perspectives on the future*. New York: M.E. Sharpe, pp. 134–150.

Zwick, D. and Cayla, J. (2011). *Inside marketing: Practices, ideologies, devices*. Oxford: Oxford University Press.

2   Postmodern marketing and beyond

Introduction

Postmodernism can be a difficult concept to comprehend because of its richness and complexity. An elaborate lexicon surrounds it, full of 'ologies', 'ities' and 'isms', that often obscures and confuses its would-be audiences. Our ambition in this chapter is to take away some of the term's mystique, by clarifying and, we hope, simplifying some of its key principles.

The postmodern era signalled a major change in Western thinking and philosophising. Leading commentators consider that it commenced around the end of the 1950s when the term 'postmodern' was first applied to describe changing characteristics in art and culture (Lyotard, 1984; Jameson, 1991). For example, it was used in architecture to describe the distinct break that occurred during the 1960s with the type of rational thinking that had given rise to modern functionalism (a perspective dictating that the design of an object or building should be determined by its function). In contrast to functionalism, postmodernism focused more on style and, indeed, a mixture of styles that also often playfully harked back to the past. As a cultural movement, postmodernism is characteristically sceptical about many of the key assumptions that have underpinned Western thinking for several centuries. Accordingly, the postmodern critique questions authority, sources of knowledge and many other cultural, social, economic and political taken-for-granted assumptions in society.

Over its fifty-year history, postmodernism spread to affect all disciplines and branches of knowledge, including marketing, where it has made its biggest impact in relation to the understanding of consumers. This has given rise to many new theories around the hedonic and experiential nature of consumption.

In this chapter we consider the implications of postmodernism for marketing and consumer behaviour. First, in order to set it in its historical context, we give a brief overview of postmodernism in relation to modernity. Next we discuss how the characteristics of what Lyotard (1984) termed 'the postmodern condition' are manifested in marketing phenomena. We then explore the influence of postmodern critique in overturning some of marketing's basic assumptions. Finally, we consider some of the criticisms that have been levelled at postmodernism and discuss how we may be moving beyond postmodernism.

Modernity versus postmodernity

As the name suggests, postmodernity marks the end of modernity – variously referred to as the *Age of Reason* or the *Enlightenment* – a period in Western history running from the mid-18th to the mid-20th century. Widespread industrialisation marked the first phase of modernity, together with the rise of capitalism and the increasing role of science and technology. Its second phase, in the 20th century, was marked by the huge proliferation of mass media. In general terms, modernity was characterised by a belief in the intrinsic power of humankind to be master of its own destiny, principally through the control of nature.

Postmodernism recognises that the modernist notion of improving human existence by controlling nature through scientific technologies is an illusion (Firat, 1991). This has been forcefully spelt out in recent decades by major scares such as Mad Cow Disease, AIDS, the thinning of the ozone layer and the many other implications of humankind's environmental pollutants. In addition, rationalist thinking has witnessed the many extremes of ethnic cleansing during the 20th century. In the face of these many disasters and tragedies there has been a loss of faith in the notion of 'progress', together with an accompanying scepticism concerning the many hopes for science and technology.

This sceptical questioning is characteristic of the postmodern era, an era that marks the disintegration of what Lyotard (1984) refers to as grand 'meta-narratives'. These are systems or ideologies, for example Christianity and the rationalist thinking of the Enlightenment (see Adorno and Horkheimer, 1973) that set standards to measure dualistic/binary values such as good and bad, high and low, true and false. Hence, a postmodernist perspective challenges traditional value systems with such dichotomous modes of thinking and merges categories in a relativistic way, thereby producing complex mixtures of those binaries. Categories of true and false, genuine and fake, high and low are blurred and mutually dependent. For example, clear demarcations between high and low art no longer exist. An advertisement is just as likely to be labelled an artwork as a Van Gogh painting. In the multicultural world of the 21st century, there is no one perspective that is privileged, or one source that provides any absolute 'truth'.

We now go on to consider all these issues in greater depth. In order to do so we have found it useful to distinguish between the *characteristics* of postmodernism and the postmodern *critique*. This follows on from Zymunt Bauman's (1988) distinction between 'a sociology of postmodernism' and 'a postmodern sociology'. Whereas the former looks at postmodernism through a lens that uses traditional sociological tools, the latter introduces new tools to analyse social phenomena. Accordingly, first we look at the characteristics of postmodernism as they are manifested by changing trends in marketing and, second, we look at how the tools of postmodern critique have influenced our understanding of marketing phenomena.

Marketing and the characteristics of postmodernism

Marketing and consumption have been pinpointed as key phenomena of the postmodern era (Baudrillard, 1988; Brown, 1995, 1998; Firat et al., 1995), to the extent that marketing, as the main purveyor of signs, symbols and images, has been identified as more or less synonymous with postmodernism (Firat and Venkatesh, 1993). Increasingly, the emphasis is on product intangibles such as brand name and overall image, the fantasy aspects that surround a product as opposed to any intrinsic, tangible value in the product itself. Thus the image becomes the marketable entity and the product strives to represent its image rather than vice versa. Firat et al. (1995) describe this as the quintessential postmodern approach. Of the various authors who have identified and discussed postmodernism's key features in relation to marketing (Firat, 1991, 1992; Firat and Venkatesh, 1993, 1995; Firat et al., 1995), Brown's (1995: 106) list of seven characteristics is the most comprehensive for our present analysis, as follows.

Fragmentation

A sense that all things are disconnected pervades our everyday experiences, particularly through the disjointed images of mass advertising and the media. This is heightened by other factors such as the demise of political stability, social organisation and mass market economy, the nature and grounds of knowledge. With the collapse of mass marketing approaches, we are witnessing the fragmentation of markets into smaller and smaller market segments. This is encouraged by the huge growth in database marketing, the increasing prevalence of one-to-one marketing and the concept of mass customisation.

De-differentiation

This involves the blurring of established hierarchies such as high/low culture, local/global marketplaces, education/training, politics/show business and so forth. Formerly clear-cut boundaries have become opaque, with one category merging into the other. On the pages of *Hello* magazine we are likely to see footballers and their wives (e.g. David and Victoria Beckham), alongside royalty (e.g. Prince William and his wife, Kate Middleton, now Duchess of Cambridge). Here we are witnessing the collapse of traditional social class distinctions into an overriding category of celebrity culture. Similarly, high and low art blur, with displays of advertising 'art' occurring regularly in the Tate Gallery in London. These have included exhibits of Bovril labels and shopping bags. During 2002 and 2003 the Tate Liverpool held an exhibition entitled Shopping – A Century of Art and Consumer Culture, which was the first exhibition to carry out an in-depth examination of the interrelationships between contemporary art and the display, distribution and consumption of goods. This included Barbara Kruger's famous photographic screen print depicting a large hand carrying a sign that reads 'I shop therefore I am'.

Andy Warhol famously predicted that 'All department stores will become museums and all museums will become department stores' (Gawker.com). We can see this prediction coming to pass with the increasing trend for large companies, such as Nike, Guinness and Coca-Cola, to develop museums devoted to their history and the development of their brand. In the following report, posted on a travel website, we can see how consumers enthusiastically communicate with each other and how their cultural sightseeing now includes such museums:

> Coca-Cola Museum – Las Vegas (*consumer report*)
> Couldn't help not miss this place as it totally stood out of its place. A semi-glass building in the shape of a Coca-Cola bottle... wow. Small entrance fee I forgot how much... 2 or 3 dollars to go in. They have a lovely coke gift shop as you enter. If you're a Coke lover, then this is Paradise! Inside there's the complete history of Coca-Cola plus a room where one can view the best Coca-Cola commercials of all time. Plus you get to try some of the different cokes from around the world. They have around 6–8 coke dispensers where you grab a little plastic coke cup and help yourself. Careful not to drink yourself silly. I honestly enjoyed myself there as I am an avid Coke bottle collector.

Hyperreality

This is the becoming real of what was originally a simulation. This is exacerbated by the dream worlds created by advertising and promotion. Nowadays alternative meanings may even be attached to many mundane products like toothpaste, soap and deodorant (i.e. sex, money, power and so forth). The many trends towards consumer fantasy, for example themed environments (pubs, shopping centres, restaurants and hotels), virtual reality and computer games, exemplify this characteristic. The Irishness conveyed in Irish theme pubs becomes what we think of as 'Irish'. In Las Vegas, the casino, New York, New York, is very similar to its 'real' counterpart's neon-lit Times Square (Firat and Dholakia, 2006).

The West Edmonton Mall in Canada, one of the world's largest shopping malls, recreates a Parisian Boulevard, Bourbon Street, New Orleans and Chinatown, among many other fantasy-evoking simulations. One of Europe's biggest shopping and leisure centres, the MetroCentre, in Gateshead, England, has themed shopping in the Roman Forum, Antiques Village, Garden Court and Mediterranean Village.

Alongside this continual simulation there is an accompanying sense of loss of authenticity, and confusion over what is real and what is not. This leads to a quest on the part of consumers to experience what is really 'real'. Farmers' markets are making a comeback to city centres as people tire of the sameness of out-of-town shopping malls. The market is burgeoning for guides (books and people) that cater for travellers who shun the managed tourism of package holidays and seek 'authentic' experiences in the countries they visit (see Caruana et al., 2008). Chapter 3 discusses in detail the importance of perceived authenticity in the development of brand culture.

Chronology

Instead of looking towards a future that it mistrusts, postmodernism adopts a retrospective perspective (see Brown, 2001 for a very detailed discussion of this). It has a nostalgic concern for the past and its representations, rather than the progressive orientation of modernism. This links very much to the desire for authenticity and the 'real' just discussed. Another manifestation of this is the trend for retro products as illustrated, for example, by the launch of the new MINI (see the case study in Chapter 3); Volkswagen Beetle cars which hark back to the 1960s/1970s; and Citroen C3s modelled on the original 2CVs of the 1950s.

Nostalgic consumption is particularly associated with the ageing baby boom generation (those born between 1948 and 1964). However, Goulding (2002) has highlighted an increasing trend for what she terms 'vicarious nostalgia', a preference for objects associated with ten to fifteen years before one's actual birth date. Evidenced by the growing numbers of 'retro' clubs and shops, this type of nostalgia focuses on the aesthetic consumption of a particular period. Her research documents many consumers who live the lifestyle as closely as they can of a decade outside their living memory. This passion pervades all their consumption experiences. For example, one young woman, Caroline, who drives a Vespa scooter and a 1960s Mini, has a flat full of 1960s memorabilia and only likes music from that era. For an evening's entertainment she goes to a 60s club where she and her friends follow the dress codes of the 60s, and dance the night away to the music of the Stones, Beatles, Sandy Shaw, Lulu and the many other pop stars of that decade. The website, retrowow.co.uk, caters for just such lovers of retro style (check it out!). Apart from including details of a vast range of retro collectibles, it also gives advice on retro lifestyles that intermingles with snippets of social history of the particular period being discussed.

Pastiche

This concerns postmodernism's tendency to mix styles, past and present, often achieving the effect of a collage. As we already saw, in the example of the West Edmonton Mall, quite incongruous styles are juxtaposed (i.e. Chinatown and New Orleans). Pastiche is done in a playful and often ironic or self-referential way with a blending of existing codes, be they architectural, musical, literary and so forth. Often these result in parody advertisements or even advertisements about advertising. A good illustration of this is the Energizer Bunny advertising series that commenced in 1989 and ran through the 1990s. The first advertisement featured the now iconic pink toy rabbit, wearing dark glasses and beating a drum. It escapes from the studio where the advertisement is being made and rampages through other commercials that are being made in adjacent studios. The concept of the Energizer Bunny was itself a parody of Energizer's arch rival, Duracell, whose advertisements at that time showed a series of toy animals playing instruments and slowly coming to a halt with only the one powered by Duracell continuing to play.

Pastiche also includes intertextuality which means that one text draws on its audience's understanding of another text to give it meaning. Advertisements frequently draw on elements from other popular culture sources such as TV programmes or music. For example, the Magners Irish Cider advertising campaign featured the husky tones of Steve Earle singing 'Galway Girl' (a song well known to its target audience for being featured in the romantic film, *PS I Love You*, which was released just prior to the advertisement's release). Such intertextuality served to enhance the brand's mystique.

Anti-foundationalism

This is postmodernism's tendency to eschew mainstream, traditional approaches and beliefs and is typified by anti-fashion movements such as grunge. It is inherently deconstructive of anything that is orthodox and representative of the establishment. In the Magners campaign referred to above, Steve Earle is a perfect example of the 'rebel' archetype in mass culture (Holt and Thompson, 2004). In his youth, the singer was a hard drinking man who refused to conform to society's norms and was revered for his anti-establishment attitude. This 'rebel sell' is discussed in more detail in Chapter 3. Developing counter-cultural brand images and advertising messages has become big business. Think of French Connection United Kingdom's infamous acronym, FCUK, which helped turn a £5 million loss (in 1992) into a £39 million profit (Spencer, 2004). There are now many subversive advertising campaigns, such as the infamous 'You know when you've been Tango'd'.

The green movement can also be identified with postmodern anti-foundationalism. This critiques the basic structures of Western social organisation and, in particular, excessive lifestyles that are encouraged by increasing consumerism. Green marketing and sustainable marketing are becoming very important areas for marketers to understand and are discussed in more depth in Chapter 7.

Pluralism

The effect of the previous six characteristics leads to an acceptance of incongruous phenomena typified by the 'anything goes' syndrome. It welcomes and embraces diversity in all areas. Postmodern pluralism is associated with relativism, a perspective that eschews any belief in absolute truth. Instead, relativism embraces the idea that knowledge is dependent on an individual's perspective which will be highly influenced by his/her sociocultural background. Reality is thus socially constructed and there can be no objective knowledge or absolute representation of reality. Multiculturalism is a manifestation of this, respecting as it does all cultural positions and religious backgrounds. In his book, *Shopping for God* (2007), James Twitchell highlights how religious pluralism is leading to a market-based approach to spiritual practice in America, where consumer choice and church competition are the order of the day (Scott and Maclaran, 2009). Twitchell uses the term 'vernacular religion' to describe how consumers either produce their own ritual objects, use traditional religious props in unintended ways, or incorporate elements from other religious traditions – to use for their creative, and highly personalised, spiritual practices.

Overall, then, our above analysis of postmodernism's seven key characteristics shows the large extent to which postmodernism and marketing phenomena are intertwined. Indeed, consumer society is at the heart of postmodernism. In the next section we go on to look at how the postmodern critique has introduced new ways for us to understand our changing, increasingly marketing-driven, consumerist world.

Marketing and the postmodern critique

The postmodern critique is usually associated with French poststructuralist thinkers such as Jacques Derrida, Michel Foucault and Jean-François Lyotard, among others, although postmodernism and poststructuralism are by no means synonymous. We are not going to attempt to give a detailed overview of this highly complex and abstract body of thinking. We will, however, discuss some of the areas in marketing and consumer behaviour that this theorising has influenced.

Poststructuralism shows how meanings are constructed through discourse (systems of expression with in-built power relations and ideological implications), and that meanings are constantly shifting and evolving. It exposes how conceptual opposites, referred to as 'binary oppositions' (e.g. male/female, reason/emotion, speech/writing, etc.), depend on each other for their meaning, meaning which is also hierarchical in that one term is usually seen as superior to the other (i.e. reason is usually privileged over emotion). Poststructuralism tries to deconstruct these paired relationships of meaning, showing how the more privileged term depends on its relationship to the other, less privileged term. For example, to be male depends on not being female and being rational depends on not being emotional. Through the act of deconstruction, poststructuralism exposes the assumptions and knowledge systems that underpin such binary, hierarchical oppositions and unsettles the idea that there are any essential meanings that stay fixed over time. Instead it shows how meaning shifts with historical and cultural contexts. What it means to be male or female in one culture, or in one period in history, varies considerably.

Within consumer research, interpretivist research has frequently been conflated with postmodernism (Sherry, 1991), although not all interpretivist research takes a postmodern perspective. Certainly this body of scholarship (now also referred to as Consumer Culture Theory, see Arnould and Thompson, 2005 for a detailed overview) has contributed many new theoretical insights that have been influenced by the postmodern critique and, in particular, by post-structuralism through its analysis of discourse. Fundamental to these insights has been the recognition of the changing relationship between the production/consumption binary. During modernism, production and the political economy were privileged over consumption and the domestic sphere. Postmodernism shifts the emphasis from production to consumption, however, privileging culture instead, and meaning creation through consumption. The consumer becomes a producer of meanings through his/her consumption acts and, hence, the binary division between production/consumption becomes blurred, with production no longer assuming the privileged position. Rather, the consumer becomes the creative hero, playfully seeking out an identity, or identities, in the marketplace. This is very much the position taken by two leading interpretivist researchers, Firat and Venkatesh (1993), who celebrate the overturning of modernist conceptions of the consumer in their seminal article on 'liberatory postmodernism'. In this highly influential article, they argue that postmodernist developments in our knowledge of consumption processes offer emancipatory potential because they release us from traditional roles and constraints (e.g. gender, class, race) and allow a multiplicity of consumption forms and identity positions. It is in this respect particularly that Firat and Venkatesh recognise the potential of individuals to 'register rebellion' (p. 260) in the marketplace, through creating identity positions that could be subversive to the meanings intended by marketers. Other interpretivist studies have shown the emancipatory potential of, and within, the marketplace, in relation to: subcultures of consumption (Schouten and McAlexander, 1995); ethnicity (Peñaloza, 1994); fashion discourses (Thompson and Haytko, 1997); and the gay community (Kates, 2000).

Experiential consumption

We have already discussed how, from a postmodern perspective, contemporary consumption is not so much to do with use value or even exchange value, but rather more to do with symbolic value. As the symbolic meanings around products and services become increasingly important to consumers, so too do the experiences that are associated with those products and services. Experiential consumption is one of the dominant theoretical themes to emerge in interpretivist research (Belk, 1995) and it has its origins in the postmodern notion of consumers as manipulating signs and symbols in the marketplace in order to communicate with those around them. An experiential consumption perspective conceptualises consumers as socially connected beings rather than merely as potential purchasers of a product or service. There is a realisation that choosing depends on using, that customer choice depends on their experiences, and that buying depends on consuming (Holbrook, 1995). This overturns traditional marketing assumptions of a rational, information-processing consumer. Instead it emphasises the primacy of emotions over rationality, experience over cognition and the subconscious over the conscious. Usage experiences become a basis for 'hedonic' consumption and the role of 'fantasies, feeling and fun' in the lives of consumers (Hirschman and Holbrook, 1982).

As consumers seek more meaningful associations from products and services, they are moving away from wanting value for money to wanting value for time. As part of this shift, they expect more experiences from the brands they buy, experiences that also link them to other like-minded consumers. Thus, rather than being interested in the use value of goods and services, postmodern consumers seek a 'linking value' (Cova, 1996: 21). For example, Liberty, the upmarket London department store, hosts 'stitch 'n' bitch' sessions in its café to help create a community around its brand. T-Mobile invites customers to 'Street Gigs' where they can try out the newest technology. Innocent Smoothies runs an event called 'Fruitstock' as a way to encourage consumers to engage with the brand. Because consumers are increasingly sceptical about brand claims made through advertising (part of the postmodern scepticism referred to above), they want to experience brands for themselves, and discuss what other consumers feel about them, before making up their minds. The influence of brand communities is discussed in detail in Chapter 3.

Many major brands are now investing in permanent brand experiences. At Cadbury World we can learn about the history of chocolate before buying it in a vast emporium dedicated to lavish displays of enticingly packaged chocolates. We can also explore the set where the television soap opera, Coronation Street, sponsored by Cadbury's, was filmed. Similarly, Volkswagen's headquarters in Germany features a complete mini town, Autostadt, with streets, train stations, marketplaces, parks, rivers and bridges. There are also plenty of other entertainment and restaurants. Here consumers can study the technology behind Volkswagen cars and see Volkswagen's vision for the future, as well as browse around a museum of vintage VWs. There is even a special centre for children where they can drive miniature Beetles.

The key to experiences such as these is that they are interactive, both consumer-to-marketer and consumer-to-consumer. These interactive experiential strategies are designed to co-create meanings with consumers. Again, this is a further illustration of the breaking down of the production/consumption binary that has been influenced by the postmodern critique. Marketers may create certain meanings around their brands, but unless these resonate with consumers they will not be accepted, or be seen as authentic, by them. Experiential marketing encourages consumers to weave their own personal and social meanings alongside those created by marketers. Of course, we need to maintain a healthy (postmodern) scepticism as to marketers' motives in empowering consumers in this way. Arvidsson (2006), for example, accuses marketers of building on the immaterial labour of consumers, namely the values, commitments and forms of community around many products and services that are sustained by consumers. In other words, in a postmodern marketplace, consumers do a lot of the work and actually pay the company to be able to do so! We now go on in our final section to consider other limitations of a postmodernist approach.

Beyond postmodernism

From a critical perspective, this emphasis on a playful, imaginative consumer, as he or she creatively appropriates marketplace signs and symbols, also reinforces the achievement of personal freedom through economic means. It must be remembered that there are many marginalised groups who cannot afford the luxury of such marketplace play. Unlike their more prosperous counterparts, consumers in poverty and those who are homeless do not have the luxury of constructing and reconstructing consumer identities at will (Hamilton, 2007; Hill and Stamey, 1990). For such destitute groups of consumers, it is survival strategies rather than identity strategies that count.

Moreover, a postmodernism lens is only relevant to advanced consumer societies and cannot be applied to the large majority of the world's subsistence and developing economies. This is the theme of a key article by Rohit Varman and Ram Manohar Vikas (2007) who focus on subaltern consumers in India. They demonstrate how consumer freedom remains, as yet, only for the elite. Highly critical of a postmodern lens whereby consumption increasingly defines human freedom, they make an important contribution to the debate by calling for a re-emphasis on production which, they argue, has become separated from consumption. Their research with subaltern consumers shows how these consumers are disempowered in the workplace and, consequently, lead wretched lives which are barely at subsistence levels. Varman and Vikas conclude that powerlessness in relation to production ensures powerlessness in the sphere of consumption.

Another criticism of postmodernism has been that, while many inter-pretivist studies have given us greater insights into consumer culture theory and individual agency through the marketplace, this has sometimes been to the detriment of the wider social landscape and its structures. Catterall et al. (2005) argue that because rebellion takes place on an individual basis in the marketplace or within market-based subcultures, this has stifled much collective critique of wider social, economic and political structures. This is in part encouraged by the relativist stance that postmodernism adopts and its reluc-tance to privilege any one perspective which also weakens its political potency.

Bearing these significant limitations in mind, there is some evidence that we are now beginning to move beyond the postmodern condition. Throughout this chapter we have highlighted the consumer quest for authentic goods and services as part of the characteristics of a postmodern era. According to Holt

(2002), what he refers to as 'the postmodern branding paradigm' relies on the fact that, when perceived as authentic, brands are viewed by consumers as key resources for identity construction (for a more detailed discussion of these issues, see Chapter 3). However, Holt warns that this paradigm is now threatened because of the core paradoxes it contains whereby marketers are taking riskier strategies to appear authentic and original. As consumers become more and more sceptical of marketing activities, they are not easily taken in by such techniques and quickly see through inauthentic, money-making gambits. Holt envisages that in the future marketers will not be able to conceal their profit-making bias and they will have to acknowledge their commercial interests more readily. In turn, consumers will view the products and services marketers provide as cultural materials for identity projects that are no different from other cultural resources such as music, theatre, film and television. Marketers will then be judged, not by the perceived authenticity of the goods they offer, but by the creativity of those goods in helping consumers express themselves.

One of the most influential writers of our time, David Foster Wallace, critiques postmodernism for the nihilistic attitudes that accompanied its ironic and sceptical view of the world. In an analysis of TV sitcoms ('The Problem with Irony' – see the Internet resources at the end of this chapter), he pinpoints the emergence of a new sincerity that moves beyond the typically ironic nature of postmodern sitcoms. Wallace identifies an earnestness and search for human connection that was missing from the latter group. Now many other commentators also agree that we are facing another cultural shift, often referred to as post-postmodernism (Cova et al., 2013), entering a new period where enthusiasm and engagement counter postmodern apathy. This enthusiasm is about reconstruction as opposed to deconstruction, alongside a more realistic perspective arising from world events like 9/11 and the financial crisis. Moreover, movements like Occupy Wall Street – 'We are the 99%' – express a new collective desire for equality and justice, and question wider economic and political structures that remained unchallenged during the more individualistic postmodern era.

Summary

In this chapter we have looked at the impact of postmodernism on our knowledge of marketing and consumer behaviour. In particular, we have looked at how a postmodern perspective conceptualises the consumer as a communicative subject who reinforces his or her identity through the marketplace. Postmodernism emphasises interpretivist, qualitative ways of knowing, rather than survey-based or experimental quantitative research. Interpretivist perspectives have given us many new ways to understand the relationship between consumers and marketing phenomena, and how marketplace cultures develop through these ongoing interactions. We have also considered some of the drawbacks of postmodernism perspectives and how we may be experiencing another cultural shift that heralds a post-postmodern era.

CASE STUDY: experiencing a postmodern marketplace

Developed out of a beautiful 18th-century building, the Powerscourt Town-house Centre opened as a festival marketplace in 1981, a short walk away from one of Dublin's busiest shopping areas, Grafton Street. The centre comprised three levels of retail outlets grouped around an enclosed courtyard. The majority of shops sold specialist merchandise, with jewellery, ladies fashion, antiques and eating places predominating. Like its American and European counterparts (e.g. Harborplace, Baltimore and Covent Garden, London), Powerscourt offered an allegedly unique shopping environment, the 'Powerscourt Experience', as it was described on promotional material. Festival malls provide an alternative to the uniformity of shopping malls which offer mass-produced goods via high street chains such as Next, Miss Selfridge, New Look and Zara. They typically occupy a refurbished building of acknowledged architectural merit, retail an eclectic mix of speciality goods and services, are tenanted by independent retailers rather than national chain stores, encourage recreational as opposed to utilitarian shopping activities and adopt an essentially aesthetic ethos involving artworks, craft activities and designer goods.

On the ground floor in Powerscourt there was a central café where shoppers could pass the time chatting or people watching. Surrounding this were small market stalls, selling an eclectic mix of products, from ice cream to bonsai trees. Rising up from the courtyard was a stage for cultural events, with a grand piano to provide special recitals and enhance the centre's ambience. More exclusive shops, on the higher levels, proffered a range of designer jewellery, clothing, antiques and paintings. Its quirky mix of shops and entertainment gave Powerscourt a special ambience that consumers loved. Its combination of arts and crafts and the sense that there was something for everyone made it very different from other high street shopping. Many people came just to sit with friends over coffee or food in the many restaurants that were interspersed throughout the centre. Visually, a plethora of colourful signs, restaurant canopies and plant greenery greeted shoppers as they entered the courtyard. Powerscourt's somewhat haphazard layout encouraged exploration and gave shoppers a sense of discovery. It was not unusual for some to actually lose their way as they wandered around the different floors.

During the 1980s and 1990s, Powerscourt typified the nature of postmodern retailing (although it has subsequently been refurbished), as we go on to show using the previously discussed seven characteristics of postmodernism identified by Brown (1995).

Fragmentation

In its espousal of unique retail as opposed to the mass market, Powerscourt offered many richly contrasting opportunities for (re)creation of the self. The centre provided much scope for imaginings that centred on changing one's image or identity and engaging in the creative exploration of many celebratory identities. The setting's many associations with arts, crafts and aesthetics encouraged consumers to seek this self-expression in many different ways and to consider the many possible variations of Belk et al.'s (1996) 'myself-that-could-be'. For example, the Design Centre with its exclusive Irish designer labels together with other designer goods shops proffered many possibilities for self-transformation, as did other smaller stores: the Colour Me Beautiful stall, Buttercups (the beauty salon), Pzazz (the hair salon), Townbride and Wigwam (the wig boutique).

De-Differentiation

The design and setting of Powerscourt challenged many traditional marketing notions around segmentation and targeting. Whereas the higher levels were devoted to designer labels, craft shops, goldsmiths, antiques and art galleries, the ground floor was characterised by an abundance of bric-a-brac shops and cheap jewellery stalls. Many consumers commented that there was something for everyone. The extremes of bric-a-brac and expensive designer outfits catered for very different budgets. Thus the boundaries between high and low culture became indistinct in an environment where you could obtain anything ranging from high-quality antiques to the downright 'kitsch'.

Furthermore, for consumers, Powerscourt represented a very local market-place that took its identity from the character of its immediate surroundings. This was in sharp contrast to the perceived uniformity of the global market-place. Hence the special significance to consumers of the localised and con-textualised nature of the symbolic meanings that were created. In turn, this meaning creation blurred boundaries between production and consumption, art and life, in a characteristically postmodern way, with consumers becoming the producers of their own meanings and dream artists of their own imaginings (Campbell, 1987).

Hyperreality

The abundance of spectacle and dreamlike images in Powerscourt encour-aged a sense of being in a world apart, and this effect contributed greatly to it being a hyperreal environment. Powerscourt looked like a Georgian resi-dence or a traditional market, depending on which entrance one looked at. In either case, once inside it was not as it had seemed from the outside. Its airy vistas opened up to a profusion of colourful and enticing shopping spectacles around the tiered courtyard. The serendipitous nature of this dis-covery frequently surprised and entranced consumers, provoking many expressions of amazement and lending a hyperreal quality to consumers' shopping experience.

The centre stage that housed the grand piano epitomised this hyperreal ambience and the notion of postmodern consumption as a symbolic activity and as a consumption of meaning. Even when unplayed, it created an air of expectancy and anticipation. Its associations with performance reminded consumers of the theatre, the concert hall and the opera house, thereby simulating a more cultured environment, an environment normally very much removed from the more mundane task of shopping.

Chronology

In its eclectic blending of the old with the new, a blending that did not attempt to make chronological sense, Powerscourt typified the postmodern tendency to adopt a retrospective perspective. With its historic setting, its sweeping mahogany staircases, the grand piano, its antiques and art galleries and other fixtures and fittings such as mock-Victorian gas street lamps, wrought iron balustrades and creaking wooden floorboards, Powerscourt evoked a strong sense of the living past in the present.

This, then, is a good illustration of our earlier point about how the very ubiquity of hyperreality stimulates a countervailing desire for authenticity. Powerscourt was considered authentic on several levels: its 'sympathetically restored' historic building with many original features preserved intact; its many hand-made products that testified to the craftsmanship that had made them unique; and the overall impression conveyed to consumers of a dedication to more subtle aesthetic values rather than blatant commercial interests. In respect of the latter, the piano in Powerscourt was a further symbolic reinforcement of the centre's long-standing traditions and cultural superiority, signifying what was lacking in other shopping environments and experiences.

Pastiche

Styles were unashamedly mixed in Powerscourt to achieve the effect of a giant collage that greeted consumers as they entered the main courtyard. With no uniformity to shopfront design or layout, an array of different codes and references intermingled both vertically and horizontally within the centre. On the ground floor more contemporary shops mixed with others trying to convey a more historical ambience. For example, Wigwam displayed its brightly coloured blue and red wigs in close proximity to Joseph Appleby Diamond Jewellers, with its mock-Georgian wooden façade that framed the opulent jewellery displays within.

The hotchpotch of small market stalls and kiosks, informally placed around the ground floor, belied the more formal Georgian lines of the courtyard in which they were housed. Its two entrances symbolised these inherent contradictions. The original front entrance with its marbled black and white floor, its empty fireplace and its high ceiling, was somewhat cold and forbidding, reminiscent of the distant aristocracy that had previously inhabited its surrounds. In sharp contrast, the original back entrance (used more frequently as the front) was a profusion of flowers and fruit that spilled out onto the street. Its welcoming earthen flagstones and cosy ambience invited consumers to enter and go beyond, to investigate and explore. Contradictions in these two entrances abounded: urban/rural, high culture/low culture, aristocracy/peasantry, coldness/warmth, temperance/indulgence.

Anti-foundationalism

In eschewing mainstream forms of shopping, the ethos of Powerscourt, as a festival marketplace, was inherently anti-foundational. Everything about the centre was read by consumers as standing in opposition to the mass market with its overcommercialisation and its loss of more traditional and aesthetic values. In addition, it symbolised a localised resistance to fears of an anonymous globalisation, a uniqueness retained despite the encroaching efficiency of mass production lines. This perceived anti-foundationalism played an important role, allowing consumers 'to live their own myths or stories (narratives) instead of otherwise enforced or imposed ones' (Venkatesh et al., 1993: 216).

Pluralism

This last characteristic can be seen reflected in all the others. The eclectic and paradoxical mix that made up the shopping experience in Powerscourt contributed to a rich diversity on which the utopian imagination could feed. There was something for everyone, and anything seemed to go. Consumers found it difficult to categorise Powerscourt in relation to other forms of shopping. With its subversive mixing of class-based ambiences under one roof – designer chic alongside tourist 'tack' – it conveyed a social ambivalence that evaded categorisation.

Seminar exercises

Discussion topics

1   Using the library and internet, discover further sources of information on modernity. What other characteristics can you identify that are not discussed in this chapter?
2   Search various media sources (magazines, TV ads, the internet) and identify a retro product. Discuss what market you think this is targeting and why.
3   Choose an advertisement that you think best illustrates an experiential approach and analyse its various experiential elements.
4   What are the key criticisms of postmodernism? Can you think of other examples besides those already discussed?

Group exercises

1 Look for an advertisement that you think could be described as postmodern.

- How many of the seven postmodern characteristics can you relate to this?
- Are there different ways the advertisement can be interpreted (i.e. depending on your sex/age/cultural background)?

2 Choose a themed consumptionscape that all your group can visit at least once (preferably alone or in pairs, but not the whole group together). Each member should write an individual account (minimum 400 words) of their experience there and the feelings and emotions that were evoked. Try not to think too rationally and be as creative as you want. You can use photographs or anything else that you feel is appropriate (brochures, advertisements, etc.).

- Compare and contrast the differing viewpoints that group members expressed about their visit.
- Are there key themes that run through these accounts and, if so, what are they?
- What are the key emotions and feelings that you all had?
- Have you found the seven characteristics useful in understanding and interpreting your experiences?
- Make a 10-minute presentation in your seminar to give an overview of your group's experiences and reactions to the consumptionscape.

Internet resources

Gawker.com website: http://gawker.com/386202/the-department-stores-have-all-become-museums

Website for lovers of retro style: www.retrowow.co.uk

Professor Stephen Brown's website (author of Postmodern Marketing): www.sfxbrown.com/

Energizer Bunny 1989 advertisement: www.youtube.com/watch?v=fILdYrxnrf8&feature=related

David Foster Wallace, The Problem with Irony: www.youtube.com/watch?v=2doZROwdte4

Key readings

Brown, S. (1995). *Postmodern marketing*. London: Routledge.

Catterall, M., Maclaran, P. and Stevens, L. (2005). Postmodern paralysis: The critical impasse in feminist perspectives on consumers. *Journal of Marketing Management*, 21(5–6): 489–504.

Cova, B., Maclaran, P. and Bradshaw, A. (2013). Rethinking consumer culture theory from the postmodern to the communist horizon. *Marketing Theory*, 13(2): 213–225.

Firat, A.F. and Venkatesh, A. (1995). Liberatory postmodernism and the reenchantment of consumption. *Journal of Consumer Research*, 22(3): 239–266.

References

Adorno, T. and Horkheimer, M. (1973). *Dialectic of enlightenment*, trans. J. Cumming. London: Verso.

Arnould, E.J. and Thompson, C.J. (2005). Consumer Culture Theory (CCT): Twenty years of research. *Journal of Consumer Research*, 31(4): 868–882.

Arvidsson, A. (2006). *Brands: Meaning and value in media culture*. London: Routledge.

Bauman, Z. (1988). Sociology and postmodernity. *Sociological Review*, 6(4).

Baudrillard, J. (1988). *Jean Baudrillard: Selected writings*, ed. M. Poster. Oxford: Blackwell.

Belk, R.W. (1995). Studies in the new consumer behaviour. In D. Miller (ed.), *Acknowledging consumption*. London: Routledge, pp. 58–95.

Belk, R.W., Ger, G. and Askegaard, S. (1996). Metaphors of consumer desire. In K.P. Corfman and J.G. Lynch, Jr. (eds), *Advances in consumer research*, Volume 23. Provo, UT: Association for Consumer Research, pp. 369–373.

Brown, S. (1998). *Postmodern marketing 2: Telling tales*. London: ITP.

Brown, S. (2001). *Marketing: The retro revolution*. London: SAGE.

Campbell, C. (1987). *The romantic ethic and the spirit of modern consumerism*. Oxford: Basil Blackwell.

Cova, B. (1996). The postmodern explained to managers: implications for marketing. *Business Horizons*. November/December: 15–23.

Caruana, R., Crane, A. and Fitchett, J. (2008). The paradox of the independent traveller. *Marketing Theory*, 8(3).

Firat, A.F. (1991). The consumer in postmodernity. *Advances in Consumer Research*, 18: 70–76.

Firat, A.F. (1992). Fragmentation in the postmodern. *Advances in Consumer Research*, 19: 70–76.

Firat, A.F. and Dholakia, N. (2006). Theoretical and philosophical implications of postmodern debates: some challenges to modern marketing. *Marketing Theory*, 6(2): 123–162.

Firat, A.F. and Venkatesh, A. (1993). Postmodernity: The age of marketing. *International Journal of Research in Marketing*, 10(3): 227–249.

Firat, A.F., Dholakia, N. and Venkatesh, A. (1995). Marketing in a postmodern world. *European Journal of Marketing*, 29(1): 40–56.

Goulding, C. (2002). An exploratory study of age related vicarious nostalgia and aesthetic consumption. *Advances in Consumer Research*, 29: 542–546.

Hamilton, K. (2007). Making sense of consumer disadvantage. In M. Saren, P. Maclaran, C. Goulding, R. Elliott, A. Shankar and M. Catterall (eds), *Critical marketing: Defining the field*. Oxford: Butterworth–Heinemann, pp. 178–192.

Hill, R.P. and Stamey, M. (1990). The homeless in America: An examination of possessions and consumption behaviors. *Journal of Consumer Research*, 17(3): 303–320.

Hirschman, E.C. and Holbrook, M.B. (1982). Hedonic consumption: Emerging concepts, methods and propositions. *Journal of Marketing*, 46 (Summer): 92–101.

Holbrook, M.B. (1995). *Consumer research*. New York: SAGE.

Holt, D.B. (2002). Why do brands cause trouble? A dialectical theory of consumer culture and branding. *Journal of Consumer Research*, 29(1): 70–90.

Holt, D.B. and C.J. Thompson (2004). Man-of-action heroes: The pursuit of heroic masculinity in everyday consumption. *Journal of Consumer Research*, 31(2): 425–440.

Jameson, F. (1991). *Postmodernism, or the cultural logic of late capitalism.* Durham, NC: Duke University Press.

Kates, S.M. (2000). Out of the closet and out on the street: Gay men and their brand relationships. *Psychology and Marketing*, 17(6): 493–513.

Lyotard, J.-F. (1984). *The postmodern condition: A report on knowledge.* Minneapolis: University of Minnesota Press.

Peñaloza, L. (1994). Crossing boundaries/crossing lines: A look at the nature of gender boundaries and their impact on marketing research. *International Journal of Research in Marketing*, 11(4): 359–379.

Schouten, J.W. and McAlexander, J.H. (1995). Subcultures of consumption: An ethnography of the new bikers. *Journal of Consumer Research*, 22(1): 43–61.

Sherry, J.F. (1991). Postmodern alternatives: The interpretive turn in consumer research. In T.C. Robertson and H.H. Kassarjian (eds), *Handbook of consumer research.* Englewood Cliffs, NJ: Prentice-Hall, pp. 548–591.

Thompson, C.J. and Haytko, D.L. (1997). Speaking of fashion: Consumers' uses of fashion discourses and the appropriation of countervailing cultural meanings. *Journal of Consumer Research*, 24 (June): 15–42.

Twitchell, J. (2007). *Shopping for God.* New York: Simon and Schuster.

Scott, L. and Maclaran, P. (2009). 'Roll your own' religion: Consumer culture and the spiritual vernacular. *Advances in Consumer Research*, 36: 60.

Spencer, N. (2004). Connecting with culture: Profit and loss. 27 August, www.licc.org.uk/culture/profit-and-loss

Varman, R. and Vikas, R.M. (2007). Freedom and consumption: Toward conceptualizing systemic constraints for subaltern consumers in a capitalist society. *Consumption Markets and Culture*, 10(2): 117–131.

Venkatesh, A., Sherry, J.F., Jr. and Firat, A.F. (1993). Postmodernism and the marketing imaginary. *International Journal of Research in Marketing*, 10: 215–223.

3 Building brand cultures

Introduction

Culture refers to the system of symbols and meanings that give human activities significance. Throughout our lives we are part of many different, often intersecting, cultures, such as national culture, music and literature cultures, lifestyle culture and so forth. These cultures can have a profound influence on the attitudes, beliefs and values that underpin our behaviours. Increasingly, it is recognised that brands too can have a powerful influence on us because of the meanings they incorporate, and the 'culture' that evolves around them. According to Jonathan Schroeder, one of the leading experts on the topic, brand culture concerns all the aspects and connotations of brands that have made them an important part of our everyday lives and experiences (Schroeder, 2007).

Brands are deeply embedded in the meaning systems that we use to make sense of our contemporary world. Take, for example, the golden arches of McDonald's or the Nike swoosh that we encounter on a daily basis. These symbols and their meanings are instantly recognisable around the globe, signifying respectively fast food Americana style and empowerment through sports. Yet, not only do brands create their own unique culture, but they also draw on other cultural phenomena such as history, myths, rituals, artworks, the film industry, theatre and television, to convey meanings that resonate in powerful ways with consumers' lifestyles (Schroeder and Salzer-Mörling, 2006). This ongoing iteration, between contributing to culture and drawing from it, makes brand culture a complex and multifaceted phenomenon. It is much more than just a clever name or logo, and also more than the implementation of a successful marketing strategy. Importantly, brand culture is a living entity that evolves and responds to the dynamics of the marketplace. Brand culture is continuously (re)created as the various parties that have an interest in the brand – companies, employees, culture industries, intermediaries, customers – relate stories around their experiences of the brand (Holt, 2004). The strength of a brand's culture lies in the collective perception about it, rather than the psychological aspects of an individual's response to the brand.

This chapter examines the building blocks of brand culture by looking at how meanings that circulate around a particular brand evolve as the brand intersects with other cultural phenomena. First, we discuss the important synergies between organisational and brand cultures together with the important role of employees in building brand culture, before looking at how brand cultures are also co-created with consumers and other stakeholders external to an organisation. We discuss the role of brand communities and how social media is driving their formation. After highlighting the importance of competing in 'myth markets' (Holt, 2004), we illustrate how many highly successful brands achieve iconic status through responding insightfully to the wider cultural environment. Finally, we explore some of the ways that a brand's culture can become tainted through negative perceptions that consumers hold about it and discuss the impact of the anti-branding movement.

Building brand culture with employees

Well-known entrepreneurs such as Phil Knight (Nike), Richard Branson (Virgin), Anita Roddick (Body Shop) and Steve Jobs (Apple) have built strong corporate brand cultures through personal dedication and passion for their enterprises. Their strong, charismatic personalities and missionary zeal have the ability to enthuse employees with a sense of their vision for the organisation, often making employees as passionate about the enterprise as the entrepreneurs are themselves. Such entrepreneurial vision intuitively connects corporate identity to organisational mission, a key factor in building a sustainable corporate brand culture.

Following the lead of such inspirational entrepreneurs, many companies are now moving towards corporate branding, as opposed to product branding, in a move to instil a clearer sense of corporate identity and brand culture into their employees, suppliers, customers and other stakeholders. Balmer (2006: 34) refers to the growth of the 'corporate brandscape', arguing that brand cultures, and the communities that they engender, are much stronger for corporate brands than those created by product brands. Whether we feel an affinity with them or not, powerful corporate brands, such as Microsoft, IBM, BMW, HSBC and Coca-Cola, convey a rich set of associations in our minds as to what they stand for and who they are. Corporate brand culture is three-dimensional, reaching not only inside and outside the organisation, but also *across* organisations (Balmer, 2006). Consider the rebellious nature of the Virgin brand and how this is conveyed across many different industries that range from mobile phones to air travel. Embodied in the figure of its flamboyant founder, Richard Branson, the Virgin brand culture is based on the idea of doing things differently, of radical rethinking and of siding with the consumer in the face of bureaucracy and monopoly.

The role of employees in enacting the corporate vision is one of the core building blocks for brand culture, together with the idea that they should 'live the brand' and be empowered to be 'brand champions' (Ind, 2007). From this perspective, the marketing role diffuses throughout the organisation, no longer resting with a specific marketing function or brand manager. Whereas in the past, marketers have been accustomed to thinking of specific externally focused marketing activities, particularly marketing communications, to convey the brand ethos and values, a corporate brand approach emphasises the customers' brand experience that comes from their dealings with an organisation's employees. From chief executive to delivery driver, all employees' actions can be seen as reinforcing the brand values. These actions are responsible for translating the corporate vision into a reality and embedding the brand culture in all employee/customer interactions, as well as throughout the organisation. In this way the organisation and all its employees provide the basis for the brand's position in the marketplace vis-à-vis its competitors (Elliott and Wattanasuwan, 1998).

Of course, all this is easier said than done. A corporate branding culture cannot simply be dreamt up in a day or be imposed on an organisation regardless of the existing organisational culture. It requires a subtle touch and a lot of patience to understand and reconcile the different meaning systems that may already exist in an organisation (for example, managerial versus shopfloor cultures). Schultz and Hatch (2006) emphasise that for corporate branding to be successful the strategic vision, organisational culture and stakeholder image must be aligned. Normally top management dictates the strategic vision, a vision that embodies their aspirations for the future direction of the company. In contrast, organisational culture is 'the internal values, beliefs and basic assumptions that embody the heritage of the company and manifests in the ways *employees* [emphasis in original] feel about the company they are working for' (p. 16). Organisational culture is much more organic than strategic vision, emanating from employees' sense of what the organisation is and their sense of identification with their employer. The culture of an organisation is often taken for granted, going unquestioned and expressed in the familiar phrase of 'just the way we do things around here'. If employees' and managements' visions of the organisation are at odds, it will be much more difficult to develop a consistent image with the organisation's customers and other stakeholders.

Successful brands go to great lengths to establish the right culture within their organisation, and to ensure that employees believe in the brand. Innocent made itself the fastest growing business in the UK's food and drink sector by building a strong organisational culture that ensures its employees share its strategic vision. In their company headquarters, 'Fruit Towers' in West London, Innocent's young and irreverent culture is reinforced by a sign saying 'Burglars' on the front window and another saying 'People' on the door (Simmons, 2006). There is a 'wall of acclaim' beside the reception where consumer praises of the brand are proudly displayed. Employees engage in communal stretching exercises at the regular Monday morning meetings where everyone updates on sales and swaps stories across departments in an informal and relaxed atmosphere that often includes sitting on cushions on the floor. Innocent treats its employees generously in order to provide the right atmosphere for them to flourish and use their own creativity in their jobs.

Of course, from a more critical perspective, we are also right to be sceptical about such seemingly enlightened employer/employee relationships which can be regarded as a form of control, a kind of 'brainwashing'. They can even be seen as establishing a quasi-cult around the brand to ensure that employees internalise the brand values unquestioningly in order to appear more committed and authentic to the consumer. This in turn helps inscribe the brand into the 'life-world of the consumer' (Arvidsson, 2006: 43) as they interact with employees. In the next section we go on to consider the consumer aspects of brand culture in more detail.

Building brand culture with consumers

We have just explained above how a key aspect of brand culture is to ensure that a common vision unites employees. The other key building block of brand culture is how well the values the organisation embodies match what its customers are seeking. Employees and management may share a similar passion but if this is not also shared with the customer then the brand will be doomed to failure. It is now well recognised that consumers no longer seek just functional benefits from products and services, they seek meanings that help them construct and maintain their identities (Elliott and Wattanasuwan, 1998). By providing us with symbolic resources, brands present us with a multitude of possible ways to express ourselves and with which to gain the approval of our peers.

Brands such as Apple, Benetton and Harley-Davidson act as quasi activists in the sense that they lead us in thinking differently about the world and ourselves (Holt, 2004). Heath and Potter (2005) see this as 'the rebel sell', arguing that it is rebellion, and not conformity, that drives desires in the marketplace as we seek to differentiate ourselves from others. A good example of this is the Volkswagen Beetle that is remembered as an iconic rebel car in the 1960s and 1970s when it was seen as a rejection of the values of mass society and the showiness of its larger competitors. This iconicity was leveraged successfully by VW in its popular relaunch of the Beetle in the late 1990s.

Social agendas, and the values they represent, can generate deep bonds with consumers who 'buy into them' both literally and metaphorically (see Chapter 7). The founders of Ben and Jerry's ice cream, Ben Cohen and Jerry Greenfield, have built a strong brand culture around a social and ecological conscience since they launched the brand in 1978. For example, their launch of a 'Fossil Fuel' ice cream was accompanied by an invite to 'Help Lick Global Warming with Ben & Jerry's New Flavour'. This contributed to their 'Lick Global Warming' campaign which raised money for climate change research (Marketing Digest, 2007). They use sustainable dairy farming programmes ('caring dairy'), achieve a carbon neutral footprint (or 'hoofprint' as they like to refer to it!) and in 2006 launched the first Fairtrade vanilla ice cream. Their consistent commitment to a social agenda has developed a following of highly loyal consumers who see the company as caring for more than just commercial gain. Once again, as Arvidsson (2006) reminds us, we need to maintain a healthy scepticism over such actions. Creating social agendas in this way also enables large corporations to better infuse themselves through every aspect of our lives. It is often how they convince us they are 'authentic' (see Chapter 7 for more on 'greenwashing').

This perceived authenticity of corporate intention and responsibility is becoming increasingly more important to consumers. This is particularly relevant in terms of what Holt (2002) describes as the postmodern branding paradigm, which is 'premised upon the idea that brands will be more valuable if they are offered, not as cultural blueprints, but as cultural resources – as useful ingredients to produce the self as one so chooses'. As people choose brands that have the right meaning for them in terms of how they want to reflect their identity, they need to be confident that the brand is not going to let them down. Choosing brands they can be sure will enhance their identity helps consumers minimise the purchase risk and, as we will see later in this chapter, they can become very disillusioned with the brand if they feel it has betrayed their trust.

Brand communities

Nowadays brands must be seen to share, rather than manipulate, consumers' passions and emotions. The brand–consumer relationship can be very powerful and include a range of strong emotions such as love, intimacy and commitment, to the extent that consumers may even experience separation anxiety (Fournier, 1998). Thus, consumers' contribution to brand culture, and their role in co-creating meanings not only with marketers but also with other consumers, should not be underestimated. Often the strength of consumer feeling is experienced collectively and a community forms around the brand, a community that is held together by mutual appreciation and loyalty to the brand. Brand communities are not restricted to any one product category and can be as diverse as the consumer groups who form them. They include commonplace car brands such as Saab, Jeep, Volkswagen and Mini, as well as more idiosyncratic media productions like *Star Wars*, *X-Files* and *Xena: Warrior Princess*.

A brand community is defined as a 'specialized, un-geographically bound community, based on a structured set of social relationships among admirers of a brand' (Muniz and O'Guinn, 2001: 412). Although they differ from traditional communities in terms of their commercial nature, brand communities are held together like their traditional counterparts by three key aspects: consciousness of kind, shared rituals and traditions and moral responsibility. Consciousness of kind is about shared values and how members form in-group/out-group categorisations (see, for example, the Mini case study at the end of this chapter). Shared rituals and traditions are about the community experience and celebrating the brand history. A sense of moral responsibility is about the commitment to other members of the community, helping them with problems or making new members feel at home. In these ways, consumers use their own labour to add cultural and emotional value as they develop interpersonal relationships around the brand (Cova and Dali, 2009). Accordingly, consumers are often drawn to products and services because of their linking value rather than their use value. From this perspective, marketing activities are more about facilitating the 'co-presence and the communal gathering of individuals in the time of the tribes: a kind of "tribal marketing"' (Cova and Cova, 2002).

Social media in particular drives the formation of brand communities, linking physically distant lovers of a brand. More than 50 percent of the top 1,000 global brands have online brand communities (Manchanda et al., 2012). Such communities enhance consumers' engagement with a brand across seven key dimensions: enthusiasm, enjoyment (affective level), attention, absorption (cognitive level), and learning, endorsing and sharing (behavioural level) (Dessart et al., 2015). These types of engagement and intra-community interactions lead to increased loyalty as well as often generating a fervent passion for the brand. Of course, community members have different levels of commitment and loyalty and not all members participate for the same reasons. A useful typology of significant distinctions in member behaviours has been developed by Kozinets (1999):

Insiders: participate actively on a regular basis and are the most influential community members. They are passionately devoted to the brand.

Devotees: are strongly attached to the brand but less dedicated to the community and they are not so involved in the social aspects.

Minglers: have strong community ties but are not so attached to the brand. They enjoy the social interactions but may not consume the brand at all.

Tourists: often they are lurkers and do not have an active relationship with either the brand or the community.

Overall, we can see how the role of the consumer is changing to take a much more active part in the production of value. The firm and the consumer have traditionally been seen as having distinct roles: the role of the firm to create brands offering benefits; the role of the consumer (the target market) being to passively consume those brands, and taking no role in actual value creation around the brand. In Chapter 2 on postmodernism we highlighted the blurred boundaries between traditional binary divisions such as production/consumption. This blurring affects the role of the consumer. Because consumers want a relationship with brands they can trust, and with whose values they can identify, they are now influencing much more directly the value systems that a brand embodies and that give it a unique culture. According to

Fournier (1998), we can form relationships with brands that are just as fulfilling as the relationships we have with other people. On this same basis, however, we can put the same pressure on brands that we do on human relationships, and we can expect a lot from them! Consequently, marketers need to spend a lot of effort to co-create brand experiences with consumers, experiences that form a crucial part of building and maintaining brand culture. Through their website, Ben and Jerry's invite customers to suggest new flavours and even to ask for a discontinued flavour or product to be reinstated. This approach shows foresight and acknowledges the power that consumers now have to make demands on a brand. For example, Wispa was an iconic 1980s chocolate bar that was discontinued in 2003, causing loyal customers to use social media to lobby Cadbury's for its return. Following this pressure from loyal customers, the bar was reintroduced in 2007. This is by no means an isolated incident. Other successful campaigns by loyal communities surrounding a brand include the Fiat 500 (ceased production 1975) and the Raleigh Chopper (ceased production 1979) that were both relaunched (2004 and 2007, respectively).

Word of mouth/mouse runs rampant in brand communities and marketers frequently try to influence consumer-to-consumer (C2C) communications in a variety of ways including viral and guerrilla marketing. Known as a 'seeding' campaign, sometimes marketers place a product with influential consumers (opinion-leading bloggers, for example) in order to encourage them to post favourable reviews and spread the word to their communities. A study on this by Kozinets et al. (2010) found that bloggers changed marketer messages to make them more relevant and palatable to their community because blatant marketing promotions risk compromising the sharing and caring aspects of communal relations. These authors revealed four key narrative strategies that bloggers used and that were significant for marketers, namely evaluation, explanation, embracing and endorsement:

Evaluation: avoids mentioning the marketer influence and focuses on product performance.

Explanation: acknowledges the marketer participation and shows awareness of the cultural tension this may produce.

Embracing: emphasises the consumer-marketer co-creation aspects but puts the focus on meeting personal needs with the product.

Endorsement: acts as a quasi-marketer for the product and is happy to pass on all marketing promotions and communications.

The commercial–cultural tension follows a continuum moving from implicit (evaluation) to explicit (endorsement). Whether the message is accepted depends on the product's perceived fit with the blog and communal norms. If there is a mismatch the community may resist the marketer influence or result in negative word of mouth. Building brand culture is a delicate balancing act between being seen as authentic (sharing the passion) and being seen as too self-interested and commercial.

Sometimes a brand community is completely controlled by consumers with no marketer interventions whatsoever. Despite being discontinued by Apple in 1998, the Apple Newton still motivates a lively community of users (see, for example, http://myapplenewton.blogspot.co.uk/) who remain dedicated to the brand. They still share knowledge about the product and help each other to maintain their Newtons. Apple launched the Newton in 1993 as the first personal digital assistant on the market. The launch was rushed and the design had many ongoing problems that eventually led to its discontinuation. However, it retained a loyal core of followers who feel abandoned by the parent brand Apple (Muniz and Schau, 2005). These enthusiasts display a quasi-religious fervour towards their Newtons and rumours even surface from time to time that the Apple Newton will be relaunched (a second coming and narrative of redemption).

Creating iconic brands

In Doug Holt's (2004) path-breaking book on cultural branding, he shows how brands become iconic. Icons are representational symbols that embody meanings that we admire and respect. They provide us with templates of what to value and how to behave. In ancient times icons were mainly religious figures (saints, gods, disciples and so forth) and stories about them were circulated mainly by word of mouth, passed down through generations in this way. Now, Holt argues, the circulation of cultural icons has become a key economic activity and takes place through mass communication (i.e. films, books, TV, sports, advertising, PR, etc.). Many icons are film stars such as James Dean and Marilyn Monroe, politicians such as John F. Kennedy and Martin Luther King, or sporting heroes such as Michael Jordan. These figures all represent certain kinds of stories, stories that convey 'identity myths' (Holt, 2004) that people use to address the anxieties and desires they have about their own identity. To illustrate, the 1950s rebel figure, James Dean, defied middle-class conventions of suburban family life and encapsulated the idea that a man could follow his own desires. This myth was especially appealing to the postwar American male who felt tied down by family responsibilities and the dull routine of working for a large and faceless corporation.

According to Holt, iconic brands are the ones that best know how to respond to key cultural tensions that are taking place in the wider socio-cultural environment. A good example of this is Brand Beckham (Milligan, 2004). As a sporting celebrity, David Beckham is also a powerful brand that embodies core values of dedication, down-to-earth humanity and an impeccable sense of style. Proud of being a loving father, Beckham is well known for being in touch with his feminine side, changing his hairstyles regularly and willing to be photographed in a sarong. The identity myth that he represents helps young men carve a path between the perceived 'sissiness' of the feminine and the widespread disapproval of the 'brutish' masculine.

Companies can now be seen as competing in myth markets rather than product markets (Holt, 2004; Thompson, 1997). Traditionally, myths make us aware of oppositions that they progressively mediate such as good/evil, life/death, science/nature, male/female and so forth; their tales take on life's big contradictions and the complexities of being human. It is in this sense they speak across cultures and similar myths and symbolic associations exist across very different religious beliefs. And so it is that commercial myths can also resonate with us at deep, unconscious levels. A successful brand creates a commercial myth that intersects with both historical and popular memory (Thompson and Tian, 2008; Arnould, 2008). Take, for example, the highly successful Magners Irish Cider campaign that is single-handedly accredited with changing consumer attitudes to cider by transforming it into a fashionable drink. In order to do this, the Magners campaign very successfully taps into beer discourse in order to position and legitimise cider as a masculine and culturally empowering drink. This discourse is about 'challenge, risk and mastery – mastery over nature, over technology, over others in good natured "combat" and over oneself' (Strate, 1992: 82). However, a crucial aspect of the campaign's success is that it also draws on nostalgic, age-old images of the Irish male as being in touch with his deeply romantic self, thereby restoring a sense of the 'intense masculinity' that has become displaced and unfashionable in 21st-century representations of masculinity. The nature/culture binary is central to the Magners campaign. Maclaran and Stevens' (2009) analysis of the Magners campaign illustrates how the Celtic soul that lies at its core is encouraging young men to negotiate a masculinity that restores ideals of manliness (culture) alongside a celebration of the feminine (nature). Thus, as a commercial myth, this conception of 'Magners Man' conveys a new mythic ideal that draws on many existing cultural myths to achieve its unique 'syncretic blending of narrative and imagistic elements' (Thompson and Tian, 2008).

When the brand eludes control

Identity myths thus have the power to forge deep bonds with consumers and they are often a crucial part of the relationship we have with a brand. Yet, similar to any meaningful relationship, people can feel very aggrieved when it does not go well. The fact that brands can engender deep emotions in us also means that we can become very dissatisfied if our trust is betrayed, or if we feel let down in some way. For example, when a well-known shopping centre in Dublin was radically refurbished, many consumers felt that they had lost a part of their heritage and were very unhappy with what the management had done to the centre. Some experienced such deep emotions over the changes that they swore never to return (Maclaran and Brown, 2005).

In the current business world it is almost impossible for a company to control its external brand image. Modern communication technologies, and in particular the internet, mean that there are very few corporate secrets and any discrepancy between a company's outward image and its internal one swiftly gets revealed. Consumers talk to other consumers all the time and with the use of email, web discussion groups and social networking sites, news can spread very quickly. Consumers also talk to employees and this brings us full circle, back to our previous discussions about the importance of good employee relations. Dissatisfied employees can set up their own websites to reveal home truths about their employer, both to other employees and consumers alike. There is a plethora of boycotting sites to be found on the web, each revealing various dissatisfactions and rallying others to join the boycott. Such actions can seriously damage a company's reputation. Because brand culture is organic, flowing as much from employees and customers as from an organisation's strategic vision, it can also be fragile and not easily controlled by marketers. Brand culture, therefore, can be adversely affected by negative associations, just as easily as it can be enhanced by positive ones.

Many well-known brands have had their reputations severely tainted. Martha Stewart was convicted of illegal stock trading in relation to her own media company. Perrier's crystal clear water with health-giving properties was contaminated with benzene. The energy company, Enron, was found guilty of accounting fraud. Indeed, transgressions of this nature have become so commonplace that terms such as 'brand rehabilitation strategy' and 'brand repair' are now in frequent use in relation to attempts to avoid irreparable damage to a brand's culture (Kahn, 2005). However transgressions do not always have to be damaging and sometimes they can form an intrinsic part of a brand's culture. Aaker et al. (2004) found that relationships with 'sincere' brands such as Coca-Cola, Ford and Hallmark, perceived to be traditional and family-orientated, suffered after transgressions. Conversely, relationships with 'exciting' brands such as Virgin, Yahoo and MTV, perceived as more youthful and irreverent, showed signs of reinvigoration.

A brand does not always have to commit a transgression to acquire negative connotations. Brand tainting can also occur because consumers' perceptions change. There was criticism of the Body Shop when L'Oréal took over the company. The Body Shop was seen as joining the 'enemy' because L'Oréal is part owned by Nestlé which has been criticised for marketing powdered baby milk in developing countries. Sometimes the most powerful sources for brand tainting exist beyond the control of those who manage the brand, as, for example, with the symbolic associations that may emanate from particular consumer groups that use the brand. The red, white, black and camel check that is synonymous with Burberry led to the brand becoming severely tainted in the UK where it is associated with a 'chav' image. This image is typified by Daniella Westbrook, the *EastEnders* soap opera star who gained notoriety for her cocaine addiction and who is a major fan of the Burberry brand. She and her baby were even photographed by the press, both dressed head to foot in Burberry check and with a matching pushchair. Because of negative associations such as these, the Burberry check has been downplayed in recent designs. The baseball cap has been discontinued by the company in an attempt to distance itself from this marginalised 'chav' group. Interestingly, this tainting did not affect the brand's international markets where Burberry is still seen as an upmarket, very British brand.

Another threat of tainting comes from the many anti-branding movements and campaigns that have been gaining momentum. Works like Naomi Klein's *No Logo* (1999), one of the most influential anti-globalisation texts, expose how branding techniques are grounded in a profit motive despite the many creative ways in which marketers may try to hide this through appeals to authenticity. In particular, Klein severely critiques such brands as Nike, Gap, McDonald's, Starbucks, Shell and Microsoft, and highlights their many exploitative practices. In addition, successful brands often work to suppress competition in the marketplace. A good example of this is Microsoft, whose software is on 80–90 percent of computers around the world (Lury, 2004). A dominant market position, such as Microsoft's, enables a brand culture to be diffused globally (see Chapter 10), with the risk that local cultures are eroded, or even extinguished, in its wake. 'Culture Jamming' has become a well-known method of resistance to the pervasiveness of brand culture, made famous by the activist magazine, *Adbusters*. Culture jamming involves transforming advertisements in an ironic way to critique the corporation behind the advertisement's message. Whereas originally these activities focused on the ways in which brands manipulated desires, now they are more likely to expose the hypocrisy 'between brand promises and corporate actions' (Holt, 2002: 85).

Summary

In this chapter we have looked at the different facets of brand culture and explored its many influencing factors. Marketers are by no means the sole source for the meanings that surround a brand and that produce its overall culture. There are as many organic influences that marketers cannot control as, for example, those that stem from organisational culture and employee perceptions of the brand. Consumers also play a major role, often co-creating meanings that can be both positive and negative and even forming communities around the brand. The most successful brands have built strong cultures that incorporate these organic influences and remain sufficiently flexible to adapt to changes in the macro environment. The best brands tell great stories with which we can identify. However, the more we look to brands to guide our beliefs and behaviours, the more they are likely to be held accountable. Activist movements against brands are likely to become more aggressive as brands play a bigger part in our everyday lives. In the future, as Holt (2002) has indicated, the most successful brands are likely to be those that provide us with the most creative cultural resources.

CASE STUDY: building a Mini brand culture

Like the Volkswagen Beetle, the Mini is an iconic car that dates back to the rebel culture of the 1960s. Just like the mini-skirt and the Beatles, the little car is an enduring symbol of the 'swinging sixties'. The Mini was designed by the British Motor Corporation in response to the increasing popularity of the smaller and fuel-efficient German 'bubble cars'. Sir Alec Issigonis, the Mini's designer, has become a legend in his own right, famed for his innovative design that allowed both performance and space despite the limitations of size. Sir Alec's history intertwines with that of the Mini and many stories circulate around him that contribute to the Mini's brand culture and reinforce it as a triumph for British design. Fans relate how Pininfarina, a famous Italian carmaker, once asked Issigonis why he did not style the Mini a little. The reply that Issigonis made to this competitor's taunt has now become part of the Mini myth: 'It will still be fashionable when I'm dead and gone' (Beh, 2008).

The Mini was marketed as a fun car with a cheeky image. 'You don't need a big one to be happy. Happiness is Mini shaped' and 'Small is beautiful' are some of its famous straplines. Its brand culture has evolved around this image, an image that made it 'cool' to drive a small, unpretentious car. In challenging prevailing notions of respectability, the Mini was very much a part of the countercultural movement that emerged during the 1960s. Heralding the idea of the 'rebel sell' that we have previously referred to, it stood for a youth culture that was hedonistic and fun-seeking. The Mini was continually associated with major celebrities throughout the decade. This enhanced its brand culture significantly, giving it celebrity status by association with stars such as Peter Sellers, Ringo Starr, Britt Ekland, Lulu and fashion designer Mary Quant. When Marianne Faithful drove to Mick Jagger's drugs trial in her Mini, and George Harrison's psychedelic Mini appeared in the Beatles' *Magical Mystery Tour*, the Mini's subversive connotations were enhanced (wikipedia.com). Well-known dare-devil racers such as Niki Lauder, Enzo Ferrari and Steve McQueen drove Mini Coopers. In 1969 three Minis featured as getaway cars in *The Italian Job*. The car chase that ensued, with its daring stunt driving that included descending a set of steps, has become a classic. In 2003 three new BMW MINIs featured in a remake of this film.

Like other iconic brands, the Mini addressed certain tensions in society at the right time. During the postwar 1950s in Britain and the US, size was regarded as a marker of status and this was particularly so in the case of cars. The Suez crisis of 1956 meant that oil prices soared and the size–status equation came under pressure from the need for fuel economy. The Mini car addressed this contradiction and, at the same time, countered the postwar climate of continued austerity with its message that linked fun and size (Beh, 2008). The Mini symbolised a unique blend of hedonism, small size and Britishness, core values that consumers quickly responded to. They bought the Mini not just for its fuel-saving capacity, but also because they were buying into these core values. In doing so they were using the Mini to say something about their own identity: they were cool!

Over the years, although it was a mass-produced car, the Mini brand culture evolved to include a highly individualistic element. This was aided by its many endorsements from celebrities who had specially designed models. It became the custom for individual owners to decorate their Minis in unique ways. Some painted Union Jacks on the roof or on the bonnet, while others painted colourful stripes or motifs on the bodywork. Still others kitted out the interior in fanciful décor, sometimes running a theme throughout the car's interior and exterior. This element of creativity and individual self-expression was added to the brand culture by consumers themselves and has now become an important part of the brand's evolving history.

The Mini car finally ceased production in 2000, having become a legend in its own right. A huge following of loyal fans still mourn its loss and remain committed to guarding the Mini's heritage in brand communities around the globe. Many fans also deeply resent the launch of the new BMW MINI in 2001 (BMW bought the Mini brand as part of their takeover of Rover) and argue that it is not an authentic Mini. They perceive one of its core values, Britishness, to have been violated by association with a German manufacturer. In terms of its size also, the design of the new MINI can no longer be regarded as particularly small. There is thus a clash of brand cultures between the values of the old Mini and the new Mini – between old and new brand communities – that is still being played out in the marketplace. Many of the classic Mini clubs that exist will not permit new MINI owners to join and refuse to admit that the new model has any links to them. Despite this opposition, there can be no doubt that the launch of the new Mini has been highly successful. The new design has taken one of the Mini's core values, fun, and used this value very successfully in conjunction with the theme of individualisation. As far as the new MINI manufacturer, BMW, is concerned, there is no disjuncture between the old Mini and new MINI and the brand has simply evolved. The new MINI website (www.mini.co.uk) invites customers to design their own MINI from hundreds of different combinations, alongside the claim that:

> Over the years MINI has changed. However the foundations of this small car, its character traits, have remained unchanged from its inception in the 1950s until today. Be it old Mini or the present-day MINI, people just can't stop talking about it.
>
> Because it's in the genes!

Seminar exercises

Discussion topics

1   Outline the three cornerstones of brand culture. Discuss which you think is the most important.
2   What are the different ways in which employees can influence a brand's culture during their interactions with customers? Thinking of your own experiences, identify an incident with an employee that has helped you form an opinion about a brand.

3 How do brands help us create and maintain our identities? Think of your own relationship with brands. What are your favourites and how do you think these are consistent (or not) with how you see yourself?

4 Identify a brand community and analyse it in terms of the three markers of community as identified by Muniz and O'Guinn (2001).

Group exercises

1 Take a brand of your choice and put together a presentation about its brand culture.

- What do you think are the different influences on its brand culture?
- What are the brand's core values and how have these evolved?

2 Search through marketing magazines, newspaper reports and marketing websites to identify a recent case of brand tainting (other than those discussed in the chapter).

- Document what happened to cause the tainting.
- How could this have been prevented?
- What should the brand do now to try to overcome the associations of tainting?

3 Investigate more about the classic Mini's history and compare this to the launch of the new BMW MINI.

- Why is there a potential clash of brand cultures?
- How do you think BMW could have used the Mini brand community to their advantage?

Internet resources

The famous activist magazine, *Adbusters*: www.adbusters.org
MINI car website: www.mini.co.uk/
Mini car forums: www.theminiforum.co.uk/forums/
Professor Jonathan Schroeder's interview: https://vimeo.com/670432
An article by Bernard Cova, Olivier Badot and Ampelio Bucci: http://visionary marketing.com/en/blog/2006/07/beyond-marketing-in-praise-of-societing-by-bernard-cova-olivier-badot-ampelio-bucci/

Key readings

Arvidsson, A. (2006). *Brands, meaning and value in a media culture*. London: Routledge.

Cova, B., Pace, S. and Skalen, P. (2015). Brand volunteering: Value co-creation with unpaid consumers. *Marketing Theory*, 15(4): 465–485.

Holt, D.B. (2004). *How brands become icons: The principles of cultural branding*. Boston, MA: Harvard Business Press.

Schroeder, J.E. and Salzer-Mörling, M. (eds) (2006). *Brand culture*. London: Routledge.

References

Aaker, J., Fournier, S. and Brasel, S.A. (2004). When good brands do bad. *Journal of Consumer Research*, 31 (June): 1–16.

Arnould, E. (2008). Commercial mythology and the global organization of consumption. *Advances in Consumer Research*, 35: 67–71.

Balmer, J.M.T. (2006). Corporate brand culture and communities. In J.E. Schroeder and M. Salzer-Mörling (eds), *Brand culture*. London: Routledge, pp. 34–49.

Beh, K.H. (2008). Unity in diversity? Relationships in the Mini brand community. Unpublished doctoral dissertation, De Montfort University.

Cova, B. and Cova, V. (2002). Tribal marketing: The tribalisation of society and its impact on the conduct of marketing. *European Journal of Marketing*, 36(5/6): 595–620.

Cova, B. and Dali, D. (2009). Working consumers: The next step in marketing theory? *Marketing Theory*, 9(3): 31–339.

Dessart, L., Veloutsou, C. and Morgan-Thomas, A. (2015). Consumer engagement in online brand communities: a social media perspective. *Journal of Product and Brand Management*, 24(1): 28–42.

Elliott, R. and Wattanasuwan, K. (1998). Brands as symbolic resources for the construction of identity. *International Journal of Advertising*, 17: 131–144.

Fournier, S. (1998). Consumers and their brands: Developing relationship theory in consumer research. *Journal of Consumer Research*, 24 (March): 343–373.

Heath, J. and Potter, A. (2005). *The rebel sell: How the counterculture became consumer culture*. Chichester: Capstone Publishing.

Holt, D.B. (2002). Why do brands cause trouble? A dialectical theory of consumer culture and branding. *Journal of Consumer Research*, 29 (June): 70–90.

Ind, N. (2007). *Living the brand: How to transform every member of your organization into a brand champion*. London: Kogan Page.

Kahn, B. (2005). Brand rehab: How companies can restore a tarnished image. Knowledge@Wharton. http://knowledge.wharton.upenn.edu/article.cfm?articleid=1279

Kozinets, R.V. (1999). E-tribalized marketing? The strategic implications of virtual communities of consumption. *European Journal of Marketing*, 17(3): 252–264.

Kozinets, R.V., de Valck, K., Wojnicki, A.C. and Wilner, S.J.S. (2010). Networked narratives: Understanding word-of-mouth marketing in online communities. *Journal of Marketing*, 74 (March): 71–89.

Lury, C. (2004). *Brands: The Logos of the global economy*. London: Routledge.

Maclaran, P. and Brown, S. (2005). The center cannot hold: Consuming the utopian marketplace. *Journal of Consumer Research*, 32 (September): 311–323.

Maclaran, P. and Stevens, L. (2009). Magners man: Irish cider, representations of masculinity and the 'burning Celtic soul'. *Irish Marketing Review*, 20(2): 77–88.

Manchanda, P., Packard, G. and Pattabhiramaiah, A. (2012). Social dollars: The economic impact of consumer participation in a firm-sponsored online community. Marketing Science Institute, *MSI report*, 11–115.

Marketing Digest (2007). Brand-ish opinion. www.ameinfo.com/news/Marketing_Digest/

Milligan, A. (2004). *Brand it like Beckham: The story of how Brand Beckham was built*. London: Cyan Books.

Muniz, A.M., Jr. and O'Guinn, T.C. (2001). Brand community. *Journal of Consumer Research*, 27(4): 412–432.

Muniz, A.M., Jr. and Schau, H.C. (2005). Religiosity in the abandoned Apple Newton brand community. *Journal of Consumer Research*, 31 (March): 737–747.

Schroeder, J.E. (2007). Video interview with Professor Jonathan Schroeder. www.revver.com/video/662442/jump-in-11-professor-jonathan-schroeder/

Schroeder, J.E. and Salzer-Mörling, M. (2006). Introduction to the cultural codes of branding. In J.E. Schroeder and M. Salzer-Mörling (eds), *Brand culture*. London: Routledge, pp. 1–12.

Schultz, M. and Hatch, M.J. (2006). A cultural perspective on corporate branding: The case of LEGO Group. In J.E. Schroeder and M. Salzer-Mörling (eds), *Brand culture*. London: Routledge, pp. 15–33.

Simmons, J. (2006). *Innocent: Making a brand from nothing but fruit*. London: Cyan.

Strate, L. (1992). Beer commercials: A manual on masculinity. In S. Craig (ed.), *Men, masculinity and the media*. Newbury Park, CA: SAGE, pp. 78–92.

Thompson, C.J. (1997). Marketplace mythology and discourses of power. *Journal of Consumer Research*, 31 (June): 162–180.

Thompson, C.J. and Tian, K. (2008). Reconstructing the south: How commercial myths compete for identity value through the ideological shaping of popular memories and countermemories. *Journal of Consumer Research*, 34 (February): 519–613.

4 Gender, feminism and consumer behaviour

Introduction

Sociologists, philosophers and feminists, to name but a few, have long been at pains to explain and differentiate experiences of men and women in order to better understand what it is to be male and what it is to be female. This ground has been trodden very carefully and rigorously in the past. So we might ask, what have marketing and consumer researchers got to bring to the table? There are two possible answers here. Firstly, the marketplace plays a central role in perpetuating norms and stereotypes of masculinity and femininity and these stereotypes have a very real impact on our everyday lives. Consider for example the role of advertising in promoting super thin female body ideals and couple this with the stream of adverts promoting diets, diet medications and low fat foods. Perhaps it is no surprise that eating disorders have increased by an average of 7 percent per year in England since 2009 (Beat, 2015). These market-driven stereotypes don't only impact on image but also on roles and expectations. Consider the average washing powder or breakfast cereal advert which presents the ideal selfless mother figure working hard to meet the needs of her family. These stereotypes and norms are not just presented to us literally in advertising but more subtly in other ways through store environments (the pink and frilly world of Claire's Accessories) or product design (Kleenex's Mansize Tissues and Gillette's 'Best a Man Can Get'). So the marketplace sends us a series of signals about what it is to be masculine or feminine and how to behave as a man or a woman in society. Secondly, the marketplace positions us hierarchically in relation to one another through the opportunities it provides (in terms of jobs, housing, education, etc.). Research shows that very often access to these opportunities is still unequal between men and women. As such gender inequalities and indeed gendered experiences are inextricably linked with marketplace dynamics. As marketers and consumer researchers we are tasked with teasing out these links and understanding how inequalities are perpetuated and how they might be changed.

In this chapter we start by exploring perspectives on gender (or how gender has been theorised) in marketing and consumer research studies. We follow this with a consideration of how gender has been understood and researched within marketing. We go on to analyse how masculinities and femininities have been portrayed and perpetuated in the marketplace through advertising. We then explore the issue of gender and roles within the family discussing how mothering and fathering are mediated by consumption practices.

Perspectives on gender: the four waves of feminist research

The way in which gender has been researched and understood has differed quite significantly over the past century. It is possible to discern a series of 'waves' of feminist research (Maclaran, 2015). Of course these waves overlap significantly and their boundaries are very blurred, but they are a useful device to help us understand the perspectives we hold about gender today.

First- and second-wave feminism: women's rights and changing legislation

The first wave of feminism began in the 1850s and was largely concerned with getting women the vote but also promoting women's rights in employment and education. This movement focused on changing legislation that militated against women. This first wave of feminism has a long history of around a hundred years and provided the backdrop to a rather more focused and formally organised *second wave* which emerged in the 1960s. This wave continued to be concerned with changing legislation notably in the areas of equal pay and access to credit but also in marital rights, abortion and childcare. However, perhaps just as importantly this wave was concerned with changing social attitudes towards women. Feminists in the second wave invented the phrase 'the personal is the political' to highlight that patriarchy and sexism had infiltrated into virtually every aspect of women's public and private lives. Here Betty Friedan's *Feminine Mystique* (1963) made an important contribution. For the book Friedan interviewed suburban housewives in America and researched the way in which women were presented in the media and advertising. She reveals how unhappy many women were in their domestic roles in the 1950s and early 1960s. She found that while imagery in the media and advertising presented women as ultimately fulfilled by domestic work and childrearing, the real experiences of women were vastly different as they reported feelings of isolation, frustration and boredom. She argues that not only did advertising present unrealistic images of women but that, much more insidiously, these adverts were intended to discourage women from having careers outside the home. Instead they were encouraged to see themselves as domestic professionals, a ready-made target market for a widening array of household products. A good contemporary depiction of this state of affairs is the 2008 film *Revolutionary Road* where Kate Winslet stars as the hapless wife desperate to escape the hopeless emptiness of American suburban life. In her book *Desperate Housewives, Neurosis and the Domestic Environment, 1945–1970* (2016), Ali Haggett also nicely captures the domestic boredom and stultification of the postwar years, but this time in the UK. In fact the image of the 'desperate housewife' continues to resonate today – for example in the contemporary American TV series of the same name where a veneer of suburban bliss hides a series of dark undercurrents. A second book that encapsulates the spirit of the second wave is Germaine Greer's (1970) *The Female Eunuch*. Greer's target was also the issue of female oppression. She argues that historically the norms that women use to measure their perception of self and their role in society were shaped by male expectations. She calls on women to challenge these norms, reject their traditional roles, question the power of authority figures and explore their own sexuality. Written in a direct, easy to read and witty style, the book is probably the most widely read feminist text ever published.

Third-wave feminism: new perspectives

The third wave of feminism in the 1990s saw an opening out of the movement to encompass a much wider range of issues including not only gender but also race, class, disability and ethnicity. This wave was also characterised by the recognition of multiple feminisms – the idea that there wasn't only one way to be a feminist. This brought with it a questioning and blurring of the binary categories of men versus women acknowledging that these boundaries were not clear cut. One key thinker who promoted a questioning of the gender binary is Judith Butler, who argued in her book *Undoing Gender* (1990) that gender, rather than being a biological given, is performed through social interaction. Thinking along these lines means that men are not automatically masculine and women feminine but that masculinity and femininity are enacted in social life. This approach to understanding gender draws attention to the instability of the categories male and female, questioning the societal norms that underpin them and highlighting the way in which they include and exclude groups and individuals. One key idea that emerged here was that of 'heteronormativity', a term first coined by Warner (1991) to describe the ways in which heterosexuality pervades institutional, cultural and legal norms in society. In heteronormative societies, gender is viewed as the outward expression of an innate, biological essence of sex wherein opposite-sex desire ultimately renders gender intelligible (Butler, 1990). For instance, the gender identity of masculine men who desire women is intelligible whereas according to 'inversion theory' men who desire men are not, as they are assumed to be women trapped in male bodies. For Butler, this coherence of sex/gender/ desire, in other words, heteronormativity, is sustained through discourse and regulatory practices that span the various institutional, cultural and daily spheres, and it is key to contemporary understandings of gender.

Thus feminist thinking began to recognise the way in which gender intersects with other categories (such as race, class, sexuality, disability and ethnicity) to include some groups in society and exclude others. This way of thinking, termed intersectionality, stemmed from the inclusion of a wider range of feminist voices in the debate to embrace for example theories of race (hook 1981) and queer studies (Sedgwick, 1990). The marketplace mirrored and harnessed this celebration of difference by tapping into the idea that identity was something that could be bought and sold. Companies began to appeal more and more to the consumer as an 'individual' that would buy their products to construct and maintain their identity. They achieved this through increasingly fine-grained and sophisticated market segmentation which not only embraced categories such as gender, age and class but identified segments on the basis of 'lifestyle'. This mode of lifestyle marketing sought out groups whose aim might have been to resist or counteract mainstream culture in order to sell to them – or perhaps harness their countercultural values and sell them to a wider audience. Feminism ultimately became the target and feminist values and dispositions were repackaged (and watered down) for mainstream consumption. Key examples of this are the idea of 'girl power' promoted by groups such as the Spice Girls and the 'pink pound' which touted female empowerment as their key selling point. On the face of it this might not seem problematic, after all it is evidence of women moving into the media spotlight and participating more fully in the marketplace. The problem though, as feminists argued, was that the market only ever appeals to the individual in its efforts to persuade them to consume. This had the effect of dispersing the collective power of feminism and other collective movements. The feminist project faltered as postfeminism (also sometimes referred to as choice feminism) took hold in popular culture (Munford and Waters, 2014) and with it came the idea that women (Western women anyway) had all the choices available to men, and thus feminism was no longer relevant to society.

Fourth-wave feminism: an online revolution?

The fourth wave of feminism which arguably emerged around 2008 represents a backlash against the idea of 'choice feminism' in making attempts to reclaim female bodies from the marketplace (Cochrane, 2013; Stevens and Houston, 2016). In many ways this wave continues the second-wave project of seeking change in social attitudes towards women, but it also embraces the idea of blurred boundaries and multiple feminisms introduced in the third wave. However, the key characteristic of this movement is that it harnesses the power of the internet and social media to create a new space in which to reorder gendered inequalities, critique and question dominant representations of women (such as those in the media and advertising) and take back power in setting the agenda for the way in which women choose to present themselves. In this sense the internet facilitates a globalised 'call-out' culture in which instances of racism and sexism can be 'called out' and challenged. There has been an explosion of feminist blogs, social media campaigns and online organising which has given form and voice to a range of thought leaders and grassroots activists. The number of women using digital spaces is on the rise. And, according to a recent report, women aged between 18 and 29 are the 'power users of social networking' (Martin and Valenti, 2012). There is also evidence that women in countries where inequalities and injustices are part of everyday life are really starting to engage with social media. In Turkey for example, women make up 72 percent of social media users (Martin and Valenti, 2012).

These initiatives act as a form of consciousness raising, building on existing debates and exposing those debates to a wider than ever range of global participants. One good example is the Doula Project which is an organisation that provides care and support for women across the spectrum of pregnancy to include birth, miscarriage, stillbirth, foetal anomaly or abortion. They use the online environment as a vital platform for their activities. The sites Women in Media and News, and the Women's Room are education and advocacy groups which work to create a space for women in the media. The F Word is an online magazine which includes debate and discussion about contemporary feminism. Very often there is a symbiosis between online and offline activity with many campaigns such as Freethenipple (a campaign which opposes sexual objectification of women), the Everyday Sexism Project (which catalogues experiences of sexism in everyday life) and No More Page 3 (a campaign opposing *The Sun* newspaper's publication of topless women), creating a seamless relation between online blogs, twitter feeds and video material and offline events such as seminars, rallies and support groups. With hundreds of new sites popping up every month it is impossible even to capture the variety of issues covered and the array of creative interventions feminists are using on this platform. Important from a marketing perspective though is the power of these groupings in calling out the big brands on their activities. Facebook were forced to deal with the hundreds of instances of gender-based hate speech and shut down offensive pages as a result of the #FBrape campaign. Critiques of Dove's Real Beauty campaign appeared all over the pages of feminist blogs and twitter feeds, as 'peddling the same old beauty standards'.

However, this communication format is not without its challenges. For example, the limited Twitter feed allowance of 140 characters and the Facebook 'like' facilities arguably encourage a shallow and binary (yes/no) engagement with debates. Also the format may be encouraging individualistic judgements as opposed to collective solidarity.

Recently the big brands have started to get in on the act themselves, perhaps another example of the way in which consumer capitalism has modified itself to subsume countercultural ideas in the pursuit of profit (Wechie, 2016). It seems that elements of fourth-wave feminism have become marketplace fodder in the guise of Femvertising. Brands have begun to use hashtag feminism to sell products by launching feminist-oriented social media campaigns. For example, the energy company EDF have launched #prettycurious, a campaign to encourage young women into jobs where they have traditionally been underrepresented such as science, technology, engineering and maths. Cosmetics brand CoverGirl's #GirlsCan campaign, fronted by Pink, Ellen DeGeneres and Janelle Monae, is aimed at breaking down barriers for girls. Pantene's #Shine Strong included a short film titled 'Sorry, Not Sorry' which highlighted how women constantly apologise in a range of situations at home and at work. The video went viral. These are just some examples of brands' use of the idea of female empowerment to sell products and services. The question remains as to whether they do in fact empower young women or really take the goal of gender inequality seriously. Instead perhaps they merely key into ideas of empowerment and solidarity that make young women feel good rather than actually doing much about the fact that they don't already feel good about themselves.

Gender, feminism and marketing

Historically speaking, gender in general has not been very well understood by marketers. Typically used as a segmentation tool it has been viewed very much as an either/or, male/female binary. Rather than seeing gender as dynamic and socially produced it has been used by marketers as just another way of ascribing people to categories with little recognition of the politics of this process. The subtleties of associated forms of sexuality have also been largely sidelined in this approach. One of the problems has been a lack of communication between marketers and sociologists and feminist theorists working on the topic of gender in the marketplace. Until a point in the late 1980s and early 1990s these lines of communication were quite closed with marketers continuing to work in isolation, which resulted in rather outdated understandings of gender. However, the last twenty years have seen dramatic leaps in the way in which gender is understood and researched. This may be attributed to the increase in women working in university business schools (Stern, 1996) and marketing organisations (Maclaran et al., 1997).

One study that really made a difference to our understanding of gender and marketing looked at the language used in academia to talk about the relationships between marketers and consumers (Fischer and Bristor, 1994). The study found that this language wasn't value free but rather that it reproduced notions of patriarchy through painting marketers in masculine terms (as patriarch) and consumers in feminine terms (as seduced by the market/marketers). This conflation of consumption with femininity and the notion that shopping is largely the preserve of women still holds sway today. Another early feminist criticism of consumer research called for a re-examination of the (very gendered) principles underlying this work, thus rejecting 'pervasive, systemic assumptions about women and about gender that reflect ungrounded stereotypes and beliefs' (Bristor and Fischer, 1993: 518). Bristor and Fischer (1993) use feminist theory to critique which topics we choose to research (problematics) and how we theorise these topics; but also how we then collect and analyse data in consumer research. For example they argue that research questions often don't fully consider the relational (feminine) aspects of consumption and that problems are often formulated to serve male interests as opposed to reflecting female experiences. They also critique the view of gender which sees differences as biologically based observing that gender is socially constructed and variable within as well as between the sexes. In data analysis they find tendencies to simplify and exaggerate sex differences. In sum their study really highlights how pervasive masculine thinking was in the discipline at this point in the early 1990s, influencing not only the *choice of* topics researched but the way in which those topics are researched.

A third key study during this period argued that it is also important to focus on the body itself as a locus through which gender (and inequality) are reproduced (Joy and Venkatesh, 1994). The authors argue in their study of body rituals such as diet and make-up that women's bodies are significantly mediated and shaped by consumer culture. They observe that marketing practitioners have colonised the human body, especially the female human body, for commercial ends. They make a call for us to deconstruct and critique marketing practices in order for women to 're-make their bodies' (p. 333).

More recent work has taken further steps to bring the body back in to better understand how the marketplace constructs and constrains gendered identity. One study (Harju and Huovinen, 2015) examines how plus-sized women cope with the marginalised identity positions offered to them by the fashion marketplace. The study reveals how this group of women use online blogging to resist and reframe normative constructions of beauty. Indeed, as we discuss above in relation to fourth-wave feminism, the online environment offers a space in which women can take control over the way in which their bodies are represented. Along these lines a study by Matich et al. (2016) has explored an example of an online campaign, #freethenipple, which attempts to disrupt patriarchal framings of the breast as inherently sexual and the associated practices of concealment and censorship. Campaigners do this by posting their own pictures of their breasts on Instagram. This diversity of images deliberately demonstrates the radically unruly, complex and non-uniform nature of the breast in attempting to interrupt patriarchal attempts to fix its meaning.

Stereotypes and gender roles in advertising

There has been a continued focus on the way in which marketing practices reinforce notions of masculinity and femininity, particularly in advertising. Visual representations of men and women, of masculinity and femininity, are complex but importantly they gain their meaning through being juxtaposed against each other.

> Within this system, iconic masculine activities such as shaving the face, driving fast cars, having a hearty appetite, smoking cigars, and drinking liquor are juxtaposed to feminine visions of applying makeup, driving a minivan, eating 'light', doing the laundry, and decorating houses.
>
> (Schroeder and Zwick, 2004: 21)

As this quotation suggests, these images are not just flat two-dimensional representations; they suggest appropriate modes of dress and appearance but also, more significantly, they suggest appropriate *activities*, ways of doing, living and being masculine and feminine. Further, as the author above argues, advertising does not act on its own, rather it is part of a *system* of meaning which involves both advertising and consumption – responding to and acting out these representations through our consumption activities reinforces them and gives them meaning.

The problem with this is that most often these images remain largely elusive to us, as they are exaggerated stereotypes and perfected images which bear little resemblance to everyday reality. Consider the heavily made-up, translucent skinned images of femininity in cosmetics adverts or the chiselled and muscled images of masculinity in aftershave adverts. These images are a long way from lived reality for most of us. The clothing retailer H&M recently tried to slim down images of the singer Beyoncé in one of their swimwear campaigns; after significant pressure from the celebrity herself they ended up running the original advert. The skincare brands L'Oréal and Olay have also been forced to withdraw adverts due to the overuse of airbrushing to remove wrinkles and make skin appear flawless. However, some brands are making real attempts to change things. Marketers have begun to address women in all of their various lumps, bumps, shapes and sizes in order to better reflect the reality of everyday life. The Dove Campaign for Real Beauty launched in 2004 used regular women in place of models. This campaign was accompanied by a whole series of associated initiatives including: an online discussion forum, fundraising to help girls with low self-esteem, self-esteem workshops and the establishment of the Program for Aesthetics and Well-Being at Harvard University. The campaign was also followed up by a series of others involving real women. Unilever defined this approach using the mission strategy: 'To make women feel comfortable in the skin they are in, to create a world where beauty is a source of confidence and not anxiety' (Unilever, cited in Vega, 2013). This approach has had mixed responses with some women finding it empowering showing that beauty comes in many guises, while other women argued that this was just another clever attempt at manipulation and that because Dove is a beauty brand, it still reinforces the message that beauty defines women.

The Dove campaign is just one example of a recent trend in advertising which has been called femvertising or pro-female advertising. These adverts have taken up the feminist mantra of female empowerment and used it to sell a range of products from energy (EDF), to yoghurt drinks (Organic Valley), clothes (JCPenney), beer (Budweiser), software (Microsoft) and shampoo (Pantene). These adverts tackle a range of issues including the objectification of women in particular, combatting stereotypical negative portrayals of women in terms of body shape, sexuality, strength and intelligence. The women's media company Sheknows Media have instituted an annual #femvertising award in order to 'honor brands that are challenging gender norms by building stereotype-busting, pro-female messages and images into ads that target women' (Sheknows Media website).

As we suggested earlier, a key criticism of advertising concerns its promotion of gender stereotypes, significantly impacting on the way we think about male and female roles within society. Think about the happy Oxo family of the 1980s and 1990s with mum serving up dinner, or the Fairy Liquid mum who is always at the kitchen sink. However, adverts have started to embrace at least some of the diversity that exists in family roles. For example, a recent Oxo advert includes Dad giving cooking advice to his son as he tries to make a stir-fry for his girlfriend. Or a McDonald's advert in which a single mum asks her boyfriend to move in with her and her two children.

However there is still a long way to go though in representing diversity in advertising. A study found that 80 percent of disabled people feel under-represented by TV and the media (Scope, 2016). Only very recently have people with disabilities appeared in mainstream advertising (see for example the Mal-tesers 'Look on the Light Side' series of adverts). In addition, LGBT people are still sorely underrepresented with Nike making a big deal of airing its first advert featuring a transgender athlete this year. The appearance of multiracial individuals in advertising is on the rise, for example celebrities such as Halle Berry, Tiger Woods and Mariah Carey. But a study which explores the representation of multiracial identity in advertising finds that these depictions are positioned as a new standard of beauty and as a racial bridge rather than an accurate reflection of everyday multiracial identity (Harrison et al., 2016).

Markets and motherhood

Pregnancy, motherhood and consumption are inextricably intertwined in contemporary Western cultures. This relationship between mothers and markets is two way – with women's experiences of mothering being significantly shaped by the marketplace but equally with women using the marketplace to shape and make sense of these experiences. Thus we might consider the making of mothers *by* the marketplace but also what mothers make *out of* the marketplace (O'Donohoe et al., 2014).

Thinking first about the ways in which mothers are made by the marketplace we might consider the role that advertising plays in shaping our conceptions and expectations of mothering (Hogg et al., 2011). A study which explored the way in which motherhood has been depicted in food advertising in *Good Housekeeping* magazine found a series of ideal archetypes that were promoted across the period 1950–2010 (Marshall et al., 2014). In the 1950s mothers were depicted in the role of nurturers very much tied to the home. In the 1960s and 1970s mothers were still tied to the domestic sphere but alongside their role of nurturers they were increasingly presented as experts – encapsulated in the phrase 'mother knows best'. In the 1980s narratives of mothering in the magazine move away from the domestic sphere; they also shift towards health and well-being – particularly in relation to child rearing. So advertising serves to shape mothering by depicting specific modes of mothering and ideal motherly types. However, it also acts in a more direct manner by appealing to the anxieties that surround mothering. A study of advertising used by Danonino (a children's dairy brand) in five European countries found that the adverts dealt with five kinds of anxieties (Coutant et al., 2011). These anxieties were linked to children's growth, intellectual development, exclusion from peer groups, family bonding relationships and lack of parental presence. The study found that once they had presented the risk the adverts then offered a resolution in the form of their own products to maintain mothers' peace of mind. This is just one example of the way in which brands routinely play on existing parental, but in particular motherly anxieties and indeed create new ones in order to sell products. As such advertising significantly shapes motherly experiences and expectations.

Turning to think about what mothers make *out of* the marketplace, mothers have increasingly been encouraged to use consumer goods to buy their way into their identity as mothers (Thomson et al., 2011). In this sense motherhood is seen as something that can be achieved or accomplished through consumption. Good, or successful, mothering is intertwined with a series of consumption projects. At the domestic level this may be as simple as creating a family meal (Cappellini and Parsons, 2012). At the public level objects themselves and the ways in which they are used, styled together and displayed may play a significant role in mothering. Here we can find examples of objects and brands which have come to stand as models of classed mothering: 'What the stigmatized dummy (or "dirty-did") is to some model of compromised working-class motherhood, the Bugaboo pram is to "achieved middle class" motherhood' (Clarke, 2014: 50). These examples highlight that choosing and using products within the practice of mothering is not as straightforward as it may first seem. The assumptions that mothering should be second nature and that knowing how to mother is a pre-existing disposition for women put significant pressure on choices of what to buy, where to buy and how to use these products and brands. This is even more the case considering that practices of mothering are often very public and open to scrutiny. There is a premium attached to getting it right and a risk of failure in getting it wrong. As Miller (2014: 161) observes: 'The contours of successful motherhood can be seen as a socially constructed performance, which is increasingly managed and "read" through the consumer goods and consumption patterns which signal and facilitate its successful accomplishment'. Therefore, products and brands don't always help in the project of motherhood. While sometimes they may act as props to the doing of mothering, at other times the array of products and brands available and their promoted uses may be bewildering and may even jeopardise attempts at managing impressions as a new mother (Miller, 2014).

Markets and fatherhood

Arguably, contemporary fatherhood is not as deeply intertwined with the marketplace and consumption as motherhood. This may well be because as yet the market of fathers for many child-focused products is simply not as big as the market of mothers. Put simply in Western contexts at least, mothers are still doing most of the shopping for child- (and family-) focused products – they are therefore still the main target for marketing activity (Coffey et al., 2006). In addition, we know much less about fatherhood per se from a marketing and consumption perspective because it has been the focus of fewer studies. This is largely due to the privileging of men in society through the operation of masculine hegemony. Studies have therefore tended to focus on the ways in which women have been marginalised and oppressed through the operation of the marketplace and studies into men and masculinity have been seen as a less pressing concern.

The relationship between men and their role as fathers may well be more complex and conflictual than between women and their role as mothers. This might be because of the deeply entrenched social and cultural link between women and mothering in many cultures. This link is weaker for men who seem to have a wider range of roles open to them, and the norms surrounding fathering that do exist often conflict with those surrounding masculinity (Gentry and Harrison, 2010). Men also feel detached and isolated from what is seen as a very woman-centred process of parenting. So, while in the discussion above about mothering we found that the marketplace tended to give mothers a series of relatively clear signals about what constitutes 'good mothering', it seems that for fathers things are more blurred. Rather than giving clear signals about fathering the marketplace offers men a tapestry of resources that they use to cope with some of the role conflicts they experience in becoming fathers. Navigating the marketplace is not that easy for fathers though. A study which explored the role of mundane caring technological objects (such as baby monitors and baby rockers) in the transition to new fatherhood found them to be largely ambivalent (Bettany et al., 2014). These technologies smoothed but also exacerbated fatherhood role conflict and gender struggles in the home.

It is still largely the case that fatherhood is linked to the public arena of paid employment whereas motherhood is still wedded to the domestic sphere. This means that stay-at-home fathers find that they occupy a marginalised role status in society that contradicts the traditional breadwinner role. A study of at-home fathers who previously were breadwinners in their homes finds that they use consumption to legitimise this marginalised status (Coskuner-Balli and Thompson, 2013). To regain some status they create a distinctive gender identity which is neither masculine breadwinner nor feminine carer and nurturer but which draws on elements of both of these positions. Thus fathers seem to engage in a form of productive domestic consumption which reproduces their socialisation into the world of work and which contrasts with the typical depiction of mothers as consuming as part of the wider project of care and nurture. A study of men and DIY in the home nicely illustrates this (Moiso et al., 2013). The study finds that men with low levels of cultural capital view their domestic DIY as a form of work likening the home to a workplace, whereas men with existing high levels of cultural capital see DIY as a leisure activity. A Finnish study examined a range of materials that offer advice surrounding fathering, including a parenting manual, a textbook, a guide for professionals and government sources on fatherhood and parenting (Eraranta and Moisander, 2011). They found that there was a wide chasm between advice and depiction of fathering in these texts and the sorts of behaviours that were required in the workplace. Depictions of good fathering included involved fathering, with ideals of caring and family-oriented parenting. However, this does not readily match with the ideals surrounding the committed employee who is available and able to work long hours. In sum this results in conflicts for men surrounding their identities as workers and as fathers.

Just as advertising shapes conceptions of mothering in direct ways it also shapes conceptions of fathering. Advertising studies have shown that male portrayals still reflect a very traditional masculine perspective (Gentry and Harrison, 2010). These hyper-masculine portrayals can be problematic because they often clash with the more caring and nurturing roles required of fatherhood. This portrayal therefore is the cause of male confusion concerning what masculine roles are expected of them. However, things do seem to be changing, as interestingly in 2016 a new category was added to the #femvertising competition mentioned earlier titled 'Dadvertising', to encompass adverts that directly target and counteract stereotypical portrayals of fatherhood.

In summary then it seems from the limited studies to date on the links between fatherhood and the market that (in Western contexts at least) fathers are not a target for marketers to the same extent as mothers are. Equally it seems that the market has nowhere near as pervasive a role in shaping expectations of fathering and indeed shaping the notion of what it is to be a good father. Undoubtedly, as society changes and fathers continue to take on a more central role in relation to parenting the market will morph and reflect these changes. In the future it is likely that we will see fathers as a target market emerging much more clearly.

Summary

This chapter has explored the range of ways in which marketing activity and the thinking (or ideology) behind it serves to impact on gendered experience. It does this by offering the resources for identity construction. Here adverts, store environments and even products themselves send often very subtle messages about what it is to be a man or woman in today's society. They send messages about what it is to be masculine, what it is to be feminine and they send more explicit messages about ideals of beauty and body shape and size. They also send messages about gendered roles within society – what it means to be a good mother or a good father. However, the relationship between individuals and the marketplace is complex. As consumers we don't blindly accept these messages but we use and reshape them in our own individual contexts to make sense of our experiences. As such the jury is out as to er, when it comes to gender at least, the consumer is ultimately duped and exploited or creative and empowered.

CASE STUDY: femvertising – selling empowerment

Feminist theory: Throwing Like a Girl

In 1980 the political philosopher and feminist Iris Marion Young wrote an essay which she titled 'Throwing Like a Girl'. In the essay Young explores the issue of embodiment, i.e. how we live in our bodies, how we move them, understand them and experience them, and how this differs between the sexes. She describes the way in which women (and girls) tend to be overcautious and self-conscious about their bodies, leading to feelings within themselves that they are incapable. She argues that this is a socially conditioned mind-set though, that women are conditioned to limit their bodily abilities. Vitally, she argues that this is because their bodies are often seen by others as mere objects (they are objectified) and that women sometimes internalise this and are therefore very self-conscious about their body, worrying about how they look to others. Thus when engaging in activities like sport women, instead of focusing on what they aim to do (e.g. hit a target), self-consciously focus on what their body needs to do.

> We often experience our bodies as a fragile encumbrance, rather than the media for the enactment of our aims. We feel as though we must have our attention directed upon our bodies to make sure they are doing what we wish them to do, rather than paying attention to what we want to do through our bodies.
>
> (Young, 1980: 146–7)

'Throwing Like a Girl' is also a phrase that has passed into common usage with negative connotations of inadequacy and lack of power and direction. In fact to do anything 'like a girl' is generally seen to be both ineffective and not to be taken seriously.

Femvertising: Always #LikeAGirl campaign

Fast forward thirty-four years to 2014 and the sanitary product brand Always release their advertising campaign #LikeAGirl. The campaign builds significantly on the ideas in Young's 1980 essay. It is a good example of a growing trend that has been called 'femvertising', which is said to draw on feminist values of female empowerment to target women and encourage them to consume (Iqbal, 2015).

The creatives at the advertising agency Leo Burnett designed what they called a 'social experiment' where they asked people of both sexes, young and old, to show them what it was like to do things 'like a girl'. So in an individual interview they asked them to 'throw like a girl', 'fight like a girl' and 'run like a girl'. What they found was that many of the older participants (male and female) ran, threw and fought in half-hearted and ineffective ways, appearing 'sissy' and putting in little effort. But when they asked the younger girls the same question they ran, threw and fought in uninhibited, energetic and determined ways. In essence the young girls gave it their best shot. The interviews were captured on film. The final cut included sequences of the older participants' half-hearted activities set against the young girls' uninhibited and determined activities. Sequences also included interview material where they asked participants to reflect on their depictions asking them what 'like a girl' meant for them. Towards the end of the advert the text 'Let's make #likeagirl mean amazing things' appears on the screen.

The campaign quickly went viral and in the year that followed notched up more than 50 million YouTube views. The advert was aired at the 2015 Super Bowl and was named by CBS as one of the top 3 Super Bowl commercials of all time. It has won a plethora of industry awards, including the 2015 Emmy Award for Outstanding Commercial, the Grand Clio Award, a Cannes Grand Prix, a Black Pencil and a White Pencil at D&AD and eleven Webby Awards. The campaign was designed at Leo Burnett, with the London, Chicago and Toronto offices collaborating on the advert. The lead creative was Judy John (CEO Canada and Chief Creative Officer North America at Leo Burnett). John has an impressive CV with over twenty-five years' experience in copywriting and creative directing in advertising. She was ranked No. 1 Chief Creative Officer in the World in *Advertising Age's* Awards Report 2015 and No. 8 in *Business Insider's* 30 Most Creative People in Advertising. Hopefully in the future John won't be an anomaly as a woman in the upper echelons of the advertising industry. To tip the balance more women are still needed in advertising creative departments.

The parent company of the Always brand (Procter and Gamble, P&G) augment the advertising campaign through a series of other initiatives. In the developed-country context P&G are focusing on providing puberty education resources for girls. Their Schools Programme has developed kits containing information on puberty for parents and lesson plans and materials for teachers. They have developed a similar set of resources to build confidence and help keep girls in sports. They launched the Always Confidence Teaching Curriculum in 2015 with conferences in ten cities around the globe featuring thought leaders, educators and inspiring young girls. The curriculum was created in partnership with confidence and education experts.

In developing countries P&G work with partners such as local ministries of education and non-governmental organisations such as Save the Children and organisations like Girlology to deliver puberty education. The programme has been endorsed by UNESCO and is active in more than sixty-five countries. Due to a lack of sanitary products, girls in underprivileged areas are often forced to skip school. P&G have partnered with the Department of Basic Education, UNICEF, the Small Projects Foundation and other stakeholders to initiate a programme which delivers sanitary towels and health education to girls in these areas to help keep them in school. P&G have also teamed up with UNESCO to offer a literacy education programme in Africa. In 2016 the programme had reached around 60,000 girls in Nigeria and Senegal, mainly through information and communication technologies. P&G intend to extend the programme to reach a further 50,000 girls and women in northern Nigeria by the end of 2019. P&G also contributed to the UN Women's 'One Win Leads to Another' programme in 2016. The programme began in Brazil offering 10–18-year-old girls free sports facilities in the Olympic villas with experts providing workshops on health, preventing violence and leadership. There are plans to expand the programme globally.

Femvertising: is it really empowering?

Questions have been asked as to whether femvertising is truly empowering. As Nosheen Iqbal (2015) from *The Guardian* noted recently, 'behind the hype who is really benefitting?' Most of these campaigns use the power of the internet to reach their target audience. They rely on creating such a resonance with women's core values and beliefs that they willingly share these adverts through their social media sites such as Facebook pages and Twitter accounts. This online presence might make this trend a possible example of fourth-wave feminism with companies cashing in on riding the wave. Is this commercialisation of the feminist movement ok if it does genuinely challenge gender norms and battle inequality? As Iqbal (2015) somewhat cynically comments:

> The idea that confidence and self-belief is what the debate and struggle is missing is seductive: it encourages sisterly encouragement – likes, shares and stories told in 140 characters are easily digestible, and a soft way to get adolescents, in particular, hooked on the movement – and, of course, your brand.

A series of key issues emerge here. First, clearly this kind of questioning of existing gendered norms and stereotypes is needed within society, but are commercial organisations in the best position to do this in a fair and balanced way? Might it be possible that they are merely just selling a different brand of femininity back to us? Second, is social media the best medium to use to engage in this struggle? It allows for short, snappy and ultimately easily sharable stories to be told, but are these always the most helpful ones? In summary though perhaps the popularity and resonance of these campaigns is a little depressing, merely evidence of how little distance we have travelled in achieving true gender equality. A comment from Laura Bates, the founder of the Everyday Sexism project, sums it up nicely:

> while I applaud progress, wouldn't it be nice to live in a world where we didn't have to celebrate ad campaigns that give children equal access to

toys or don't present women in a sexist way because [those things were] just the norm?

(Davidson, 2015)

Seminar exercises

Discussion topics

1   Discuss the range of ways that the marketplace has shaped our conceptions of motherhood and fatherhood (think about the role of advertising, products and the wider media).
2   Choose a brand or product which specifically targets male or female consumers and discuss the values it promotes and how it achieves this (think about advertising, packaging, price, etc.).
3   Discuss the range of ways that feminists are making use of the internet to support their cause (see the section above on 'Fourth-wave feminism: an online revolution?' for examples). Which ones do you think are most effective and why?
4   Having read the case study above consider the ways in which Femvertising might be seen as empowering.

Group exercises

1   Ask each group member to bring in an example of an advert that they particularly like or dislike that draws on gendered norms or stereotypes (think about role portrayals as well as representations of masculinity and femininity).

    • Discuss why you particularly like or dislike the advert.
    • Explore which particular stereotype or gendered representation the advert is drawing on.
    • Discuss how you think the advert promotes the wider values of the brand.
    • Discuss whether you think the advert is likely to be successful and why.

2   Read the chapter by Marshall et al. (2014), 'Images of motherhood: Food advertising in Good Housekeeping magazine 1950–2010'.

    • Identify the different ways in which motherhood is represented in the magazine across the period studied.
    • Discuss how representations of motherhood have changed since the 1950s.
    • Discuss whether you think the depictions of motherhood are accurate and reflect real mothers. If not, why not?
    • Build a picture of a contemporary mother from your home country context. What do you think are her everyday concerns?
    • Drawing on your own experience how do you think motherhood has changed over the past twenty years?

Internet resources

Everyday Sexism project, an online platform which encourages people to post their experiences of sexism: http://everydaysexism.com/
Women's lifestyle digital media company Sheknows Media: www.sheknowsmedia.com/

Key readings

Arsel, Z., Eräranta, K. and Moisander, J. (2015). Theorising gender and gendering theory in marketing and consumer research. Special issue of *Journal of Marketing Management*, 31(15–16).
Catterall, M., Maclaran, P. and Stevens, L. (eds) (2000). *Marketing and feminism: Current issues and research*. London: Routledge.
O'Donohoe, S., Hogg, M., Maclaran, P., Martens, L. and Stevens, L. (2014). *Motherhoods, markets and consumption: The making of mothers in contemporary Western cultures*. London: Routledge.

References

Beat (2015). The costs of eating disorders: Social, health and economic impacts. PwC, February. www.beat.co.uk/assets/000/000/302/The_costs_of_eating_disorders_Final_original.pdf?1424694814
Bettany, S.M., Kerrane, B. and Hogg, M.K. (2014). The material-semiotics of fatherhood: The co-emergence of technology and contemporary fatherhood. *Journal of Business Research*, 67(7): 1544–1551.
Bristor, J.M. and Fischer, E. (1993). Feminist thought: Implications for consumer research. *Journal of Consumer Research*, 19(4): 518–536.
Butler, J. (1990). *Gender trouble and the subversion of identity*. New York: Routledge.
Cappellini, B. and Parsons, E. (2012). (Re)enacting motherhood: Self-sacrifice and abnegation in the kitchen. In R. Belk and A. Ruvio (eds), *Identity and consumption*. London: Routledge, pp. 119–128.
Clarke, A.J. (2014). Designing mothers and the market: Social class and material culture. In S. O'Donohoe, M. Hogg, P. Maclaran, L. Martens and L. Stevens (eds), *Motherhoods, markets and consumption: The making of mothers in contemporary Western cultures*. London: Routledge, pp. 43–55.
Cochrane, K. (2013). *All the rebel women: The rise of the fourth wave of feminism*. London: Guardian Shorts.
Coffey, T., Siegel, D. and Livingstone, G. (2006). *Marketing to the new super consumer: Mom and kid*. Ithaca, NY: Paramount Market Publishers.
Coskuner-Balli, G. and Thompson, C.J. (2013). The status costs of subordinate cultural capital: At-home fathers' collective pursuit of cultural legitimacy through capitalizing consumption practices. *Journal of Consumer Research*, 40(1): 19–41.
Coutant, A., de La Ville, V.I., Gram, M. and Boireau, N. (2011). Motherhood, advertising, and anxiety: A cross-cultural perspective on Danonino commercials. *Advertising and Society Review*, 12(2). Advertising Educational Foundation. Retrieved 26 September 2016, from Project MUSE database.
Davidson, L. (2015). Femvertising: Advertisers cash in on #feminism. *Telegraph*, 12 January. http://www.telegraph.co.uk/women/womens-life/11312629/Femvertising-Advertisers-cash-in-on-feminism.html

Eraranta, K. and Moisander, J. (2011). Psychological regimes of truth and father identity: Challenges for work/life integration. *Organization Studies*, 32(4): 509–526.

Fischer, E. and Bristor, J. (1994). A feminist poststructuralist analysis of the rhetoric of marketing relationships. *International Journal of Research in Marketing*, 11(4): 317–331.

Friedan, B. (1963). *The feminine mystique*. New York: W.W. Norton.

Gentry, R. and Harrison, R. (2010). Is advertising a barrier to male movement toward gender change? *Marketing Theory*, 10(1): 74–96.

Greer, G. (1970). *The female eunuch*. London: Harper Perennial.

Haggett, A. (2016). *Desperate housewives, neurosis and the domestic environment, 1945–1970*. Oxford: Routledge.

Harju, A.A. and Huovinen, A. (2015). Fashionably voluptuous: Normative femininity and resistant performative tactics in fashion blogs. *Journal of Marketing Management*, 31(15–16): 1602–1625.

Harrison, R.L., Thomas, K. and Cross, S. (2016). Visual representations of multiracial women. Paper presented at the 13th Conference on Gender, Marketing and Consumer Behaviour, 4–6 July, ESCP Europe, Paris.

Hogg, M., Maclaran, P., Martens, L., O'Donohoe, S. and Stevens, L. (2011). Special issue: (Re)creating cultural models of motherhoods in contemporary advertising. *Advertising and Society Review*, 12(2), Advertising Educational Foundation. Retrieved 26 September 2016, from Project MUSE database.

hooks, b. (1981). *Isn't I a Woman*. Boston, MA: South End Press.

Iqbal, N. (2015). Femvertising: How brands are selling #empowerment to women. *Guardian*, 12 October. www.theguardian.com/lifeandstyle/2015/oct/12/femvertising-branded-feminism

Joy, A. and Venkatesh, A. (1994). Postmodernism, feminism, and the body: The visible and the invisible in consumer research. *International Journal of Research in Marketing*, 11(4): 333–357.

Maclaran, P. (2015). Feminism's fourth wave: A research agenda for marketing and consumer research. *Journal of Marketing Management*, 31(15–16): 1732–1738.

Maclaran, P., Stevens, L. and Catterall, M. (1997). The 'glasshouse effect': Women in marketing management. *Marketing Intelligence and Planning*, 15(7): 309–317.

Marshall, D., Hogg, M., Davis, T., Schneider, T. and Peterson, A. (2014). Images of Motherhood: Food advertising in Good Housekeeping magazine 1950–2010. In S. O'Donohoe, M. Hogg, P. Maclaran, L. Martens, and L. Stevens (eds), *Mother-hoods, markets and consumption: The making of mothers in contemporary Western cultures*. London: Routledge, pp. 116–128.

Martin, C. and Valenti, V. (2012). *New feminist solutions. Volume 8: #FemFuture: Online feminism*. New York: Barnard Center for Research on Women, Columbia University.

Matich, M., Ashman, R. and Parsons, E. (2016). #Freethenipple: Embodied resistance in the fourth wave feminist movement. Paper presented at the 13th Conference on Gender, Marketing and Consumer Behaviour, 4–6 July, ESCP Europe, Paris.

Miller, T. (2014). Engaging with the maternal: Tentative mothering acts, props and discourses. In S. O'Donohoe, M. Hogg, P. Maclaran, L. Martens and L. Stevens (eds), *Motherhoods, markets and consumption: The making of mothers in contemporary Western cultures*. London: Routledge, pp. 159–170.

Moisio, R., Arnould, E.J. and Gentry, J.W. (2013). Productive consumption in the class-mediated construction of domestic masculinity: Do-it-yourself (DIY) home improvement in men's identity work. *Journal of Consumer Research*, 40(2): 298–316.

Munford, R. and Waters, M. (2014). *Feminism and popular culture: Investigating the postfeminist mystique*. New Brunswick, NJ: Rutgers University Press.

Schroeder, J.E. and Zwick, D. (2004). Mirrors of masculinity: Representation and identity in advertising images. *Consumption Markets and Culture*, 7(1): 21–52.

Scope (2016). *Disability in the media*. London: Scope.

Sedgwick, K.E. (1990). *Epistemology of the closet*. Berkeley: University of California Press.

Stern, B.B. (1996). Textual analysis in advertising research: Construction and deconstruction of meanings. *Journal of Advertising*, 25(3): 61–73.

Stevens, L. and Houston, S. (2016). Dazed magazine, fourth wave feminism, and the return of the politicised female body. Paper presented at the 13th Conference on Gender, Marketing and Consumer Behaviour, 4–6 July, ESCP Europe, Paris.

Thomson, R., Kehily, M.J., Hadfield, L. and Sharpe, S. (2011). *Making modern mothers*. Bristol: Polity Press.

Vega, T. (2013). Ad about women's self-image creates a sensation. *New York Times*, 18 April. www.nytimes.com/2013/04/19/business/media/dove-ad-on-womens-self-image-creates-an-online-sensation.html

Warner, M. (1991). Introduction: Fear of a queer planet. *Social Text*, 9(4[29]): 3–17.

Wechie, T. (2016). A 'post' post feminism: The utopian possibilities of a fourth wave of feminism and its intersections with the continued dominance of a tyrannical consumer capitalism. Paper presented at the 13th Conference on Gender, Marketing and Consumer Behaviour, 4–6 July, ESCP Europe, Paris.

Young, I.M. (1980). Throwing like a girl: A phenomenology of feminine body comportment motility and spatiality. *Human Studies*, 3(1): 137–156.

5 Psychoanalysis in marketing theory and practice

Introduction

Psychoanalysis is a 'form of inquiry, a theory of mind and a mode of treatment concerned, above all, with the unconscious mind' (Pick, 2015: 19). Many of the key concepts of psychoanalysis were developed by Sigmund Freud (1856–1939), the 'father of psychoanalysis', but have since been redeveloped and substantially revised by many key figures including Melanie Klein, Jacques Lacan, Wilfred Bion, Donald Winnicott and Carl Jung, among others. As a consequence, contemporary psychoanalysis offers a very large repertoire of tools and concepts that have inspired both therapeutic work and the broader realms of arts, humanities and social sciences.

Psychoanalysis has a long and rather fluid relationship with marketing theory and practice. It begins with Sigmund Freud's nephew Edward Bernays (1891–1995), the pioneer of public relations, propaganda and, for some, of Western consumer culture. Bernays employed many of his uncle's ideas for the benefit of promoting commodities as diverse as cigarettes, soap and the bacon and egg breakfast. In his autobiography, he claims to be the agent behind the first psychoanalytic application to advertising: that is a long-standing campaign for American Tobacco, starting in 1929, that successfully repositioned cigarettes as 'torches of freedom' in women's battle for socio-economic liberation. As a result, cigarettes became a far more popular consumption habit for women in America and beyond. No wonder then that during his visit to the US, Freud was somewhat amused by his nephew's aggressive marketing campaigns, including, for instance, an undertaker's advert saying 'Why live when you can be buried for only $10?' (Freud and Freud, 1960).

In this chapter, we introduce some key psychoanalytic ideas and explain their relevance to marketing and consumer behaviour. We begin with a short discussion of three key figures of psychoanalysis, that is Sigmund Freud, Melanie Klein and Jacques Lacan. Subsequently, we discuss applications of psychoanalysis in marketing, focusing on three distinct areas: advertising, marketing research and consumer behaviour.

The return of the 'repressed' in marketing

Psychoanalysis originally entered the field of marketing under the guise of 'motivational research' and most famously through Ernest Dichter's promotion of new methods of understanding and influencing the increasingly affluent consumers of post-World War II. Also known as the 'Freud of Madison Avenue' and 'Mr Mass Motivations' (Fullerton, 2007), Dichter has been credited with the rise of various famous household brand names, such as Chrysler and General Mills. He introduced many innovative approaches to marketing research, including 'focus groups', 'depth interviews' and projective techniques. At times, he had a rather outlandish take on the symbolic meaning of everyday consumption acts: smoking was 'comparable to sucking at the nipples of a gigantic world breast'; whereas cake mixes that did not involve adding eggs were a threat to women's fertility. For critics of motivational research, Dichter's research programme had unprecedented moral implications:

> All this probing and manipulation has its constructive and its amusing aspects; but also, I think it fair to say, it has seriously antihumanistic implications. Much of it seems to represent regress rather than progress for man in his long struggle to become a rational and self-guiding being.
>
> (Packard, 1957: 34)

Ironically however, such criticisms made Dichter even more influential, not least because of the numerous TV and radio invites to talk about his research to the general population.

Despite the early affair of psychoanalysis with marketing communications and consumer research, subsequent decades experienced what Cluley and Desmond (2015) describe as the 'repression' of psychoanalysis whereby psychoanalytic understandings of the consumer to some extent continued to take place outside the marketing discipline but firmly not within it. This mirrored the evolution of the fields of psychology and psychiatry more broadly (e.g. Pick, 2015), with more sanitised and less speculative forms of inquiry, as exemplified in the emergence of Cognitive Behavioural Therapy and the consolidation of biological (as opposed to psychoanalytic) psychiatry (O'Shaughnessy, 2015), earning a significantly higher status. Past the 1970s, psychoanalysis began to be viewed as outdated, largely reliant on reductivist ideas, empirically unsubstantiated and sexist, among others.

More recently however the 'repressed' psychoanalysis has returned, according to Cluley and Desmond (2015). For some, this is not surprising: in one sense, the return to psychoanalysis reflects the relative failure of other disciplines to account for human and social behaviour on the basis of what is commonly understood as 'scientific proof'. There is increasing awareness that human behaviour is far less rational and 'measurable' in the sense that experimental psychologists and quantitative marketers wish it would have been. Psychoanalysis, with its focus on the unconscious and inherent critique of outcome testing (Pick, 2015), is in a very good place to explicitly confront more conventional and tried understandings of consumer behaviour. Beyond questions of empirical validity, it provides a rich vocabulary, a series of sensitising concepts that can prove very useful in developing alternative accounts of marketing and consumption. As we will illustrate below, psychoanalytic applications can be particularly creative and counterintuitive. Psychoanalysis has also played a key role in so-called psychosocial studies, which is an emerging stream of research that attempts to overcome dualisms of inner versus outer, individual (consumer) versus society and to develop more nuanced accounts of how individuals' inner and outer realities are mutually constitutive (Frosh, 2010). For example, rather than pathologising and individualising notions such as narcissism and autism, psychosocial approaches would attempt to view them instead as products of the sociocultural, discursive and material environments that we inhabit.

Key figures: Freud, Klein, Lacan

Sigmund Freud

Freud is the founder of psychoanalysis, coining the term in 1896. Attempting to understand 'hysteria', a common mental illness at the time that Freud witnessed being treated with hypnosis, he developed a new technique called 'free association'. That involves asking patients to talk freely about their thoughts and emotions without any self-censorship or prohibition. His belief was that patients with symptoms of hysteria suffered from repressed memories and thoughts and by bringing them to consciousness in a safe environment, effective treatment was possible. As his technique began to bring positive outcomes, Freud developed a series of terms and concepts that have since become part of the psychoanalytic vocabulary, embraced by specialists and laymen alike.

In accounting for how repression operates, Freud originally developed the so-called topographical model of the mind, comprising the unconscious (thoughts that are completely repressed and cannot be recalled), the preconscious (thoughts that can be recalled) and the conscious (thoughts that are recalled). Later on he significantly revised his observations in what was now called the structural model (Freud, 1923), comprising the id, the ego and the superego. The id is the completely unconscious part of the brain that contains instinctual sexual urges and aggressive drives. But equally far from conscious awareness may lie the superego, an internalised authority that watches and judges often in extremely punitive and sadistic ways. For Freud, the superego is constituted through the internalisation of parental prohibitions and demands. Finally, the ego is what is more commonly associated with common sense, what perceives and mediates internal and external reality, and which for Freud has to strike a very fine balance in fighting 'three dangers': the external world, the superego, and the id. Accordingly, a key purpose of psychoanalysis is 'to strengthen the ego, to make it more independent of the super-ego, to widen its field of perception and enlarge its organisation, so that it can appropriate fresh portions of the id' (Freud in Pick, 2015: 46).

The Freudian vocabulary still informs everyday understandings of people's personalities and psychological states. Terms such as the Oedipal complex, Freudian slip, the unconscious, narcissism, repression, fetishism, neurotic obsession and displacement remain in regular use across various parts of the world.

Melanie Klein

Melanie Klein (1882–1960) is relatively less well known but very influential, especially in the UK and other countries where 'object-relations theory' has become a popular alternative to traditional Freudian psychoanalysis. Klein viewed herself as the ultimate successor of Freud, leading to an infamous conflict with Freud's daughter, Anna, who also claimed the same in a series of meetings called the 'controversial discussions' (1942–4). Despite considering herself a faithful adherent to Freud's ideas, she significantly departed from him, not least by locating the emergence of unconscious conflict way before the formation of the Oedipal complex (around six months as opposed to three to five years old). Klein was the first to use traditional psychoanalytic theory and practice with children, often as young as two years old, and in doing so she developed various innovative techniques such as play therapy.

Klein is mostly known for her formulation of the *paranoid-schizoid* and *depressive* positions. The paranoid-schizoid position represents a primitive mode of mental organisation, located during the infant's early developmental stage (from birth to six months old) and characterised by their inability to experience the mother (or caregiver) as a whole object. Instead, the caregiver is split into a 'good breast' and a 'bad breast', with corresponding feelings of love and hate (Klein, 1946, 1948). These early affective states are *schizoid* because bad and good objects are split. They are *paranoid* because of the threat entailed in realising that the good object associated with satisfaction (the feeding breast) is also a frustrating object (non-feeding breast) that cannot be relied upon; hence why infants often attack the mother's breast. The *depressive* position reflects a later developmental stage in which the infant moves from a part-object to a whole-object relation and becomes capable of recognising good and bad aspects in the loved and loving object (first of all, the mother or caregiver). For Klein, these positions persist into adulthood: for example, we are often able to see both the good and bad in other objects (be it people, institutions or actual consumption items), whereas at other stages we may be overwhelmed by irrational feelings and thoughts of excessive love or hate.

Jacques Lacan

Jacques Lacan (1901–81) has become very popular within a small milieu more recently, especially through his influence on celebrated contemporary social theory scholars, most notably Slavoj Žižek. He is associated with the application of psychoanalysis to the realm of language and, by implication, broader sociocultural processes. Lacan's mantra has been that the 'unconscious is structured like a language', at least since his famous essay titled 'The instance of the letter in the unconscious, or reason since Freud' (Lacan, 2010; originally written in 1957). Central to his thinking is the development of the 'mirror stage', the time in which a baby progressively moves away from the fantasy of a fragmented and disorderly body to recognising its image in the mirror. It is important to recall here that, like Klein, Lacan recognises that prior to this stage (around six months old) the baby does not experience its body as whole and complete. Seeing its image as a whole and the synthesis of this image threatens the child with fragmentation; in other words, the distance between the subject and its image is profoundly traumatising until the ego is formed. But what constitutes the ego is a misunderstanding as the 'me' becomes alienated from itself through an *imaginary* dimension. In Lacan's thinking, the imaginary contrasts with the *symbolic*, the realm of law and language and the *real*, what is left outside language and resists symbolisation.

Another key and strongly interrelated concept in Lacan's writings is the idea of desire, here always viewed as lack and forever unsatisfied as it is expressed through language that always leaves a leftover or surplus. Accordingly, for Lacan, the aim of psychoanalysis is to make the analysand (a term used for someone who is undergoing psychoanalytic treatment) realise and uncover the truth about his/her desire:

> what is important is to teach the subject to name, to articulate, to bring desire into existence. The subject should come to recognize and to name his/her desire. But it isn't a question of recognizing something that could be entirely given. In naming it, the subject creates, brings forth, a new presence in the world.
>
> (Lacan, 1988: 228–9)

Psychoanalysis outside the clinic and into marketing

There has been ongoing controversy as to whether psychoanalysis can be applied beyond the clinic, let alone outside the particular historical and spatial context in which it was developed and practised. Indeed, the links between modernity and the specific notion of the inner self that psychoanalysis offered have been extensively documented (Zaretsky, 2005), as has the specific geographical-cultural context of psychoanalysis. Even for Freud (1916: 431) psychoanalysis was the product of a very particular European city:

> psychoanalysis, especially the assertion that the neuroses can be traced back to disturbances in the sexual life, could only have originated in a city like Vienna, in an atmosphere of sensuality and immorality not to be found in other cities.

Likewise the therapeutic method is always undertaken within a specific spatial context (including the analyst and the analysand) and within particular time intervals, aiming altogether for a 'consistent frame' (Pick, 2015). With this in mind, it is remarkable how readily and often unreflectively psychoanalytic concepts have been applied to arts, humanities and social sciences.

Psychoanalysis, therefore, still holds a rather precarious status within social sciences more generally and the field of marketing in particular. On the one hand, psychoanalytic applications rely on 'evidence' that is the product of subjective interpretation and thus are too questionable for the type of logical empiricism that predominates in disciplines such as marketing and consumer research. On the other hand, interpretivist and social constructivist researchers often reject psychoanalysis because of the 'innerness' it involves, the employ-ment of a totalising, 'expert' discourse that is inherently reductionist. That is to say, it imposes frameworks and ways of thinking that are self-fulfilling. Between these two positions lie more sympathetic views that see something in the ability of psychoanalysis – or at least in some versions of it – to fill the 'gaps' left in the language and methodologies employed by other research paradigms. According to Michael Rustin (2010; see also Frosh, 2010), for example, psychoanalysis, with its focus on the unconscious and seemingly irrational, has the capacity to 'disrupt' or 'unsettle' more normalised and taken-for-granted understandings: 'The assertion is that, where psychoanalysis has something valuable to say … it will mostly be where its contribution is counter-intuitive or even paradoxical' (p. 472).

Accordingly, in the remainder of this chapter, we review some psycho-analytic applications with a two-fold aim. First, we address questions around empirical validity as well as the moral debates that followed some of the more prominent examples of psychoanalytically inspired marketing. Second, we attempt to illustrate psychoanalysis' broader ability to inspire more dis-ruptive and creative modes of thinking. We begin with some psychoanalytic premises on 'how to sell sex' before moving on to discuss Dichter's ambitious programme to uncover consumers' hidden motivations. Last, we discuss some psychoanalytic understandings of contemporary consumption and consumer culture.

Selling sex (and other primal instincts)

The idea that much communication passes below our conscious radar and that aspects of our mind will always remain obscure was bound to have a major influence on those interested in manipulating them, not least marketers and advertisers. As vividly explained in the award-wining documentary series by Adam Curtis, *The Century of the Self* (also mentioned in Chapter 7), psychoanalytical techniques have been widely and systematically employed at least since the end of World War II, when the consumerist way of living was for the first time promoted to a mass audience. According to this account, previously insignificant and mundane objects, such as cigarettes, cars and power detergents, were now psychically and sexually charged, unconsciously linked with 'phallic symbols', narcissistic objects or alleviators of women's 'penis envy', among others. As critics saw it, consumers were duped by an extremely sophisticated and professionalised body of marketers and advertisers that, having mastered major Freudian works such as 'The interpretations of dreams', were able to manipulate the symbolic imagery of consumer objects and via these to arouse sexual fantasies in socially acceptable ways. This was often accompanied with a 'knowing wink' to those in the know (i.e. other advertisers and communications experts) and quickly became the paradigm for the communication of all kinds of otherwise controversial messages (Desmond, 2012).

Meanwhile, the unconscious approach to advertising and promotional communication was most notoriously exposed in Vance Packard's (1957) *Hidden Persuaders* (also mentioned in Chapter 7). By 'hidden' Packard meant 'beneath our level of awareness', also known as subliminal, that is stimuli that are below the individual's absolute threshold of awareness and cannot be experienced at a conscious level. The same year, exploiting the popularity of Packard's book, James Vicary, owner of a marketing research firm invested in motivation research, published the famous Coca-Cola experiment. According to this hoax, the messages 'Drink Coca-Cola' and 'Hungry? Eat Popcorn' were flashed at 1/3000th of a second every five minutes to over 45,000 people in a New Jersey cinema, resulting in a sales increase of 18 percent and 58 percent of Coca-Cola and popcorn, respectively. However, a series of subsequent experiments refuted his claim, showing that persuasion at the sub-threshold or subliminal level is not possible (e.g. Moore, 1982; Beatty and Hawkins, 1989). This echoed the views of advertisers, with the vast majority of them claiming strong disbelief in the potential effectiveness of subliminal advertising (Rogers and Seiler, 1994). Altogether, further consumer research on subliminal advertising effects stagnated despite the fact that the possibility of subliminal persuasion continued to capture the general public's imagination (Bargh, 2002).

Part of the reason why the notion of unconscious advertising went out of fashion throughout the 1980s and the 1990s was because the very idea of a less rational and non-agentic consumer was in direct contrast to the models of deliberate consumer decision making promoted in positivistic marketing research (Desmond, 2012). However, more intense experimentations with the unconscious processing information continued elsewhere, including the fields of clinical and cognitive psychology and neuroscience (Albanese, 2015). Therein, numerous studies have consistently shown subliminal effects on consumption and product evaluation (Bargh, 2002). Unlike earlier consumer research, this stream of literature concludes that consumers' goals (e.g. to satisfy one's hunger) can be activated unconsciously but only when they are pre-existing (that is, only if one is indeed hungry in the first place). Meanwhile, studies relating more directly to advertising effects have consistently shown that unconscious manipulation is possible, especially when focused on more realistic outcome measures such as brand-name recall and brand-name liking as opposed to hard measures such as changes in actual behaviour or intention (Albanese, 2015).

As John Bargh (2002) observes, this makes uncomfortable reading for contemporary consumer and advertising researchers who are still largely ignorant of recent advances in knowledge of non-conscious processes, not to mention the very real possibility that these are already exploited by marketplace and governmental actors. Furthermore, he points to the additional influence of supraliminal effects, that is cues or primes that consumers may be aware of but grossly underestimate their influence. For instance, we may watch an advert that is obviously 'dirty' or manipulative by using negative stereotypes and although consciously we will reject it, we may still be influenced at an unconscious level. For Bargh, this form of persuasion is far more pervasive in contemporary advertising. His observation is even more pertinent today where the dream-like qualities of advertising are often downplayed by empowered and confident consumers whilst at the same time everyday life is increasingly commoditised in ways that would have perhaps been unimaginable in Freud's era.

Indeed, it is arguably within the realm of what experimental scientists call supraliminal effects, rather than subliminal ones, that psychoanalysis can showcase greater explanatory power. After all, what is often cited as research on unconscious or subliminal processing is primarily concerned with 'non-conscious' processing. The latter assumes that thoughts remain non-conscious only until a need or want is activated and then they become conscious. In contrast, psychoanalysis assumes that unconscious thoughts are goal directed and can influence behaviour without ever becoming conscious. In this sense, Freud's (and his followers') observations on how unconscious wish fulfilments can be projected into (consumer) objects and feed into narcissistic anxieties and self-destructive instincts are not fully compatible with the experimental studies on non-conscious effects.

Elsewhere, however, such as in the fields of cultural and visual studies, psychoanalytic concepts have been frequently employed with a view to account for what happens in relation to an image and how we may be influenced by it. For instance, drawing on Lacan, Judith Williamson (1978) focuses on the mirror-like qualities of advertising and their ubiquity, forcing us to engage intimately with 'a sort of independent reality that links them to our own lives' (Williamson, 1978: 11). For Williamson (p. 65), advertising is a signifying system within the symbolic and is also able to represent to the subject his place in the imaginary:

> Ads set up, in your active relationship towards them, the fictional creation of an impossibly unified self: an 'Ego-Ideal'. They show you a symbol of yourself aimed to attract your desire; they suggest that you can become the person in the picture before you.

Lacan's imaginary is not of course the only psychoanalytic concept that can explain the visual rhetoric of advertising. For instance, Freud's ideas around psychic displacements and Melanie Klein's understanding of projective identification can be readily employed in advertising images with a view to account for their production of meaning and symbolism (cf. Oswald, 2010) and more broadly, for the creation of the fantasy space(s) of contemporary consumerism.

Researching the unconscious with Dr Dichter

As mentioned in the introduction, psychoanalysis also implies a particular method of understanding the mind, one that goes beneath the surface with a view to uncover the hidden (unconscious) motivations of human thoughts and actions. Likewise, when applied outside the clinic, psychoanalytic methods share in common a more 'penetrative' outlook, the belief that by somehow researching beneath the surface (e.g. Clarke and Hoggett, 2011) there is scope for uncovering psychodynamic processes and mechanisms that are inaccessible in other research methods.

Within marketing and consumer research, psychoanalytically inspired methods are highly interconnected with so-called depth or motivational research, pioneered in the 1930s by Paul Lazarsfeld but more commonly associated with Ernest Dichter (see Schwarzkopf and Gries, 2010). Born in Vienna to a working-class Jewish family, Dichter fled to the US to escape Nazi prosecution. His rather flamboyant, if not narcissistic, personality helped him cause widespread sensation by fiercely criticising what he considered largely outmoded and blunt methods of consumer research, such as conventional interviews and surveys. He began his career by sending a simple (and rather overconfident) letter to six big corporations of his choice, stating that: 'I am a young psychologist from Vienna and I have some interesting new ideas which can help you be more successful, effective, sell more and communicate better with your potential clients' (Dichter, 1979: 33). Amongst them, Esquire was the first one to reply positively. From then on, he moved from strength to strength, developing a programme of motivational research that sought to understand three distinct categories of motives in their entirety: 1) those that consumers are consciously aware of, 2) those consumers are aware of but unwilling to reveal and 3) those motives that consumers are unaware of (Tadajewski, 2006).

Despite common misunderstandings, the purpose of motivational research was neither to apply psychoanalytic tools comprehensively on the consumer, nor in any sense to 'cure' them. Rather, the relationship between psychoanalysis and motivation research could be summarised in their common insistence on 'psycho-detective work' (Tadajewski, 2006), which is also described above as penetrative. His observational techniques and 'depth interviews' identified consumer motivations beyond the ones revealed in classical survey or interview-based questions. For instance, he found that men, when directly asked, would state that women did not influence their car-buying habits. In standard surveys, they would also cite additional rational buying criteria, such as reliability and price. For Dichter, however, in reality men preferred convertibles over sedans and that is why they purchased them far more frequently before getting married rather than after. And once again after they passed 45 or 50. Dichter's psychodetective explanation was that the sedan represented the wife,

> comfortable and safe. The convertible, the 'mistress', youthful, was the dreamer … the wind blows through your hair, you feel much closer to the road and the landscape. Many men have a secret wish for a mistress. This wish becomes stronger as they get older. Buying a convertible represented the realization of this wish, without the expense and the guilt feeling of having a live mistress.
>
> (Dichter, 1979: 38)

Although Dichter was personally in favour of individual rather than group interviews his consulting company also trained a large number of first generation 'focus group' researchers, developing the so-called 'depth group interview' (Stewart and Shamdasani, 2014). Dichter was rather more instrumental in introducing a variety of projective techniques to marketing research. Drawing on Freud's idea of projection as a defence mechanism by which individuals unconsciously attribute their own negative personality traits to others, his 'non-directive interview technique' (Dichter, 1960) allowed interviewees to project themselves onto another person (e.g. by asking them to comment on other consumers' behaviour) and by doing so reveal some of their own thoughts, feelings and fears. Although projective techniques have since played a central role in the marketing research industry (e.g. Boddy, 2005), the extent to which Dichter directly contributed to their development and dissemination remains questionable. For Fullerton (2007), other motivational researchers, including Lazarsfeld, had much more meaningfully and extensively engaged with projective techniques and in fact with motivational research more broadly. However, no one was a master myth maker in the way that Dichter proved to be: 'The very hyperbole and imaginative verve expressed in his "discoveries" transcend those of any other marketing figure of the 20th century' (p. 380).

In a similar vein, Schwarzkopf (2015: 41) notes the far wider-reaching, sociocultural consequences of Dichter's work in so far as 'he helped bring about in the public imagination of what consumer desire was and what significance "libidinal drives" had for the political economy of consumer capitalism'. In other words, Schwarzkopf (2015) argues, Dichter's pro-hedonistic outlook was very much in line with the promotion of the 'consumer' as the central form of human existence; Freud's 'pleasure principle', aiming for immediate, libidinal gratification, was for the first time pushed ahead of the 'reality principle', aiming for self-control and delayed gratification for the purpose of longer-term individual and collective well-being. In Dichter's words at the Institute for Motivational Research (Packard, 1957: 74): 'One of the main jobs of the advertiser in this conflict between pleasure and guilt is not so much to sell the product as to give moral permission to have fun without guilt'.

Consumers in the clinic

Beyond potential commercial applications and their ethical implications, psychoanalysis remains a body of knowledge vested in understanding human subjectivity, conceptualising it as fundamentally ambivalent: both loving and hating, altruistic and selfish, rational and irrational. It invites us to reconsider taken-for-granted ideas that individuals are rational, have stable identities and are free to exercise their 'choice', be it in the marketplace and/or other spheres of social life. This section reviews some illustrative attempts to psychoanalyse the 'consumer', acknowledging that the possibilities are as rich as the history of psychoanalysis with its variety of different traditions and therapeutic outcomes.

One of the key Freudian concepts that have been applied to understand contemporary consumers and consumerism is that of a narcissist personality. This is no coincidence given the well-explored link between consumer culture and the emergence of more hedonistic and self-absorbed lifestyles. Most famously, Christopher Lasch's (1979) bestselling book *The Culture of Narcissism* illustrates how the creation of what can be called narcissistic consumption was a necessary turn in the evolution of capitalism, circa post-World War I, as the increasingly expanding domain of production had to meet corresponding levels of consumer demand for conspicuous and experiential goods. Freud (1991) theorised narcissism as a tendency to withdraw from one's external world and redirect desire into oneself; in other words excessive redirecting of one's sexual libido from external objects (here understood more broadly as other people and/or material objects) into herself. For Lasch (1979), such tendencies are pervasive in modern societies the more paternal (or authority) figures lose their credibility. Therefore, 'the superego in individuals increasingly derives from the child's primitive fantasies about his parents, fantasies charged with sadistic rage – rather than from internalised ego ideals formed by later experience with loved and respected models of social conduct' (p. 12). Lasch, therefore, does not use narcissism as a metaphor or synonym for selfishness, a common assumption in lay accounts of our narcissistic culture. Rather he insists on a psychoanalytic understanding of narcissism, viewing it as a common pathology that is produced by the sociocultural conditions of our times.

Interestingly, Freud himself rarely spoke directly about notions such as 'consumption' and 'identity'. One notable exception was in relation to narcissism and in particular parents' consumption practices. He argued that seemingly affectionate parental actions towards their children may instead be a revival and reproduction of their own narcissism, for example when buying one's child the most exclusive shoes. For Freud (1991: 91), such examples of consumption show us that 'parental love, which is so moving and at bottom so childish, is nothing but the parents' narcissism born again, which, transformed into object-love, unmistakably reveals its former nature'. Through consumption, let alone purchasing for others, narcissistic behaviours that would otherwise be viewed as socially unacceptable become acceptable. Cluley and Dunne (2012) extend this argument to account for the darker and more sadistic instances of consumer behaviour, such as ignoring the exploitative social relations that underline commodity production. Arguing against conventional accounts of unethical and unsustainable consumption that draw on Marx's notion of commodity fetishism, they point to the repressed narcissistic pleasure in knowing that one is better than others, the idea that the only good neighbour may indeed be the dead neighbour.

Consumption, of course, serves more than just a narcissistic function. For Gabriel (2015), the idea of consumers' freedom to choose and construct their own identities also serves a disciplining/controlling function and a therapeutic function. The former becomes clear when considering how in contemporary societies, those who fail to enjoy the pleasures of consumerism (due to lower incomes) are considered as largely responsible for their choices and thus examples for others to avoid. Consumption also serves a therapeutic function in so far as it can compensate us when things go wrong and reward us when things go well. From a Freudian point of view, consumers' identities and choices can therefore be viewed as wish fulfilments or fantasies. They are unconscious defences to the challenges that contemporary civilisations place on individuals.

Psychoanalysis also provides ideas and concepts that can help explain our preoccupation with particular commodities. Most commonly, Freudian readings emphasise how consumers displace their desires (mostly of a sexual nature) into material goods, ultimately defending themselves against deeper anxieties and contradictions. Somewhat alternative readings of the relationship between people and material artefacts can be provided by object-relations traditions. Melanie Klein, for instance, began her work by studying the interaction of infants with their toys. Although she moved on to consider images of people as the most significant psychic 'objects', her work enabled later psychoanalysts to reconsider the relationship between subjects and (some of their) material objects. Most famously, Donald Winnicott (1971) developed the term 'transitional object' to account for the relationship children develop with their first comfort objects such as a toy or a blanket. These objects mediate children's relationship with external reality and become part of the processes of separating the 'me' from the 'not-me'. Such transitional objects have often been considered in consumer research. Further, later work on anthropology and material culture has reconsidered the significance of object-relations theorists, arguing that processes of projection, introjection and projective identification provide the basis for the development of a more sophisticated understanding of the subject–object relationship (e.g. Miller, 1997).

Psychoanalysis, particularly in its Lacanian guises, also provides powerful concepts for understanding our contemporary culture's obsession with the screen. For example, focusing on mobile phone usage, Reyes et al. (2015) argue that Lacanian concepts not only help us understand the pleasures of looking, but also the underlying anxieties that are a precondition for such pleasure. In doing so, the authors draw on Lacan's distinction between the 'look' and the 'gaze'. Whereas the former is more in line with the notion of commodity fetishism (in line with Cluley and Dunne, 2012) and the pleasures of seeing and constructing identities via the mediation of (consumer) objects, the latter addresses the more disruptive and anxiety-inducing aspects associated with Lacan's symbolic. Ultimately, the authors argue that beyond commonplace understandings of contemporary culture's obsession with the 'screen', there is something more profound and anxiety inducing, associated with Lacan's real. That is, our inescapable existential dilemmas associated with a lack of being and being gazed at by the 'other'.

Summary

Psychoanalysis has a long and rather contentious relationship with marketing theory and practice. Despite the early enthusiasm of post-World War II marketers, interest in understanding and influencing the consumer's unconscious waned throughout the 1970s–2000s. More recently, however, we have been witnessing some kind of return to psychoanalysis, not least because of its renewed infusion into contemporary social theory; and from there to more specific applications to marketing and consumption. Key figures of psychoanalysis that continue to be highly influential are Sigmund Freud, Melanie Klein and Jacques Lacan. Their theories and concepts have been applied in one way or another to all areas of marketing, from advertising and marketing research to consumer behaviour and consumer culture.

Psychoanalytic approaches continue to be controversial, not least because of their incompatibility with the (still) dominant project of logical empiricism. However, there is increasing recognition of the ability of psychoanalysis to provide a rich vocabulary and a series of sensitising concepts that are particularly useful for multiperspective and multimethod approaches to understanding consumers (e.g. O'Shaughnessy, 2015). Besides, we should also note that psychoanalytically inspired ideas have always been in heavy use, albeit under different labels, in various fields of research, from social anthropology to neuroscience. Notwithstanding, for some advocates of psychoanalysis it does not necessarily matter if some of the underlying premises prove to be 'true' or 'false'. Rather, as Stuart Hall, one of the foremost social theorists used to say, what matters is that they remain 'good ideas to think with'.

CASE STUDY: unethical and self-harming consumers

Chapter 7 discusses the emergence of ethical consumption and the adjoining observation of the so-called 'attitude-behaviour gap', that is the tendency of most consumers to behave in ways that are in apparent contradiction to their expressed ethical and environmental concerns. Psychoanalysis, with its focus on the unconscious, offers an entirely different explanation for why we may behave in ways that are far removed from our moral ideals (Chatzidakis, 2015).

For Freud, the key explanatory concept when it comes to ethical and moral wrongdoing is the presence of unconscious guilt. Distinguishing it from conscious feelings of guilt (the ones commonly experienced when we do something wrong), unconscious guilt arises as part of the Oedipal configuration. It is a 'reaction to the two great criminal intentions of killing the father and having sexual relations with the mother' (Freud, 1916: 333). Subsequently, through the establishment of the superego, the fear of the father (and later of any kind of authority) becomes internalised and regulates our everyday behaviour. Sometimes, however, the superego can be so punitive and torturing that unconscious guilt becomes unbearable. In these instances, one may commit actual misdeeds with a view to releasing some of these feelings into more conscious or 'real manifestations'. As Freud (1916) wrote in *Criminals from a Sense of Guilt* (p. 332):

> various wrongdoings were done principally because they were forbidden, and because their execution was accompanied by mental relief for their doer. He was suffering from an oppressive feeling of guilt, of which he did not know the origin, and after he had committed a misdeed this oppression was mitigated. His sense of guilt was at least attached to something.

Therefore, the underlying presence of guilt may not only be unconscious, but also so extreme that individuals may harm themselves or others with a view to releasing some of its otherwise unbearable presence.

With Freud's development of the superego, guilt took centre stage in psychoanalytic accounts of morality. However, for many subsequent psychoanalysts (see Hughes, 2008), it was Melanie Klein that provided a more comprehensive understanding of everyday morality. For Hughes, Melanie Klein significantly extended Freud by locating the emergence of unconscious guilt in earlier developmental stages, that is during the child's dyadic relationship with its mother (or caregiver). Klein's paranoid-schizoid position resembles Freud's understanding of unconscious guilt in so far as the splitting of the self into good and bad objects (first being the mother's breast) results in persecutory anxiety and fear of revenge in the same way that the formation of the superego does. However, Klein's understanding of unconscious guilt significantly departs from Freud's in her conceptualisation of the depressive position. Here the child moves from a part-object to a whole-object relation and becomes capable of recognising good and bad aspects in the loved and loving object (first being its mother) that it has previously inflicted harm upon. Subsequently it experiences anxiety and a different kind of guilt that

Klein calls 'depressive guilt'. This guilt primarily aims at reparation and is qualitatively different from the 'persecutory' guilt that characterises the paranoid-schizoid position. For Klein and her followers it signifies entry into a more advanced model of morality during which we can see the good and the bad as co-existing in many aspects of our lives. More importantly still, we can constructively engage with it; perhaps try to do our bit in 'repairing' the various social and environmental injustices underlying contemporary life.

Psychoanalytic readings of morality contrast significantly with the dominant tradition of understanding consumer (and marketing) ethics as a largely instrumental and cognitive process (see Chapter 7). Likewise, the widespread observation of 'attitude-behaviour' gaps is less surprising from a psychoanalytic point of view. The presence of unconscious guilt may mean that a certain amount of inconsistency between moral beliefs and actions is necessary in order to release conscious guilt and therefore serves an important adaptive function. In other words, 'a certain amount of conscious consumer guilt, as an outcome of moral attitude-behaviour inconsistency, is necessary so that unconscious guilt finds both periodic relief and a more rationalised, cognitive explanation' (Chatzidakis, 2015: 86). What are the practical implications of this? For instance, the presence of unconscious guilt may be the reason why some people consistently do harm to their bodies (through excessive alcohol consumption, smoking, etc.), feel guilty about it and still fail to change their behaviour. Others may avoid harming themselves but may still experience guilt for harming others, for example through socially and environmentally harmful behaviour. Here Chatzidakis (2015) also notes the relevance of 'depressive guilt' which is more explicitly linked with a capacity to care for rather than harm oneself or others. Many altruistic and solidaristic behaviours, from a Kleinian point of view, may be viewed in the light of a profound need for 'reparation', at first towards important others but once extended, it could be a broader will to make the world a better place after realising all the harm we have inflicted upon it.

Seminar exercises

Discussion topics

1   Discuss the controversy around the application of psychoanalytic techniques to marketing. What are the key arguments in favour of and against psychoanalysis? What is your opinion?
2   Select one advertisement and try to apply a psychoanalytic reading. What are your insights?
3   Think of a particular object that is very important to you. Can you provide a psychoanalytic interpretation?
4   How does narcissism play out in contemporary consumer culture? Give examples where you can.

Group exercises

1   Read the article by Chatzidakis (2015) in the Key readings section.

- In what ways is unconscious guilt different from conscious guilt? Explain the key difference between psychoanalytic models and more conventional understandings of (consumer) guilt.
- Consider the attitude-behaviour gap discussed in Chapter 7. How (if at all) can it be reduced from a psychoanalytic point of view?
- Consider other examples of 'virtuous' and morally degrading consumption. How could you reinterpret them on the basis of Freud and Klein?

2   Projective techniques are widely employed in contemporary marketing research. In surveys, one common example includes asking participants to fill incomplete sentences (e.g. 'Mary bought a new iPhone because ____'), whereas in depth interviews, participants are often asked to project their thoughts and feelings to a third party (e.g. 'What would your friends think of people who are driving SUVs?').

- Ask two members from your group to respond to these questions. How are their responses different?
- To what extent do these questions make participants reveal more about themselves rather than others?
- Can you apply a psychoanalytic interpretation to their responses? What are your key insights? To what extent can you consider these to be 'valid'?

Key readings

Chatzidakis, A. (2015). Guilt and ethical choice in consumption: A psychoanalytic perspective. *Marketing Theory*, 15(1): 79–93.

Cluley, R. and Desmond, J. (2015). Why psychoanalysis now? *Marketing Theory*, 15(1): 3–8.

Cluley, R. and Dunne, S. (2012). From commodity fetishism to commodity narcissism. *Marketing Theory*, 12(3): 251–265.

Pick, D. (2015). *Psychoanalysis: A very short introduction.* Oxford: Oxford University Press.

Schwarzkopf, S. and Gries, R. (eds) (2010). *Ernest Dichter and motivation research.* Basingstoke: Palgrave Macmillan.

References

Albanese, P.J. (2015). The unconscious processing information. *Marketing Theory*, 15(1): 59–78.

Bargh, J.A. (2002). Losing consciousness: Automatic influences on consumer judgment, behavior, and motivation. *Journal of Consumer Research*, 29(2): 280–285.

Beatty, S.E. and Hawkins, D.I. (1989). Subliminal stimulation: Some new data and interpretation. *Journal of Advertising*, 18(3): 4–8.

Boddy, C. (2005). Projective techniques in market research: Valueless subjectivity or insightful reality? *International Journal of Market Research*, 47(3): 239–254.

Clarke, S. and Hoggett, P. (eds) (2011). *Researching beneath the surface: Psycho-social research methods in practice*. London: Karnac Books.

Desmond, J. (2012). *Psychoanalytic accounts of consuming desire: Hearts of darkness*. Basingstoke: Palgrave Macmillan.

Dichter, E. (1960). *The strategy of desire*. Garden City, NJ: Doubleday and Company.

Dichter, E. (1979). *Getting motivated by Ernest Dichter: The secret behind individual motivations by the man who was not afraid to ask why?* New York: Elsevier.

Freud, S. (1916). The history of the psychoanalytic movement. *Psychoanalytic Review*, 3: 406–454.

Freud, S. (1923). The ego and the id. In *The standard edition of the complete psychological works of Sigmund Freud, Volume XIX (1923–1925): The ego and the id and other works*. London: Hogarth Press, pp. 1–66.

Freud, S. (1991). On narcissism. In J. Strachey (ed.), *On metapsychology: The theory of psychoanalysis*. London: Penguin, pp. 59–99.

Freud, S. and Freud, E.L. (1960). *Letters of Sigmund Freud*. North Chelmsford, MA: Courier Corporation.

Frosh, S. (2010). *Psychoanalysis outside the clinic: Interventions in psychosocial studies*. Basingstoke: Palgrave Macmillan.

Fullerton, R.A. (2007). Mr. MASS motivations himself: Explaining Dr. Ernest Dichter. *Journal of Consumer Behavior*, 6(6): 369–382.

Gabriel, Y. (2015). Identity, choice and consumer freedom: The new opiates? A psychoanalytic interrogation. *Marketing Theory*, 15(1): 25–30.

Hughes, J.M. (2008). *Guilt and its vicissitudes: Psychoanalytic reflections on morality*. London: Routledge.

Klein, M. (1946). Notes on some schizoid mechanisms. *International Journal of Psychoanalysis*, 27: 99–110.

Klein, M. (1948). A contribution to the theory of anxiety and guilt. *International Journal of Psychoanalysis*, 29: 114–123.

Lacan, J. (1988). *The seminar. Book II. The ego in Freud's theory and in the technique of psychoanalysis, 1954–55*. Cambridge: Cambridge University Press.

Lacan, J. (2010). The instance of the letter in the unconscious, or reason since Freud. In I. Szeman and T. Kaposy (eds), *Cultural Theory: An Anthology*. Chichester: Wiley.

Lasch, C. (1979). *The culture of narcissism: American life in an age of diminishing returns*. New York: Norton.

Miller, D. (1997). How infants grow mothers in North London. *Theory, Culture and Society*, 14(4): 67–88.

Moore, T.E. (1982). Subliminal advertising: What you see is what you get. *Journal of Marketing*, 46: 38–47.

O'Shaughnessy, J. (2015). Note on the marginalizing of psychoanalysis in marketing. *Marketing Theory*, 15(1): 17–19.

Oswald, L.R. (2010). Marketing hedonics: Toward a psychoanalysis of advertising response. *Journal of Marketing Communications*, 16(3): 107–131.

Packard, V. (1957). *The hidden persuaders*. New York: Pocket Books.

Reyes, I., Dholakia, N. and Bonoff, J.K. (2015). Disconnected/connected: On the 'look' and the 'gaze' of cell phones. *Marketing Theory*, 15(1): 113–127.

Rogers, M. and Seiler, C.A. (1994). The answer is no: A national survey of advertising industry practitioners and their clients about whether they use subliminal advertising. *Journal of Advertising Research*, 34(2): 36–45.

Rustin, M. (2010). Looking for the unexpected: Psychoanalytic understanding and politics. *British Journal of Psychotherapy*, 26(4): 472–479.

Schwarzkopf, S. (2015). Mobilizing the depths of the market: Motivation research and the making of the disembedded consumer. *Marketing Theory*, 15(1): 39–57.

Stewart, D.W. and Shamdasani, P.N. (2014). *Focus groups: Theory and practice*, Vol. 20. London: SAGE.

Tadajewski, M. (2006). Remembering motivation research: Toward an alternative genealogy of interpretive consumer research. *Marketing Theory*, 6(4): 429–466.

Williamson, J.E. (1978). *Decoding advertisements: Ideology and meaning in advertising*. London: Marion Boyars.

Winnicott, D. (1971). *Playing and reality*. London: Tavistock Press.

Zaretsky, E. (2005). *Secrets of the soul: A social and cultural history of psychoanalysis*. New York: Vintage Books.

6 Ethical debates in marketing management

Introduction

In the context of the recent global economic downturn, marketers are perhaps under more scrutiny than ever before in their role as 'persuaders' of consumer spending (Woodall, 2012). In addition, as the key form of communication between organisations and the general public, marketing is subject to a significant amount of societal scrutiny. Marketing also plays a central role in organisational attempts to engender the values of commitment, trust and loyalty amongst employees, customers and the public. While marketing ethics have been a cause for concern for some time, recent developments in new communications technologies, coupled with the opening up of previously closed economies in the transformation of some countries to free market systems, have undoubtedly exacerbated ethical challenges. Examples of this can be seen in the controversial promotion of cigarettes in developing countries and in the case of Nestlé, who were accused of misleadingly promoting milk formula in developing countries as better for babies than mothers' milk. However, as Brenkert (2008: 4) observes, 'we harbour, as a society, a deeply divided consciousness over marketing'. Many of those living in developed countries readily embrace the array of goods that are the consequence of the efficient operation of markets, while at the same time some feel a sense of unease at the cost of this abundance. This chapter first considers the definition and scope of research on marketing ethics. This is followed by a discussion of the role of marketing ethics in contemporary society that explores how marketing ethics might offer practical guidelines to both organisations and the individuals working within them. The chapter then examines some ethical criticisms of marketing practice including: new media marketing, marketing research, advertising, and product and brand management. In closing, the chapter draws together these debates in a case study which explores the marketing of cosmetics.

Marketing ethics: a definition and scope

Surprisingly few authors offer an actual definition of marketing ethics. Drawing from Aristotelian moral philosophy for inspiration, Gaski observes that marketing ethics could be considered as 'standards of conduct and moral judgement applied to marketing practice' (1999: 316). Murphy et al. open this out to include institutions themselves, defining marketing ethics as 'the systematic study of how moral standards are applied to marketing decisions, behaviours and institutions' (2005: xvii). However, ethical standards typically vary from one institutional environment to the next and from one culture to the next, which makes a universal application of a set of ethical marketing codes problematic. Complications also emerge from differing perspectives on ethics. In this respect Laczniak et al. (1995) found that the views of American consumers and CEOs differed widely, with consumers being far more pessimistic than CEOs about the ethical climate of businesses.

Defining the scope of marketing ethics is also difficult as the literature is both complex and extensive. At several intervals over the past thirty years scholars have made attempts to summarise and review this body of work. Murphy and Laczniak (1981) locate an initial debate on marketing ethics in the 1930s, although they observe that more significant developments occurred in the 1960s (i.e. Bartels, 1967). This latter work was largely concerned with highlighting a general, global approach to marketing ethics. It was not until the 1970s that work began to focus on specific issues such as marketing research, consumer issues, managerial issues and marketing education issues. In a review of studies, Nill and Schibrowsky (2007) identify a series of topics that have been covered in published work on marketing ethics (see Table 6.1) and note that studies may typically encompass more than one of these categories. They observe a lack of work on pricing and discrimination. They also find a worrying reduction of publications on marketing ethics in the top journals, leading them to surmise that marketing ethics is 'no longer an integral part of marketing discourse' and that, instead, it has 'evolved into a specific sub-discipline' (2007: 272).

What role for marketing ethics?

The role marketing ethics ought to play, both in relation to the individual and the organisation, has been a key topic for debate. Authors have questioned the extent to which marketing ethics might offer guidelines to marketers (Gaski, 1999, 2015; Smith, 2001). They have also been concerned with how theories of marketing ethics might translate into application (Robin and Reidenbach, 1987, 1993; Smith, 1995; Thompson, 1995). In addressing these issues, studies have been undertaken from two key perspectives: the normative approach, which aims to prescribe ethical standards and offer guidelines regarding marketing practice; and the positive approach, which aims to describe and understand ethical practices through empirical work. Before exploring these perspectives, however, it is useful to summarise their underpinning philosophies, these being primarily deontological and teleological theories.

Table 6.1 Topical areas of marketing ethics

	Issues related to
Functional areas	Product Price Placement Promotion
Sub-disciplines of marketing	Sales Consumers/consumption International marketing Marketing ethics education Marketing research Social marketing Internet marketing Law and ethics
Specific ethics-related topics	Ethics and society Ethical decision-making models Ethical responsibility towards marketers' stakeholders Ethical values Norm generation and definition Marketing ethics implementation Relationship between ethics and religion Discrimination and harassment Green marketing Vulnerable consumers

Source: Nill and Schibrowsky, 2007: 258

Deontological theories

Deontological theories focus on the behaviours of the individual, specifically the principles used to arrive at the ethical decision. Murphy and Laczniak (1981: 252) give the example of Kant's categorical imperative as a deontological theory 'that persons should act in such a way that their maxim for action could be a universal law'. In this perspective the focus is on the behaviour itself and actions are judged by their inherent wrongness or rightness. As Hunt and Vitell observe, 'For deontologists the conundrum has been to determine the "best" set of rules to live by' (1986: 6). The principles for these rules may come from a range of sources such as the family, religion, politics, etc.

Teleological theories

In contrast teleologists place emphasis on perceived outcomes rather than behaviours. They propose that individuals should make judgements based on an evaluation of the likely consequences of their actions. Teleological theories differ, however, on the issue of whose good one ought to promote:

- *Ethical egoism* suggests that individuals should act in their own interests, i.e. choose an act that results in the most favourable consequences for the individual.

- *Utilitarianism* strives to produce the greatest good for the greatest number of people. Here, an act should be judged on an evaluation of the balance of good consequences over bad consequences it provides for all individuals (Hunt and Vitell, 1986: 6–7).

Although this discussion of the two sets of theories is a simplification, it is important to understand their principles, as they provide the basis for most normative work, and some positive work, on marketing ethics. This work is explored below.

A normative role for marketing ethics

Authors working from a normative perspective have been concerned to provide a series of recommendations regarding marketing practice (Laczniak, 1983; Laczniak and Murphy, 1985, 1993, 2006a; Smith and Quelch, 1993; Chonko, 1995; Murphy et al., 2005). These recommendations are concerned with 'what marketing organizations or individuals ought to do or what kinds of marketing systems a society ought to have' (Hunt, 1976: 20). Laczniak and Murphy, in describing normative marketing ethics, observe that 'exchange, because it is *social*, must have its outcomes evaluated in terms of fairness or rightness on all marketplace parties' (2006a: 154). In examining the role of ethics in marketing management, Smith (1993) observes that the marketing manager often has little direct authority and has to rely on the cooperation of other functions within the organisation. This means that marketing managers are typically exposed to a range of competing pressures. Chonko (1995) explores how marketing professionals might deal with unethical behaviour. In his evaluation it seems that whistle blowing (or threatening to blow the whistle) and negotiation are potentially the most advantageous courses of action. He also usefully identifies some reasons why professionals sometimes engage in unethical behaviour. The first reason is diffusion of responsibility, where elaborate organisational structures mean that responsibility is so diffuse that accountability is difficult to pinpoint. A second reason is rationalisation, through which wrong decisions can often easily be explained away. Chonko observes that four commonly held beliefs about behaviour might facilitate this:

- A belief that the behaviour is within reasonable ethical and legal limits – that is, the behaviour is not really immoral or illegal.
- A belief that the behaviour is in the best interests of the individual, the organisation or both – the individual would somehow be expected to undertake the behaviour.
- A belief that the behaviour is safe because it will never be found out or published, the classic crime and punishment issue of discovery.
- A belief that because the behaviour helps the organisation the organisation will condone it and even protect the individual who engages in the behaviour. (Gellerman, 1986, cited in Chonko, 1995: 114)

A key issue is that managers are not aware that marketing ethics can be learnt. Instead they seem to think that ethics are merely a product of their upbringing, religious beliefs and social circle. To this end theorists (particularly normative theorists) are at pains to develop marketing ethics education at the business school level. As Laczniak and Murphy observe:

> The role of relativism and the attitude that all marketing practices are flexible depending on circumstance and personal opinion – views often expressed by business students – seem overstated given the articulated norms and values of marketing professionals, as well as specific codes developed through the consensus of peer practitioners.
>
> (2006a: 171)

They argue further that these codes ought to be taught in business schools, although students should be taught to improve the ethical cultures of their organisations rather than merely to preach ethics (2006a: 172). To try and bridge the gap between seemingly abstract codes of ethics and the everyday decisions that marketing managers face, Laczniak and Murphy have developed a set of perspectives to guide marketing activity. The seven basic perspectives (BP) are as listed below:

- BP1: Ethical marketing puts people first.
- BP2: Ethical marketers must achieve a behavioural standard in excess of the law.
- BP3: Marketers are responsible for whatever they intend as a means or ends as a marketing action.
- BP4: Marketing organisations should cultivate better (i.e. higher) moral imagination in their managers and employees.
- BP5: Marketers should articulate and embrace a core set of ethical principles.
- BP6: Adoption of a stakeholder orientation is essential to ethical marketing decisions.
- BP7: Marketing organisations ought to delineate an ethical decision-making protocol.

(Laczniak and Murphy, 2006a: 157)

Laczniak and Murphy observe that taken in isolation these perspectives are difficult to apply. For example, in the societal perspective in BP1, whose interests ought marketers to put first? They suggest that this can be addressed by referring to BP6, the adoption of a stakeholder orientation. They highlight a series of further relationships between the perspectives and suggest that while each basic perspective is a useful guideline in itself, they work together to form a holistic approach to marketing management. Overall, in taking a normative approach to marketing ethics, Murphy et al. (2005: 47) chart a middle path between ethical theory, individual judgement and societal standards:

In the final analysis, ethics still requires considerable prudential judgement that comes from the intuition of the marketing manager (hopefully, grounded in virtue ethics), but it is tempered by a knowledge of ethical theory as well as corporate, industry and societal standards.

Clearly the normative approach is not without its challenges; as Gaski (2015) observes, the multiplicity of perspectives it embraces can lead to conflict between norms and ambiguity in offering guidance.

A positive role for marketing ethics

While normative marketing ethics seeks to provide guidelines regarding marketing practice, positive marketing ethics is concerned with describing and understanding ethical practices. Over the years, authors have developed a series of frameworks in order to better understand ethical decision making in marketing (Ferrell and Gresham, 1985; Hunt and Vitell, 1986; Thompson, 1995). The most widely used of these frameworks has undoubtedly been Hunt and Vitell's (1986, 2006, see also Vitell and Hunt, 2015) 'General Theory of Marketing Ethics'. The model attempts to 'explain the decision making process for problem situations having ethical content' (1986: 5). Since publication, the framework has been applied in a range of contexts, with most authors finding significant support for the model (Mayo and Marks, 1990; Hunt and Vasquez-Parraga, 1993; Menguc, 1998; Vitell et al., 2001).

In their 'General Theory of Marketing Ethics', Hunt and Vitell recognise that, when making decisions, marketers draw on both teleological and deontological evaluations and, thus, they build both of these elements into their model (see Figure 6.1). They observe that the cultural, industrial and organisational environments, as well as past personal experiences, impact upon the individual's perception of the ethical problem. These factors also impact on the perceived alternatives available to them. They suggest that both a deontological and teleological evaluation of these alternatives takes place. In the deontological evaluation, they posit that the individual evaluates alternatives against a set of norms including personal values and beliefs. They also observe that these norms include issue-specific beliefs such as 'deceptive advertising, product safety, sales "kickbacks", confidentiality of data, respondent anonymity and interviewer dishonesty' (1986: 9). In the teleological evaluation, four constructs are considered, namely '(1) the perceived consequences of each alternative for various stakeholder groups, (2) the probability that each consequence will occur to each stakeholder group, (3) the desirability or undesirability of each consequence, and (4) the importance of each stakeholder group' (p. 9). They also note that individuals will differ in the stakeholder groups they identify and the relative importance of these.

The key part of the model is the combination of these two sets of evaluations. The model posits that 'an individual's ethical judgement (for example, the belief that a particular alternative is the most ethical alternative) is a

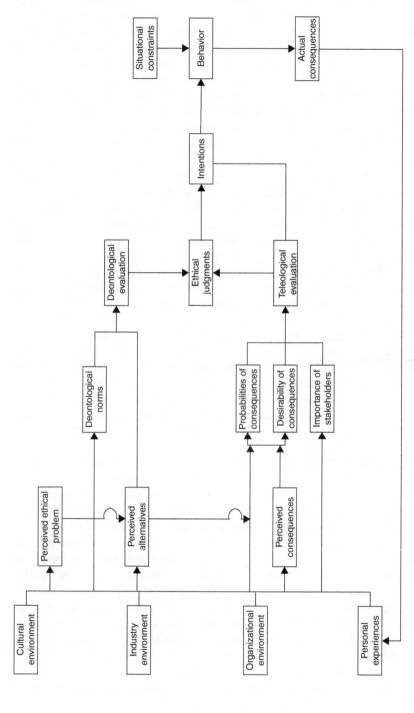

Figure 6.1 General theory of marketing ethics (Hunt and Vitell, 1986: 8)

function of the individual's deontological evaluation (i.e. applying norms of behaviour to each of the alternatives) and the individual's teleological evaluation (i.e. evaluating the sum total of goodness versus badness likely to be produced by each alternative)' (1986: 9). Hunt and Vitell then introduce an intentions construct, 'the likelihood that any particular alternative will be chosen' (p. 9), which intervenes between ethical judgement and actual behaviour. They argue that intentions may often differ from ethical judgements due to the influence of teleological evaluations. For example, an individual may reach a conclusion regarding the most ethical course of action but choose another course due to preferred consequences, either to themselves or perhaps to the organisation. In these cases the individual may well feel guilt depending on their individual ethical norms and beliefs. The action taken is also dependent on situational constraints, such as opportunities, and these may result in behaviours that do not match intentions and ethical judgements. Hunt and Vitell also include a learning construct, the 'actual consequences' of the chosen alternative. These actual consequences feed back into personal experiences and, therefore, highlight the possibility that individuals may, to an extent, become conditioned by their organisational context, i.e. through the operation of punishments and rewards. It is important to note that the cultural, industrial and organisational environments, and past personal experiences, as well as affecting the perceived ethical problem and alternatives available, also affect deontological norms, perceived consequences, probability of consequences, desirability of consequences and importance of stakeholders. Thus the model takes account of situational and contextual factors both in the formulation of the problem and the resulting action or behaviour. In fact, more recently, Vitell and Hunt (2015) argue that the model needn't be confined to marketing managers; if we exclude the industrial and organisational environments, the model may apply to understand the ethics of consumer behaviour more generally.

Thompson (1995) introduces a further model of marketing ethics arguing that 'the current models of marketing ethics do not sufficiently address the multitude of contextual influences that, from a contextualist perspective, are intrinsic to ethical reasoning' (p. 177). While there is not space here to adequately describe Thompson's contextualist model, an overview of its key components is useful in understanding some critiques of earlier perspectives on marketing ethics. In particular Thompson highlights the 'multiplicity of cultural meaning and value systems' and the fact that the marketing agent is 'culturally situated'. He posits that culturally shared beliefs influence marketing managers' identification of ethical issues, interpretations of the relevant community of stakeholders and evaluations of marketing actions (Thompson, 1995: 183–5). More recently Ferrell et al. (2015) have provided an overview of a wide range of ethical decision-making models. They develop a synthesised model (p. 57) which suggests that perceptions of ethical issues, individual factors and organisational culture and compliance all impinge on ethical decision making and subsequent ethical behaviour.

Ethical criticisms of marketing practice

The marketing practices undertaken by organisations have been criticised for a range of reasons. Four areas of particular contemporary concern are explored below.

New media marketing

New media is at the centre of the recent marketing revolution. However, it poses a series of very significant ethical challenges in terms of consumer privacy and truth and authenticity. New media is a broad and ever evolving term. We can only guess at its future meanings, but at present it is used to describe the array of content that is available on the internet. This content can be accessed through a range of devices including mobile phones, computers and games consoles. New media tends to be interactive and multivocal, allowing users to create content themselves. It also allows consumers to come together to communicate and bond around topics of interest. The format embraces video streaming, online news and virtual-reality environments; it also includes social media such as Facebook, YouTube and Twitter. Consumers use these platforms to connect with others through the sharing of photos, advice, recipes, etc., creating what has been called 'user-generated content'. Arguably, then, new media is empowering for consumers, allowing them to connect with others and giving them a platform for creativity and self-expression.

The problem arises though with what marketers and corporations are doing with the huge amounts of data that this activity generates. Developments in the area of 'big data' and consumer tracking have given companies access to increasingly intimate areas of consumers' lives (Nill et al., 2015). Data-mining techniques enable the extraction of information which may be scattered across a range of data pools to produce detailed individual consumer profiles. This means that there is a growing archive of information on individual consumers detailing their purchases and linking this to their personal data such as gender, age, life stage and even address. Worryingly, these profiles are then sold on to a range of other interested parties. Therefore we can't be sure who is using our data and who has access to it (see Laczniak and Murphy, 2006b). This is problematic in terms of invasiveness and consumer privacy, but also, on a much grander scale, in terms of consumer control. In a paper which looks in frightening depth at the capabilities of corporations to track our activities online and then use this data to segment and target us as consumers, Cluley and Brown (2014: 116) observe:

> The function of marketing in the new society of control is to identify data points and reconstruct data in clustered segments that define what products people have access to, what advertising offers are made to them and what content they see.

Instead of framing the consumer in traditional terms as an individual, Cluley and Brown (2014: 108) argue that these capabilities create a series of 'dividuals', a dividual being a 'cybernetic subject made up of data points, codes and passwords'. They further surmise that the lives of these dividuals are increasingly controlled and managed by marketers. Zwick and Denegri-Knott (2009) liken this increasingly sophisticated mode of database marketing to the 21st-century factory in which customers are manufactured as commodities. They observe that it not only facilitates a high level of continuous consumer surveillance but that it also literally 'produces' consumers through representations. The problem lies, however, in that these representations have very real effects as they define who does, and (more importantly) who does not, inform the shaping of future marketing and production activities.

The rise of social media as a platform for communication, social bonding and creative meaning making can arguably be seen as a good thing. Some commentators have argued that these platforms can significantly enrich people's lives, especially those with low self-esteem who struggle with everyday forms of social communication. However, a study of Facebook (Forest and Wood, 2012) found that while consumers with low self-esteem were attracted to this platform, the negative tone of their disclosures means that they are less liked than disclosures from those with high self-esteem. This suggests that some of the obstacles faced by people in forming solid friendships in the offline environment may transfer to the online environment. It also suggests that social media is not as democratic and value free as is often depicted and raises questions about the mental well-being of social network users. A second serious issue pertaining to social networking sites such as Facebook is the security and privacy of the information that users share on these sites. Facebook has a long-standing series of controversies over user privacy which have resulted in users being exposed, outed and emotionally manipulated (Hoffmann, 2016). Examples include gay users being unintentionally outed to their parents after being added to a queer choir's Facebook group which then automatically informed all their Facebook friends; and a disabled user losing her disability insurance benefits for depression after she posted photos of her having fun on the beach and at a nightclub. Examples also abound of companies who have either refused employment contracts or even fired staff on the basis of information gleaned from social networking sites. One of the key issues here is the perceived privacy of information by users which impacts on the level of information they share. A study found that the more control users perceive themselves as having the lower they perceive the risks associated with information sharing (Hajli and Lin, 2016). This encourages them to be more open in sharing information on social networking sites. The problem arises, however, when users' perceived control is inaccurate, while social networking sites such as Facebook provide ways to control information through privacy settings and policies; due to their complexities often users only have a limited understanding of how these operate. In addition sites seem to make regular changes to the types of personal information automatically shared which are almost impossible to predict. There will always be scenarios which users could not easily predict and which are largely beyond their control – such as the example above where a user's membership of a gay choir was posted on their Facebook site.

Problems also arise when companies start to use social networking tools such as blogs and online forums to promote their brands. There are issues here connected with truth and authenticity. While the law has been changed now to embrace social media, companies have been found in the past to be paying or compensating bloggers to endorse their products or brand. In 2006 it was revealed that Wal-Mart had paid expenses for two bloggers to undertake a road trip across the US writing positive blog entries about Wal-Mart as they went. Brands have also been known to instruct their agencies to comment on online forums promoting their products and raising questions about competitors. Finally there is the ever present issue of exploitation in the guise of user-generated content. As we discussed in the introductory chapter to this book the whole concept of co-creation, which is often supported by social networking sites, involves the user in working for free for the company. For example, brands hold online contests where ordinary consumers are encouraged to submit copy, designs or even commercials they have produced. The winner receives a prize and the company uses the creative for their own promotional purposes. Aside from the overarching issues of consumer exploitation, it is also very often the case that it is freelance or unemployed creatives (rather than ordinary consumers) who win. Thus these competitions act as a source of support for professionals who should be properly paid for their work.

Marketing research and segmentation

The above section explores how data and information in the online world can be subject to abuse, but more traditional marketing research methods are also open to abuse. Ethical issues in relation to marketing research are numerous, embracing both the practices of data collection and the subsequent use of this data. Murphy et al. highlight a series of issues relating to the professional conduct of market researchers that includes the duty not to engage in deceptive practices, the duty not to invade privacy and the duty to manifest concern for respondents (2005: 52–7). In reality, using the data collected, organisations have been accused of inappropriate stereotyping and the passing on of personal details to other organisations. Data can also easily be manipulated and/or presented in a particular light to tell the story the organisation wants to tell. Statistics are well known to be powerful agents in creating arguments because in general people tend to believe them.

The general public are now so used to requests for their personal information that they often fail to question the use to which this data will actually be put. Personal details are requested in relation to a wide variety of circumstances, ranging from returning goods to a store to completing guarantees for goods purchased, and applying for store loyalty cards. This also applies to a range of occasional services, from hotel stays, to visiting the hairdresser, or taking the car to the garage. This is in addition to the range of financial and home services which hold details about their customers from credit card, pension, insurance and mortgage companies and electricity, gas, internet and telephone providers. In fact, there are undoubtedly hundreds of organisations that hold data about each one of us. Some individuals would say that this is not a problem. It is a problem, however, when data is used to the consumer's disadvantage, as, for example, when organisations pass details on to other service and goods providers, or bombard individuals with promotional telephone calls, post, emails and text messages. These messages can be very carefully tailored to the individual. By linking purchase histories with personal details, organisations build up a relatively clear picture of the consumers' daily lives, not only their age, gender, occupation and place of residence, but also what they eat and drink, and even the personal hygiene products they use.

This fine-grained targeting becomes more of an issue where vulnerable segments are involved. Indeed, a study by Smith and Cooper-Martin (1997) found significant public disquiet over the ethics of some targeting strategies. Vulnerable groups might include children, teens, older consumers and those which Murphy et al. term 'market illiterates' (2005: 74). This last group includes those that for one reason or another are not familiar with the workings of the market; this may be due to cultural illiteracy in the case of immigrants but it may also be due to poor access to educational and financial capital. However, Baker et al. point out that 'consumer vulnerability is multi-dimensional, context specific and does not have to be enduring' (2005: 128). They refute the commonly held assumption that some individuals, because of membership in a particular group, are always vulnerable, and observe that all individuals may experience vulnerability at some point in their lives due to family death, illness, etc.

Advertising

Advertising is the area of marketing activity which has attracted the most criticism over the years. Research suggests that consumers innately distrust advertising. A review of consumer surveys on beliefs about advertising since the 1930s found that '70% think that advertising is often untruthful, it seeks (perhaps successfully) to persuade people to buy things they do not want, it should be more strictly regulated, and it nonetheless provides valuable information' (Calfee and Jones Ringold, 1994: 236). Broadly speaking, advertising has been criticised on two levels: at the micro level the content and type of some messages has been cause for concern, and at the macro level the wider effects of advertising on society has been questioned.

On the micro level, advertisements have been criticised for excessive portrayal of violence, the use of sex and profanity and the elicitation of negative emotions such as shock, fear and guilt (LaTour and Zahra, 1988; Huhmann and Brotherton, 1997; Dahl et al., 2003). In general authors warn against some of the outcomes of using negative emotions in advertising. For example, LaTour and Zahra (1988) express concern for the consumer's psychological well-being in the case of fear appeals. Advertising to vulnerable groups such as children, the elderly and those on low incomes has also come under criticism. Authors have expressed concern about young consumers, in particular young children's ability to comprehend and interpret advertising (Moore, 2004). They also observe that the blurring of advertising and leisure entertainment makes it particularly difficult for even older children to distinguish what is, and what is not, an advert (Lindstrom and Seybold, 2003). Carrigan and Szmigin (2000) address the issue of advertising and ageism, arguing that elderly consumers are substantially discriminated against, not only by being marginalised generally in marketing activity, but also by being negatively stereotypically portrayed in advertisements. Advertisements have been accused of promoting increased levels of anxiety and insecurity in society because they typically encourage processes of social comparison against idealised images. The negative influence of advertising on young women's body image has been a particular cause for concern, and the use of very thin models in fashion advertising has been blamed for an increased incidence of anorexia amongst this group (Fay and Price, 1994).

On the macro level the key issue for critics is the role that advertising might play in manipulating consumers. Packard's (1957) book *The Hidden Persuaders* is often cited in this context. Packard explores the subliminal techniques used by advertisers to manipulate consumer expectations and desire for products and services. More recently, Pollay (1986) posits that 'Advertising is without doubt a formative influence within our culture'. He goes on to conclude that scholars 'see it as reinforcing materialism, cynicism, irrationality, selfishness, anxiety, social competitiveness, sexual preoccupation, powerlessness and/or a loss of self respect' (p. 18). A key strand in subsequent debate about the role of advertising in society is whether it merely reflects a pre-existing reality or whether it actually moulds this reality. Holbrook, for example, observes that 'most advertising appears to mirror or reflect rather than to mould or shape the values of its target audience' (1987: 100).

Product and brand management

Murphy et al. (2005: 82) identify a series of issues in relation to product and brand management. In particular, 'what *degree of disclosure* does a product manager owe consumers who will be using the organization's branded product? What responsibilities do product managers and retailers have related to the *social ramifications* of their products?' The issue of social responsibility becomes obvious when we think about potentially harmful products such as alcohol, tobacco and fast foods.

One of the central ethical issues in relation to both tobacco and alcohol is misleading and deceptive advertising. This has been a particular problem in the tobacco industry where several lawsuits have been filed, accusing the industry of deceptive marketing practices, which have led to mistaken beliefs about smoking. A series of cases have been made against tobacco manufacturers that attempt to hold them responsible for injury, premature death or medical expenses related to tobacco use. Concerns have also been raised over marketing cigarettes to young people. Several studies have observed that adolescents are particularly susceptible to both tobacco and alcohol advertising (Hastings and Aitken, 1995; Pollay et al., 1996). In this respect, the infamous Joe Camel campaign has been the subject of much debate with commentators arguing that the cartoon character directly targeted the youth market (Calfee, 2000; Cohen, 2000). In an attempt to revive flagging sales, R.J. Reynolds introduced the Joe Camel cartoon character in 1988. As a result of the controversy that followed, the company agreed to cease using the character in 1997. Conversely, Calfee (2000) observes there is little evidence that the campaign did actually precipitate an increase in youth smoking. He also observes that the 'idea' that the advertisements were targeted primarily at underage smokers travelled far and fast in the popular press, government and the public health community. He argues that 'This putative role for Joe Camel appears to have substantially increased the level of public and political support for the most important anti-smoking activities of the 1990s' (p. 179).

Questions have also been raised regarding manufacturers' and retailers' responsibilities in relation to unhealthy (and fast) foods (Jackson et al., 2015). Debate has raged in the context of a rising obesity problem in the adult population, but more worryingly, the child population, in the UK and America. A series of lawsuits have been filed against fast food restaurants in which litigators have tried to draw lessons from the successes of tobacco litigation. The central argument has been that the information provided regarding the nutritional value of fast food products is misleading, leading to over-consumption and eventually obesity. Allegations have also been made that fast food is addictive. However, as Robinson et al. (2005: 305) observe in their analysis of a recent lawsuit against McDonald's, 'those who try to hold food companies legally liable for the costs associated with obesity have a difficult road ahead'. Instead they recommend alternative approaches, such as social marketing, as a solution to combat obesity (see Stead et al., 2007).

The question remains as to what extent manufacturers and marketers might be held responsible for the effects of their products on society. Overall it appears that the key elements in the marketing of potentially harmful products relate to addiction, deception and duty to warn. The first of these is very difficult to militate against, but in relation to the last two issues, deception and duty to warn, perhaps the key issue is one of information and, in particular, the type and level of information provided on packaging and in advertising. Undoubtedly manufacturers have come a long way in this respect. Fast food retailers and restaurants now produce detailed breakdowns of the fat and nutritional content of their foods for customers. Cigarette and tobacco packaging also contains significant health warnings, and alcohol advertising (in the UK at least) comes with warnings regarding sensible drinking.

CASE STUDY: the marketing of cosmetics

Female beauty is a major cultural and financial industry in Western democratic countries. Advertising spend in the cosmetics industry is proportionally higher than in any other sector. Perhaps, then, it is not surprising that ethical breaches occur with some regularity in an industry that is so fiercely competitive and where the stakes are so high. The case study below explores two key ethical elements of cosmetics marketing: deceptive advertising and consumer manipulation.

Deceptive advertising: realistic claims?

The bold claims of cosmetics manufacturers have been the cause for much controversy over the years. Claims such as skin rejuvenation and repair, improved elasticity, smoothing of wrinkles and the reduction of fine lines are routinely made by the industry. One of the key weapons in the industry's advertising armoury is the language of science. Cosmetics advertisements often call upon the authority of scientific research for 'proof' that their products are effective. However, consumers can easily be misled by this scientific 'jargon' (Sims, 2007). For example, the cosmetics company Olay gives the following description of their anti-ageing skincare product in their online advertising:

> Regenerist reclaims the lifted look of your youth. Phase 1 is specially formulated to ignite cellular regeneration and infuse skin with repairing moisture. Phase 2 helps fill wrinkles with polishing micro-powders and hydrating moisture. The high concentration of (manufacturer name) peptide-B3 complex also improves skin's moisture barrier, giving you stronger skin structure and a more youthful glow.

Another cosmetics company, Avon, offers the following description of their Anew Alternative skin cream:

> For the first time, we can encourage skin to fight the ageing process using Glycation-Reversing Technology. This breakthrough formula helps reverse existing damage and rebuild its support structure. Helps reverse the signs of ageing, restores youthful contours and redefines facial features.

The language used here is a careful mixture of scientific sounding terms such as 'Glycation-Reversing Technology' and complex ingredients such as 'peptide-B3 complex'. These phrases are used alongside the active terminology of fighting, polishing, hydrating, repairing, redefining, reversing and restoring. Impressive results are also claimed such as a 'stronger skin structure and a more youthful glow'.

The industry has made questionable claims not only in relation to its advertisements but also its labelling. For example, sunscreen makers have been accused of making misleading health claims on their labelling which overinflate the sun-protection abilities of their products. This is a particular problem in products designed for use on young children. In fact the power of language is central to the cosmetics industry's promotional efforts. In the UK, the Advertising Standards Agency has reprimanded the manufacturers of skincare creams for using misleading terminology in their advertising campaigns, making assertions such as 'the home alternative to surgery' and 'steering hearty cells to the base of wrinkles'. The use by skincare manu-facturers of science to bias the opinion of consumers regarding their products might easily be seen as exploitative, in particular by taking advantage of the lack of scientific and technological knowledge of the general public. A second issue relating to deception is perhaps more straightforward with some cos-metics manufacturers digitally manipulating advertising images, airbrushing out skin imperfections, lengthening eye lashes and enhancing eye colour. A range of major cosmetics manufacturers in the UK have been censored by the Advertising Standards Agency for using false eyelashes on models in their advertisements for mascara.

Consumer manipulation: playing on anxieties?

Although individual advertisements might be charged with making unrealistic claims and inflating the properties of products, taken as a whole these types of advertisements also impact significantly on wider consumer society. Cosmetics advertising relies on the consumer's desire to look young and attractive and plays a role in setting the tone and extent of these desires. One of the most powerful techniques of persuasion used in cosmetics advertising is the sugges-tion that a sense of improved self-esteem will result from using the products. As Reventós observes, 'Hidden beneath the glamorous ideals in beauty ads there are subtexts that play on women's anxieties and feelings of inadequacy, while promising a sense of self-worth' (1998: 32). To this end, the industry promotes a range of problems, many of which women did not even know they had, such as pale skin or thin eyelashes, and to which they are offered the ideal magical solution. As Reventós suggests 'many beauty ads appeal specifically to our sense of magic, to the "Cinderella syndrome": the magic of personal transformation that is part of the imaginative life of most women' (p. 34).

Whilst relying on men and women's anxieties surrounding appearance, these advertisements arguably play a role in actually impacting upon our everyday practices of personal hygiene. For example, women and some men are now generally persuaded that having a 'skincare routine' involving several different products is now essential for healthy and attractive skin. Of course, this takes time as well as costing money. There is a similar trend in haircare products where manufacturers have created a number of product niches based on new hair styling techniques such as straightening, curling and colouring hair. An array of gels, mousses, creams, lotions and serums have emerged, each one creating a different hair fashion. The cosmetics industry (as have many other industries) has relentlessly pursued a policy of niche product diversification and extension. Sales of these products rely on creating a consumer need for a wider array of products. Another way in which manufacturers have achieved this is by dividing the body up into an increasing number of discrete zones and persuading the consumer that each zone requires a different type of cosmetic product. For example, skincare products are sold in the form of eye creams, as well as neck and face creams. Research suggests that the ingredients of these creams do not differ very significantly between product types, and that in fact the main way in which they differ is through price and packaging size.

Who is responsible?

The Advertising Standards Authority (ASA) is the chief regulator of advertising in the United Kingdom. The mission of the agency is to 'apply the advertising codes and uphold standards in all media on behalf of consumers, business and society' (ASA website). The main principles of these codes are that advertisements should not mislead, cause harm or offend. Recently the ASA surveyed 445 cosmetic advertisements appearing on television, radio, direct mailings, online, on posters and in the press. In assessing the advertisements, using the ASA codes, they found that thirty-two (7 percent) represented obvious breaches of the codes. Three of these thirty-two advertisements were investigated by the ASA after receiving complaints and all three were found to be unacceptable. The survey found that the key problems were 'unsubstantiated cumulative beneficial effect claims and physiological claims for skin creams for women' (Advertising Standards Authority, 2007: 2). Within the cosmetics category advertisements for skin creams were a particular cause for concern, with a breach rate of 19 percent.

Seminar exercises

Discussion topics

1   Discuss the pros and cons of taking a deontological approach versus a teleological approach to decisions surrounding marketing ethics.
2   Using examples, discuss the extent to which you think manufacturers and marketers might be held responsible for the effects of their products on society.
3   Discuss the importance of ethics in marketing research. Identify the ethical factors that need to be taken into consideration at each stage of research design, data collection and the reporting of findings.
4   Drawing on your own experience of using social networking sites such as Facebook, discuss the ways in which you attempt to control the information you share. Discuss the ethical issues surrounding companies having access to this information for marketing purposes.

Group exercises

1   Using one of the examples below prepare a presentation summarising the key ethical debates in the case concerned. Use real-life examples from marketing magazines, newspaper reports and marketing websites to illustrate your discussion.

- The promotion and sale of unhealthy or harmful products.
- The targeting of vulnerable segments in advertising campaigns.
- The invasion of consumer privacy in social networking sites.

2   Look up the Advertising Standards Association's (ASA) top ten most complained about advertisements in their annual report (this can be found on their website). For each advert discuss:

- Why the advert might be seen as unethical.
- Which groups you think the advert is most likely to offend.
- Whether or not you agree with the ASA's ruling and why.

3   Consider the following scenario:

> Sarah Jones is the marketing manager of a large building company. She is designing an advertisement for a new housing development her company is about to start building. The development is located in a low area which has flooded in the past. The company has recently done some work to reduce the danger of flooding in the future. The fact is that if a flood occurs, the homes are still likely to be flooded with up to 5 feet of water.
>
> (Adapted from Lund, 2000: 334)

- Identify the alternatives available to the marketing manager. For each of these alternatives:
- Identify the stakeholders that would be affected.
- Identify the probable consequences of the decision for each stakeholder group.
- Identify the desirability of these consequences for each stakeholder group.
- Given the above considerations identify which alternative you would choose and why.

Internet resources

Academy of Marketing, Marketing and Ethics Special Interest Group: www.academ yofmarketing.org/sigs/ethics-marketing-sig/
Advertising Standards Authority: www.asa.org.uk/
Market Research Society's code of conduct: www.mrs.org.uk/standards/code_of_conduct/
Society for Business Ethics: http://sbeonline.org/

Key readings

Laczniak, G.R. and Murphy, P.E. (2006a). Normative perspectives for ethical and socially responsible marketing. *Journal of Macromarketing*, 12(26): 154–177.

Nill, A. (ed.) (2015). *Handbook on ethics and marketing.* Cheltenham: Edward Elgar.

Robin, D.P. and Reidenbach, E. (1993). Searching for a place to stand: Toward a workable ethical philosophy for marketing. *Journal of Public Policy and Marketing*, 12(1): 97–105.

Vitell, S.J. and Hunt, S.D. (2015). The general theory of marketing ethics: The consumer ethics and intentions issues. In A. Nill (ed.), *Handbook on ethics and marketing.* Cheltenham: Edward Elgar, pp. 15–37.

References

Advertising Standards Authority (2007). *Compliance report: Cosmetics advertising survey.* London: ASA.

Baker, S.M., Gentry, J.W. and Rittenburg, T.L. (2005). Building understanding of the domain of consumer vulnerability. *Journal of Macromarketing*, 25(2): 128–139.

Bartels, R. (1967). A framework for ethics in marketing. *Journal of Marketing*, January: 20–26.

Brenkert, G. (2008). *Marketing ethics.* Oxford: Blackwell.

Calfee, J. (2000). The historical significance of Joe Camel. *Journal of Public Policy and Management*, 19(2): 168–182.

Calfee, J.E. and Jones Ringold, D. (1994). The 70% majority: Enduring consumer beliefs about advertising. *Journal of Public Policy and Marketing*, 13(2): 228–238.

Carrigan, M. and Szmigin, I. (2000). Advertising in an ageing society. *Ageing and Society*, 20: 217–233.

Chonko, L. (1995). *Ethical decision making in marketing.* Thousand Oaks, CA: Sage.

Cluley, R. and Brown, S.D. (2014). The dividualised consumer: Sketching the new mask of the consumer. *Journal of Marketing Management*, 1–2: 107–122.

Cohen, J.B. (2000). Playing to win: Marketing and public policy at odds over Joe Camel. *Journal of Public Policy and Marketing*, 19(2): 155–167.

Dahl, D.W., Frankenberger, K.D. and Manchanda, R.V. (2003). Does it pay to shock? Reactions to shocking and non-shocking ad content among university students. *Journal of Advertising Research*, 43(3): 268–280.

Fay, M. and Price, C. (1994). Female body shape in print advertisements and the increase in anorexia nervosa. *European Journal of Marketing*, 28(12): 5–18.

Ferrell, O.C. and Gresham, L.G. (1985). A contingency framework for understanding ethical decision making in marketing. *Journal of Marketing*, 49 (summer): 87–96.

Ferrell, O.C., Ferrell, L. and Sawayda, J. (2015). A review of ethical decision-making models in marketing. In A. Nill (ed.), *Handbook on ethics and marketing.* Cheltenham: Edward Elgar, pp. 38–60.

Forest, A.L. and Wood, V.J. (2012). When social networking is not working: Individuals with low self-esteem recognize but do not reap the benefits of self-disclosure on Facebook. *Psychological Science*, 23: 295–302.

Gaski, J. (1999). Does marketing ethics really have anything to say? A critical inventory of the literature. *Journal of Business Ethics*, 18(3): 315–334.

Gaski, J. (2015). The trouble with marketing ethics... In A. Nill (ed.), *Handbook on ethics and marketing*. Cheltenham: Edward Elgar, pp. 111–124.

Gellerman, S.W. (1986). Why 'good' managers make bad ethical choices. *Harvard Business Review*, July/August: 85–90.

Hajli, N. and Lin, X. (2016). Exploring the security of information sharing on social networking sites: The role of perceived control of information. *Journal of Business Ethics*, 133(1): 111–123.

Hastings, G.B. and Aitken, P.P. (1995). Tobacco advertising and children's smoking: A review of the evidence. *European Journal of Marketing*, 29(11): 6–17.

Hoffmann, A.L. (2016). Facebook is worried about users sharing less – but it only has itself to blame. *Guardian*, 19 April.

Holbrook, M.B. (1987). Mirror, mirror, on the wall, what's unfair in the reflections on advertising? *Journal of Marketing*, 52 (July): 95–103.

Huhmann, B.A. and Brotherton, T.P. (1997). A content analysis of guilt appeals in popular magazine advertisements. *Journal of Advertising*, 26(2): 35–45.

Hunt, S.B. (1976). The nature and scope of marketing. *Journal of Marketing*, 40 (July): 17–28.

Hunt, S.B. and Vasquez-Parraga, A. (1993). Organizational consequences, marketing ethics and salesforce supervision. *Journal of Marketing Research*, 30 (February): 78–90.

Hunt, S.B. and Vitell, S.J. (1986). A general theory of marketing ethics. *Journal of Macromarketing*, 6(5): 5–16.

Hunt, S.B. and Vitell, S.J. (2006). The general theory of marketing ethics: A revision and three questions. *Journal of Macromarketing*, 12(26): 143–153.

Jackson, M., Harrison, P., Swinburn, B. and Lawrence, M. (2015). Marketing ethics in context: The promotion of unhealthy foods and beverages to children. In A. Nill (ed.), *Handbook on ethics and marketing*. Cheltenham: Edward Elgar, pp. 354–386.

Laczniak, G.R. (1983). Framework for analyzing marketing ethics. *Journal of Macro-marketing*, 6(3): 7–18.

Laczniak, G.R. and Murphy, P.E. (1985). *Marketing ethics: Guidelines for managers*. Lexington, MA: Lexington Books.

Laczniak, G.R. and Murphy, P.E. (1993). *Ethical marketing decisions: The higher road*. Toronto: Allyn and Bacon.

Laczniak, G.R. and Murphy, P.E. (2006). Marketing, consumers and technology: Perspectives for enhancing ethical transactions. *Business Ethics Quarterly*, 16(3): 313–321.

Laczniak, G.R., Berkowitz, M., Brooker, R. and Hale, J. (1995). The ethics of business: Improving or deteriorating? *Business Horizons*, 38(1): 39–47.

LaTour, M.S. and Zahra, S.A. (1988). Fear appeals as advertising strategy: Should they be used? *Journal of Services Marketing*, 2(4): 5–14.

Lindstrom, M. and Seybold, P.B. (2003). *Brandchild: Remarkable insights into the minds of today's global kids and their relationships with brands*. London: Kogan Page.

Lund, D.B. (2000). An empirical examination of marketing professionals' ethical behaviour in differing situations. *Journal of Business Ethics*, 24: 331–342.

Mayo, M. and Marks, L. (1990). An empirical investigation of a general theory of marketing ethics. *Journal of the Academy of Marketing Science*, 18(2): 163–171.

Menguc, B. (1998). Organizational consequences, marketing ethics and salesforce supervision: Further empirical evidence. *Journal of Business Ethics*, 17(4): 333–352.

Moore, E.S. (2004). Children and the changing world of advertising. *Journal of Business Ethics*, 52(2): 161–167.

Murphy, P.E. and Laczniak, G.R. (1981). Marketing ethics: A review with implications for managers, educators and researchers. *Review of Marketing*, Chicago: American Marketing Association, pp. 251–266.

Murphy, P.E., Laczniak, G.R., Bowie, N. and Klein, T. (2005). *Ethical marketing*. Upper Saddle River, NJ: Pearson Prentice Hall.

Nill, A. and Schibrowsky, J.A. (2007). Research on marketing ethics: A systematic review of the literature. *Journal of Macromarketing*, 27: 256–273.

Nill, A., Aalberts, R.J., Li, H. and Schibrowsky, J. (2015). New telecommunication technologies, big data and online behavioral advertising: Do we need an ethical analysis? In A. Nill (ed.), *Handbook on ethics and marketing*. Cheltenham: Edward Elgar, pp. 387–424.

Packard, V. (1957). *The hidden persuaders*. London: Longman, Green.

Pollay, R.W. (1986). The distorted mirror: Reflections on the unintended consequences of advertising. *Journal of Marketing*, 50 (April): 18–36.

Pollay, R.W., Siddarth, S., Siegel, M., Haddix, A., Merritt, R.K., Giovino, G.A. and Eriksen, M.P. (1996). The last straw? Cigarette marketing and realized market shares among youths and adults, 1979–1993. *Journal of Marketing*, 50: 1–16.

Reventós, D.M. (1998). Decoding cosmetics and fashion advertisements in women's magazines. *Cuardernos de Filologia Inglesa*, 7(1): 27–39.

Robin, D.P. and Reidenbach, E. (1987). Social responsibility, ethics and marketing strategy: Closing the gap between concept and application. *Journal of Marketing*, 51 (January): 44–58.

Robinson, M.G., Bloom, P.N. and Lurie, N.H. (2005). Combating obesity in the courts: Will lawsuits against McDonalds work? *Journal of Public Policy and Marketing*, 24(2): 299–306.

Sims, P. (2007). Cosmetic firms mislead women over skin creams with sci-fi jargon. *Daily Mail*, 21 December.

Smith, C. (1995). Marketing strategies for the ethics era. *Sloan Management Review*, 36 (summer): 85–97.

Smith, C. (2001). Ethical guidelines for marketing practice: A reply to Gaski and some observations on the role of normative ethics. *Journal of Business Ethics*, 32(1): 3–18.

Smith, N.C. and Cooper-Martin, E. (1997). Ethics and target marketing: The role of product harm and consumer vulnerability. *Journal of Marketing*, 61 (July): 1–20.

Smith, C. and Quelch, J. (1993). *Ethics in marketing*. Homewood, IL: Irwin.

Stead, M., McDermott, L. and Hastings, G. (2007). Towards evidence-based marketing: The case of childhood obesity. *Marketing Theory*, 7(4): 379–406.

Thompson, C.J. (1995). A contextualist proposal for the conceptualization and study of marketing ethics. *Journal of Public Policy and Marketing*, 14 (Fall): 177–191.

Vitell, S.J., Singhapakdi, A. and Thomas, J. (2001). Consumer ethics: An application and empirical testing of the Hunt-Vitell theory of ethics. *Journal of Consumer Marketing*, 18(2): 153–178.

Woodall, T. (2012). Driven to excess? Linking calling, character and the (mis)behaviour of marketers. *Marketing Theory*, 12(2): 172–191.

Zwick, D. and Denegri-Knott, J. (2009). Manufacturing customers: The database as new means of production. *Journal of Consumer Culture*, 9(2): 221–247.

7 Ethical consumers and the moralised brandscape

Alongside globalisation of markets and the spread of consumer culture, there is a heightened awareness of the social and environmental effects that consumerism brings. Nowadays there are few who would argue against the many known consequences of contemporary lifestyles in terms of pollution and destruction to the natural world. Documented effects, such as the hole in the ozone layer and global warming, have led to a major growth in campaign pressure groups who attempt to influence business and government to take steps to become more socially responsible. Nor is it only in relation to environmental issues (e.g. sustainability); many consumers now espouse a wide range of causes from human rights and animal protection to many other charitable concerns and ethical behaviours. This has given rise to the notion of the Ethical Consumer (a concept that we will question later in this chapter) who uses buying patterns to support certain companies and react against others. Such is the extent of moralistic concerns played out in the marketplace that ethical consumption can no longer be regarded as a quirky niche market. From the mainstreaming of Fairtrade, to Coca-Cola's recent advertising campaign designed to ease the India/Pakistan conflict, there are many brands taking up social causes and putting forth moral agendas. This 'moralised brandscape' (Salzer-Mörling and Strannegård, 2007) is also explored in the chapter, as well as more critical voices that scrutinise and challenge corporate claims and activities. First, however, we consider the phenomenon of ethical consumption.

The growth of ethical consumer behaviours

The increasing globalisation of markets has brought about a weakening of national government controls on business. Now many non-governmental organisations represent millions of workers around the world, spanning borders and uniting their employees within a corporate identity that is often independent of nationality. Major technological advances have made actual geographic location decline in importance. Global business networks now use sophisticated information systems to bypass traditional links between production, place and the nation-state. This makes it more difficult to hold global corporations to account by any one nation. Lack of accountability has fuelled much consumer mistrust and led to the rise of campaign pressure groups who harness the power of technology to advance their aims.

A shift in marketing power towards consumers has facilitated the effectiveness of market campaigning. The quest for greater differentiation in an overcrowded marketplace has seen value creation move from a focus on the product or firm to personalised consumer experiences (Prahalad and Ramaswamy, 2004). The marketing role is increasingly about facilitating conversations and interactions between consumers, as well as between a firm and its customers. Amazon.com and eBay illustrate how consumers are creating value for other users through the sharing of information, ideas and advice. As consumers become more knowledgeable, they are also putting more pressure on companies to behave in socially responsible ways. In addition, because nowadays products and services are often consumed as part of individuals' identity projects, consumers have a vested interest in ensuring that brands and corporations do not tarnish their identity.

Thus, in tandem with increasing consumer concerns over the ethical conduct of companies, there has been a concomitant rise in Corporate Social Responsibility (CSR) policies in the wider corporate environment. CSR is about how companies manage the business processes to produce an overall positive impact on society and has been shown to influence buying behaviour (e.g. Mohr et al., 2001). It implies a rethinking of many aspects of marketing. Ken Peattie (2006) identifies a number of core marketing principles that need to change in order to pursue a sustainable agenda. Although markets are now seen as the most effective way of allocating scarce resources, unfortunately markets ignore ecological distinctions and market-less resources are given no worth. Such a perspective treats environmental issues as externalities beyond the control of marketers and considers use of the environment as 'free'. Take the case of long-haul transport: marketers ensure their prices reflect the costs of fuel, labour, vehicle maintenance and so forth but treat the environmental pollution that this type of transport causes as a non-cost.

At the heart of the marketing concept is the principle of consumer sovereignty. Customer needs and wants are often used as an excuse to justify marketers' lack of initiative in response to sustainability issues. In order to work successfully, the principle of sovereignty depends on customers having access to all the appropriate knowledge and information to make sound judgements. This is almost impossible in a fast changing world where we are bombarded with new information every day. Think about buying a mobile phone and the maze of products and deals on offer that make it impossible to compare like for like across the many different permutations of free texts, calls and internet access, as well as the aesthetic qualities and design features.

Peattie (2006) also questions the principles of targeting and segmentation, crucial ingredients in the marketing mantra to satisfy customers. Because marketers are normally only interested in those who can afford their product, these key elements of marketing strategy can cause inequity and dissatisfaction. Many who do not have the appropriate financial resources are likely to have frequent exposure to advertising that stirs their desires for goods and services that will remain out of reach. It is a staggering fact that four fifths of the world's population have no disposable income. Customer satisfaction is continually monitored but never beyond the target market. This begs the question, how satisfied are other members of any given society? Marketers currently have no interest in answering this question. Yet society is another important constituent that needs to be taken into consideration when assessing the potential impact of marketing activities, particularly in relation to the idea of the 'common good' and how they may or may not contribute to this.

Following on from this logic, many product benefits need to be rethought. When we buy a super-fresh baguette at lunchtime, reassuring ourselves that this is the healthiest option, we need to remember the wastage that the current vogue for fresh food is causing. It is a sobering statistic that more than 6 million tonnes of food from retail outlets ends up in landfill sites every year. Similarly, when we enjoy the warmth of a patio heater instead of putting on an extra pullover, it is salutary to reflect on the huge environmental damage that these heaters cause. In fact, it is estimated that patio heaters cause more than 1 million tonnes of CO_2 emissions per year. In response to a call for a ban on their sales, the *Telegraph* reported a B&Q spokeswoman as saying:

> We will continue to sell outdoor heaters to customers who wish to purchase them, alongside our range of outdoor fire pits and chimineas. We want to ensure that by providing the right information our customers can make informed decisions; we do not dictate what customers buy and do at home.

Here we can quite clearly see how the B&Q spokesperson draws on the notion of consumer sovereignty and the consumer's right to choose in justifying B&Q's decision to continue selling these environmentally destructive heaters.

Consequently, it is unsurprising that comparisons between sustainability thinking and marketing thinking reveal major discrepancies (see Table 7.1). Such comparisons reinforce the need for a major rethink at the level of business education, as well as for changing expectations on the part of businesses, their stakeholders and consumers.

Table 7.1 Differences between sustainability and marketing thinking

Sustainability thinking	Marketing thinking
Future orientation	Short termism
Welfare of society	Gratification
An equable society	Consumer sovereignty
Needs	Wants and desires
Global environmentalism	Globalised production and consumption
Environmental limits	Economic hyperspace

Source: Peattie, 2006

Profiling the ethical consumer

It is against this background, then, that there has been a rise in ethical and green consumerism, defined as 'Any conscious and deliberate decision to make certain consumption choices due to personal moral beliefs and values' (Crane and Matten, 2004). In other words, ethical consumers use their buying patterns to react against certain companies and support others. They may make their decisions to select particular products or services in terms of a company's human rights record, animal protection, environmental friendliness, support for charities, to name but a few of the common reasons. The ethical consumer usually has political, religious, spiritual, environmental, social or other motives for choosing particular products and brands. Hence, the ethical consumer tries to align their moral values with what they purchase, rather than being guided by price, convenience or whim. Importantly, ethical consumers recognise that we are consuming too much at too great a rate and thus are more likely to question whether a product is needed in the first place.

Despite consumers' best intentions, there is a well-documented attitude–behaviour gap in ethical consumerism. Consumers frequently say they support ethical motives but do not follow through in their purchasing decisions. One reason for this is that old habits die hard and marketers, of course, have worked hard in the first place to build these habits. Our kitchen cupboards are likely to contain a variety of cleaning products – different ones for different rooms and purposes (bathrooms – showers, etc.) – that contain toxic materials. These are likely also to be familiar brand names – Jif, Mr Muscle, Ajax, etc. – brands that we have come to rely on to clean our work surfaces and make the jobs easier. Such habits make it difficult for consumers to break out of existing routines and to find less harmful, natural substitutes like baking soda, white vinegar or lemon. All of these will require a learning curve to use correctly, and may not be nearly as easy or efficient as the brands on which consumers are dependent.

In addition there is still little regulation in relation to ethical consumerism and misleading labels also compound the difficulty of assessing what is actually in a product. For example, around one in ten supermarket products contain palm oil which is a major contributor to land clearance. Palm oil is used in a huge range of diverse products from chocolate, margarine and oven chips to cosmetics. The cost to the environment of this consumerist demand is enormous. Tropical rainforests and peatlands in South East Asia are being completely destroyed to make way for huge swathes of palm oil plantations. But in order to avoid the consumption of palm oil we need to spend time educating ourselves about where it is used and scouring labels for ingredients. This is likely to be time that in our contemporary culture of speed (Tomlinson, 2007) we do not perceive ourselves to have.

Consumers may therefore condemn a corporation's actions but continue to buy the brand. A good example here is Nike, a brand that for many years has faced allegations of sweatshop labour and other employee abuses. Even Phil

Knight, its founder and CEO, has said, 'The Nike product has become synonymous with slave wages, forced overtime and arbitrary abuse'. Despite its tarnished image, consumers still continue to buy the Nike brand, keeping the production and consumption sides of the brand separate in their minds. Consequently, someone wearing a pair of Converse trainers will believe he or she looks cool, and not think that the wearing of Converse indicates his or her support for child labour. In their book, *The Myth of the Ethical Consumer*, Devinney et al. (2010) discuss how ethical consumption is often contextual and based on social pressure. If those around us are behaving ethically – e.g. recycling practices – then we are more likely to conform. Similarly, if our friends are wearing Nike, we are more likely to covet the brand despite its poor labour record.

The importance of space and place to ethical consumer behaviours is emphasised in a study undertaken by Chatzidakis et al. (2012). The authors illustrated how Exarcheia, a neighbourhood in Athens, Greece, encouraged a wide range of ethical and green marketplace behaviours. The extent of these ethical behaviours was made possible by the overall ethos of the area, renowned for its spirit of revolt and anti-capitalist feelings, an ethos that fostered experimentation and innovation to challenge mainstream ways of thinking. Many social movements flourish in Exarcheia, all with ideological aims and objectives that reflect an inherently anti-consumption mindset and that have led to widespread ethical consumption practices in the area. Sporos (Greek for seed) is a collective that imports coffee directly from the Zapatistas – a liberation movement based in Chiapas, Mexico that seeks to control local resources in the face of exploitation by the Mexican state and global capitalism. Skoros (Greek for 'clothes moth'), is another anti-consumerist collective where people can leave items for which they no longer have use and others can take what they need. Ventures such as Sporos and Skoros bypass mainstream economic systems and set up alternative ways to lead an ethical life.

The ethical brand

Nowadays many brands differentiate their identity through focusing on ethical values and social responsibility issues: Ben & Jerry's ice cream, Innocent smoothies, Green & Black's organic chocolate, Benetton, Dove beauty products and Ecover to name but a few of the best-known ones. The ethical brand espouses values such as equality, justice, freedom and environmental protection. For example, Ben & Jerry's values revolve around natural ingredients, employee respect and quality of life. The company also supports a range of causes including climate justice, fair trade and marriage equality. Innocent smoothies puts sustainable nutrition as its core aim, while Green & Black's are dedicated to ethical sourcing and sustainable cocoa production. Benetton is well known for its social, environmental and economic responsibility and taking a stance to campaign for disadvantaged groups. Dove campaigns against idealised body images for women. Ecover makes cleaning products that replace chemicals with plant- and mineral-based ingredients. These are just a few of the best-known ethical brand names, but there are many others with numbers continuing to proliferate.

One of the oldest and best-loved ethical brands is without doubt the Body Shop. No high street or shopping centre is complete without one. Founded by the famous entrepreneur and human rights activist, Anita Roddick, the Body Shop's first store opened in 1976. By 1982 shops were opening at the rate of two per month, eventually growing to 2,500 franchises in sixty-one countries. The brand's ethical reputation was initially established around selling environmentally friendly cosmetics and bodycare products in recyclable containers. In 1986 the Body Shop allied itself to Greenpeace's save the whale campaign and, thereafter, the brand became associated with social activism. Roddick supported many varied causes, championing environmental issues, challenging traditional beauty ideals and fair trading with the developing world. Her quotes are legendary and include: 'There are 3 billion women in the world who don't look like supermodels and only 8 that do'; and 'If you think you're too small to make a difference, you've never been to bed with a mosquito'. Indeed, she was an early pioneer of what is now thought of as Corporate Social Responsibility and continued to be highly critical of standard corporate practices throughout her lifetime (she died in 2007). Amid huge controversy, the Body Shop was sold in 2006 to French corporation L'Oréal for £652.3 million. The chain's green credentials were not seen as a good match with those of L'Oréal, often accused of perpetuating false beauty ideals and animal testing (although this latter accusation is strongly denied by L'Oréal). Roddick defended her decision to sell, revealing that she saw herself as a 'Trojan horse' that was now positioned to influence the cosmetics giant from within. Sadly she died before she could achieve much in this respect.

The other most instantly recognisable ethical brand around today is Fairtrade. Unlike the Body Shop, however, Fairtrade did not set out originally to be a brand, nor is it comprised of just one organisation. The Fairtrade movement originated after World War II as a charity sponsored by religious organisations. Its name comes from the fair terms of trade the company ensures for farmers and workers in developing countries. Initially, the ethical ethos of Fairtrade harked back to pre-capitalist notions of a moral economy that linked to 18th-century initiatives focusing on producer rights and boycotting slave goods. The range of products was based mainly around handicrafts and sold through charity shops which meant the brand had a rather dowdy, marginalised image. From the 1990s onwards, however, the movement consciously strove to become more market-orientated, establishing itself more clearly as a brand through the adoption of the Fairtrade Certification Mark and aiming to appeal to mainstream consumer markets.

As a result of this repositioning strategy, Fairtrade has had a dramatic growth over the last two decades and now has over 4,500 products across a range of categories from flowers to coffee. During this time it has moved from the margins (Oxfam charity shops) to mainstream retailing (Tesco's supermarkets).

Although a core aim is still to restructure capitalist relations of production, replacing abstract marketing channels with social connections, the idea is to do this from inside rather than outside the market. Fairtrade's success is due in part to the brand now using a wider variety of marketing channels. There are still the dedicated Fairtrade brands like Café Direct and Day Chocolate but the Fairtrade certification system has given the brand more flexibility. The Fairtrade label is now a common sight in well-known supermarket chains like Sainsbury's, Marks & Spencer and Tesco, who have all adapted some of their own-brand products to meet Fairtrade standards. Major manufacturers like Procter & Gamble, Kraft and Nestlé all now include Fairtrade brands in their product portfolios. In 2010 Nestlé's KitKat received Fairtrade certification, a move that resulted in Nestlé being accredited with bringing a better standard of living to Ivory Coast farmers and enabling them to invest in longer-term community-development projects. Fairtrade's expansion has given the brand much higher visibility and it is now instantly recognisable as the leading brand to espouse trading practices based on economic justice and sustainable development. Of course, there is also criticism and Fairtrade has been accused of helping companies like Nestlé acquire a 'cleaner' image to overcome past tainting from unethical behaviours. Nestlé has long struggled to overcome its 'baby killer' image from the 1970s when multinational milk companies were judged to be causing infant illness and death in the developing world by promoting bottle feeding and discouraging breastfeeding.

Fairtrade is not just about decent prices and working conditions, one of its central aims is to ensure local sustainability on the basis that 'trade rather than aid' (a mantra also espoused by Roddick) is a better long-term solution to helping the developing world. Fairtrade requirements ensure that small farmers not only obtain a fair price for their produce, but also receive a social premium to invest in social, economic or environmental improvements. Thus, by asserting a strict certification system over supply chains to authenticate its moral claims, Fairtrade has managed to translate values of social, economic and environmental justice into standards that consumers feel they can trust. The restructuring of interactions right along Fairtrade's supply chains has ensured that economic exchange is embedded in social relations and placed the 'politics of re-connection' (Dolan, 2011: 37) at the heart of its value creation. Affluent consumers in industrialised countries are linked to poor producers in developing economies and, hence, consumers feel they are making a more meaningful contribution towards a just society through what they consume. Consumers buy into 'a vision of global social justice' (p. 42), a vision that aligns with their own moral identity.

Dolan problematizes this consumer vision. Marketing strategies are designed to ensure the lives of developing world producers become less remote. Typically marketers personalise promotional campaigns with depictions of Fairtrade producers who give testimonials relating how Fairtrade has transformed their lives. These provide a type of myth for middle-class consumers to incorporate into their own identity projects, a myth that they are helping to save the world. Following Holt (2004), this may resolve certain tensions they are experiencing – the guilt of contemporary materialism possibly – but may actually mean the same consumers are less likely to act in other respects to fight for global justice through major structural changes like supporting higher taxes for more aid to the developing world. It may also mean that they impose their own (middle-class) value systems on producers in developing countries, values that may not be relevant there or that may have a trade-off. For example, consumers here are likely to be horrified that child labour may be involved in the production of an item they are purchasing. Yet, in poverty-ridden developing communities, there may be nothing else for the children to do anyway, as one local informant in Dolan's study (2007: 252) of Kenyan flower growers expressed:

> If people took time to look at the issues, they would understand that not all [standards] are appropriate in the developing country context... For example, child labour – if there are no schools, what's the point of them staying at home when they could be contributing to family income? So long as the work is not dangerous, [it] shouldn't be a problem for children to work in school hols or weekends.

Part of the scepticism around Fairtrade going mainstream is related to the idea of *green washing*, a term given to those companies who just make a token gesture to green concerns in order to boost their image and find another way to attract consumers. Many are suspicious that the Nestlé example above is one of green washing. Superficial green claims by many brands are frequently put to the test and found wanting by the media in the form of newspaper reports, television exposés and websites. Greenpeace has its own dedicated website (www.stopgreenwash.org) where it regularly takes to task the green claims made by big brand names such as American Airlines and Shell. Green washing comes in several forms. *Green spinning* is a PR exercise to manage corporate reputations, usually undertaken in industry sectors that are seen as environmentally polluting such as oil, chemicals and transport. *Green selling* occurs when a company promotes an existing product feature as green to climb on the environmental bandwagon and without any intentional development. Finally, *Green harvesting* refers to whenever a company saves money by cutting back on packaging, energy costs or some other 'green' aspect without passing the savings to consumers. It has now become customary in many hotels, for instance, to ask customers to think about whether they need clean towels each day and to encourage reuse in order to save energy costs. Some hotels offer guests a reward system for compliance but many do not.

The moralised brandscape

The concept of a brandscape refers to the range of brands available in the market, or a particular market segment, when the brands are considered collectively as a cultural phenomenon (Sherry, 1986). The contemporary brandscape increasingly incorporates political and social issues into a multitude of values displayed therein. In this way the market becomes the main domain for social action. Consumers can celebrate some brands and critique others, using their likes and dislikes to achieve social and political ends (see Chapter 8). As the brandscape becomes steadily more infused with ideological and ethical values, it becomes what Salzer-Mörling and Strannegård (2007) refers to as the 'moralised brandscape', 'a cultural landscape imbued with images and signs where focus increasingly is put on the expressive side of the brand and where moral statements seem to be an issue in the discourse of both consumers and producers'.

Hence many brands not previously associated with ethical or green values are espousing moral causes and blurring the boundaries of what is, and what is not, an ethical brand. Coca-Cola's 'Open Happiness' campaign running from 2009 is a prime example of this. As part of their global marketing message, in 2013 Coca-Cola launched their 'Coca-Cola Small World Machine – Bringing India and Pakistan Together' campaign. This saw Coca-Cola taking the role of global peacemaker by setting up vending machines in India and Pakistan, two countries with a long history of animosity and violence towards each other. Fitted with high-tech cameras, the vending machines permit consumers to see their counterparts in the neighbouring country. They can then join 'virtual' hands and exchange messages if they wish. Coca-Cola's advertising claims that 'A moment of happiness has the power to bring the world closer together'. Although many sceptics argue that this dispensing of happiness around the world is only dispensing money into Coca-Cola's coffers, it has proved highly popular with consumers. The success of the campaign earned Coca-Cola twenty awards at the 2013 Cannes Lions International Festival of Creativity, including the much coveted Creative Marketer of the Year Award.

New offerings that link to a moral agenda in unexpected ways are popping up more and more on the contemporary brandscape. Dans le Noir is a restaurant chain that offers a unique dining experience. Diners eat in the dark without being able to see what they are eating or where they are. It was established by the Ethik Investment Group which funds ventures that are socially or environmentally responsible. In the case of Dans le Noir, the restaurant employs a large number of blind staff. Inspired by the creation of diners by blind people for sighted people in the 19th century, in 2004 the group created the first Dans le Noir restaurant in Paris. After this proved a successful formula, other restaurants were opened in London, Moscow, Barcelona and, most recently, New York in 2011. The logo is Dans le Noir? with a question mark and, thus, intended to be ambiguous about who exactly is 'in the dark'. This questioning theme is continued through the website where the question posed alerts potential customers to the nature of the experience available: 'What if sight, the dominant sense, suddenly disappeared for a few hours, would that awaken an unbelievable world of sense, touch, taste and smells?' Research conducted into the experience has shown that customers experience a role reversal when they enter the darkness: it is they who become disabled, whereas the blind staff move with ease and confidence in the black environment (Tissiers-Desbordes and Maclaran, 2013).

Adding to the blurring boundaries referred to above is the rise in Cause-Related Marketing (CRM) which is evident all around us. CRM is whenever a partnership is established between a corporation and a non-profit organisation. By linking to charities or causes marketers give consumers a more meaningful reason to purchase their products or services. American Express is credited with first using the phrase in 1983 to describe its campaign which donated 1 cent to the Statue of Liberty every time a customer used their card. Highly successful as a promotional tool, this sponsorship gained American Express 45 percent of new customers and card usage increased by 28 percent. The company has continued to support historic preservation initiatives and uses these to emphasise its involvement in the community. Since 1990, CRM has gone from a $120 million industry to a $1.62 billion one in 2010. One survey reported that as many as 89 percent of respondents said they would switch brands to support a cause if price and quality were the same.

Tesco's 'Free Computers for Schools' is a more recent well-known cause-related partnership enabling parents and friends to collect vouchers to help their local school have new equipment. Pampers and its Unicef partnership is another high-profile partnership whereby the manufacturer, Procter and Gamble, donates 4p for every pack of Pampers bought, money that has already given more than 300 million vaccines to children in developing countries. Cadbury's donates a percentage of proceeds from its Wishes chocolates to children's charity Make-a-Wish Foundation. Innocent smoothies has had a partnership with Age UK for more than eight years. Age UK volunteers knit imaginative hats for Innocent bottles which often feature in promotional campaigns. Every November Innocent contributes 25p to Age UK for each bottle with a hat.

CRM is seen as a win–win strategy for both profit and non-profit organisations, with the business gaining a halo effect and the cause benefitting from both the donations and, in many cases, the higher profile that big corporation sponsorship can drive. It is not without criticism, however, and charities are warned to be careful how easily they give their name to a cause. Often it is not clear to the consumer how much the charity will receive and often percentages donated are hard to establish (i.e. often couched as percentages of overall profits). In addition, consumers need to believe that a company's good intentions are authentic and not just another instance of green washing. By putting its head above the parapet in this way, a company may leave itself open to criticism if it is found to be wanting in terms of other ethical behaviours. The power of the internet – particularly social media – to expose firms that do not act in accordance with their stated values is enormous.

Anti-branding and consumer resistance

The rise in anti-branding, boycotting and activist movements mirrors the growth of the moralised brandscape. Brand behaviours are monitored more closely than ever by the media as well as on internet forums. The word boycott can strike fear into even the most established brands. Lessons have been well learned from the 1990s global boycotting campaign of Nike. Nike was targeted for its labour malpractices and lack of workers' rights in supplier factories, with numerous boycotts and media criticism. The negative publicity was substantial and although it is not proven that boycotts hit a firm's bottom line (see Koku et al., 1997), the pressure was sufficient to bring about change in this brand Leviathan. Thereafter, Nike sought to rebrand itself as socially responsible and ethically aware. In 2011 Greenpeace launched its Detox Challenge which aimed to stop brands like Nike, Adidas and Puma from polluting waterways with their toxic chemical waste. These three major brands responded within weeks, drawing up plans to go toxic free over the next decade and leading the way for other companies who followed suit. This quick response to a potentially damaging accusation for their corporate image testifies to the current power of consumers to act to change corporate behaviour.

Since Vance Packard's (1957) hard-hitting exposé of marketers' use of motivational research to tap into consumers' subconscious desires – *The Hidden Persuaders* – the media has played a crucial role in fuelling consumer fears over corporate manipulation. More recently Adam Curtis' award-winning television documentary series in 2002, *The Century of the Self*, rekindled these fears by highlighting the sinister role of psychoanalysis in modern consumerism, especially its intertwining with political ambitions to keep the masses docile and malleable. Likewise, journalist Naomi Klein has been one of the leading voices in exposing brand hypocrisy. Her book, *No Logo: Taking Aim at the Brand Bullies* (1999), made a huge impact and became – in her own words – 'a cultural manifesto for the critics of unfettered capitalism worldwide'. Klein highlights the many misdeeds of huge corporations such as Nike, Pepsi, Gap, McDonald's, Shell, Microsoft and others. Her central thesis is that nowadays the marketing of a brand name is more important than the manufacture of the physical product and hence the shift of production to cheaper labour regions. This move from local to foreign production leads to increasing lack of regulation by any one government and exacerbates corporate mis-behaviours, sweatshops being a typical example. In her follow-up, *Shock Doctrine: The Rise of Disaster Capitalism*, she makes the provocative claim that major disasters such as the devastation of New Orleans by Hurricane Katrina or the Iraq War destroy the existing economic order and pave the way for laissez-faire capitalism.

Critiques such as these have helped make consumers ambivalent about marketing and led to a growing mistrust of advertising.[1] Adbusters is one of the most famous anti-consumerist organisations, known for their spoof ads and outspoken magazine. They support many subversive anti-marketing campaigns and regularly expose the policies of multinational corporations to widespread scrutiny. Adbusters have long espoused the idea of 'culture jamming', a tactic that disrupts media and marketing messages to protect 'our mental environment' from being polluted through corporate communications. Culture jammers protest against the appropriation of public spaces by commerce and often deface billboard advertising, adding political messages or corporate critique.

Ecofeminist critique

Ecofeminism – a branch of feminist thought exploring the relationship between humankind and the natural environment – provides a strong theoretical lens with which to critique marketing's green credentials. A major part of Ecofeminism's critique, as its name suggests, concerns the gendered nature of rights and responsibilities in Western culture which is related to the separation of nature from culture, with femininity being associated with the former and masculinity with the latter. Ecofeminists try to give nature and animals positive worth to challenge the negative value that is attributed to them in our society, whereby nature is seen as secondary to humankind and in service to it. Accordingly, as a body of thought, Ecofeminism seeks to address the disconnection between humans and the nature that surrounds them and on which they depend. It also tries to counter dualistic thinking that privileges culture and devalues nature, instead conceiving of all life as interconnected. As a result of women's connection with nature (and the body), however, it is often seen as women's work to protect the environment.

To this end Dobscha (1993: 37) accuses marketers of reinforcing stereotypes through the creation of advertising discourse that depicts women as 'wood nymph' and 'earth mother'. With such a limited repertoire of images for ethical consumers, she argues that marketers effectively draw women into 'romanticised servitude', making it seem their responsibility to save the planet through associating green consumerism with femininity rather than masculinity. Because Western culture emphasises a sense of self that is separate from the environment (an anthropocentric worldview) rather than a self that is interconnected, this results in a lack of both empathy for nature and a sense of responsibility for the planet.

Another ecofeminist study in marketing looks at anthropomorphic images in advertising, specifically in relation to brand mascots that have human traits and personalities attributed to them (Stevens et al., 2014). Taking the case of Elsie, the brand mascot for Borden Dairies, the authors illustrate how advertisements can transmit dominant ideologies about nature, animals, humanity and gender. Specifically, they carry out a case study analysis of Elsie the Borden cow. Analysing advertisements and publicity materials spanning Elsie's first appearance in 1936 to 2007, when she was brought out of retirement to mark the 150th anniversary of Borden, they identify how three key themes reinforce a Western, masculinist worldview that considers it acceptable to dominate nature and the feminine, a worldview that ultimately sets humans apart from the natural environment around them. The first of these themes, *Disconnection from Nature*, reveals how technological aspects surrounding the spectacle of Elsie – the 'rotolactor' milking machine and Elsie's 'cowdillac' transportation truck – served to separate Borden's brand mascot from her natural environment, turning her into a star set apart from her species. The second theme, *The Monstrous Feminine*, is about the more carnivalesque side of Elsie, especially the cartoon depictions of her in advertising. In addition, however, the theme is also about the attraction and repulsion elements of this quasi-human figure. For example, the birth of Elsie's first calf was turned into a spectator sport when Elsie (a 'real' cow as opposed to her caricatures) gave birth in front of crowds in Macey's department store. And finally, the third theme, *Mastering the Other*, highlights how Elsie's frequent appearances with white-coated male 'experts' emphasise traditional mastery over nature and further isolate her as a freak of nature and a human caricature.

Trade-offs in ethical consumption

One of the reasons that it is so hard to be an ethical consumer is because what is viewed as ethical in any given circumstance is often subjective and depends from whose point of view the situation is being considered. A study carried out by Visconti et al. (2014) into how farmers' markets contribute to sustainability, identified key ethical trade-offs, highlighting how what seems ethical at a micro level may not be so ethical when a more macro picture is included. The number of farmers' markets in the UK has been steadily growing, following their success in the US. Indeed, it is estimated that there are now over 800 farmers' markets with sales of more than £250 million. Farmers' markets sell food stuffs from farmers directly to consumers with participation in markets usually restricted by proximity of production to the site. For example, London Farmers' Markets is an organisation that manages a network of markets across London. Usually held once or twice a week in car parks, school playgrounds or local squares, produce must be grown (or made) within a 100-mile radius. Apart from being local (loosely defined in the case of London Farmers' Markets), produce must also be seasonal and middlemen are not permitted. Typical participants are farmers, nursery growers, fishermen, cooks, bakers, preserve makers and beekeepers but various handicraft makers or local services may also be present, such as the Mobile Bike Workshop, a cycle repair facility which tours the London markets. Their commitment to local, seasonal production means farmers' markets are hailed as a highly sustainable market form that also reinvigorates urban environments. Most cities have lost their traditional markets, and farmers' markets help to regain a lost sense of community.

Assessing the contribution of farmers' markets to sustainability is not as straightforward, however, as it first appears and further analysis reveals intersocial, international and intergender trade-offs. In relation to intersocial trade-offs, farmers' markets often operate in richer neighbourhoods and, consequently, there are implications for social inclusion. First, poorer people may not be able to afford the travel costs to access the market. Second, prices are often higher because of the limited economies of scale attainable, and sometimes pricing policies aim at the tourists such markets attract, particularly when they have acquired a fashionable image. Similarly, if local enterprise is privileged over international trade – 'farmers markets are often represented as a form of local fair trade system' (Visconti et al., 2014: 14) – how does this reconcile with the idea of aiding developing countries through international (fair) trade? From this perspective, farmers' markets may be more indicative of the entrepreneurialism encouraged by neoliberalist policies (i.e. allowing the 'free market' to dictate), rather than providing a resistance to globalisation. Finally, there is the intergender trade-off as a result of the nostalgia that surrounds farmers' markets and the idea that they are a return to more pastoral ways of living. This pastoral idyll usually relies on prescribed gender roles that consign women to the care of the home (and vegetable garden!). In addition, food shopping has traditionally been seen as a feminine role and the extra time that it takes to attend and browse a farmers' market is not conducive to changing this perception. Indeed, the statistics on the gender balance in farmers' markets show a majority of women in most cases.

Similar trade-offs can be seen in many other areas of ethical and green consumption: palm oil is increasingly used in biofuels which are seen as an ethical alternative to burning fossil fuels but, as discussed earlier, palm plantations come at huge environmental costs; since smoking bans, pubs are now free of indoor pollution, but the patio heaters provided for smokers to keep warm outside cause a different type of pollution. This then brings us back to the idea of more ecologically holistic perspectives (like Ecofeminism) that look at the interconnectedness between humans and their natural world and call for an analysis of the interrelationships between each element of an ecosystem. Such perspectives mean challenging the dominant social paradigm in our society, a paradigm that prioritises economic growth and possessive individualism, together with the harnessing of the natural world to satisfy these ends (see Kilbourne, 2004).

Summary

There is increasing concern over the environmentally detrimental effects of today's consumerist lifestyles. Many of the fundamental principles of marketing need to be rethought to encourage more sustainable standards of living. Despite a significant growth in companies espousing more ethically orientated values, there is still a large attitude–behaviour gap in relation to consumers' ethical consumption. The social and spatial contexts of ethical consumption are usually ignored although they can play a major role in influencing ethical consumer behaviours, often more so than individual value systems. The complexity of assessing consumers' ethical behaviours is further compounded by the increasingly blurred boundaries around what constitutes an ethical brand. As more companies seek to link themselves to ethical values and causes, the contemporary brandscape is becoming more 'moralised'. Although on the one hand this may be considered admirable, on the other there is more risk of 'green washing'. The number of anti-consumerist movements is steadily growing, partly as a response to the global economic disasters from 2008 onwards, but also because of the hypocrisies of many corporations. Critiques of corporate and consumer actions, together with an assessment of future ethical paths, should consider the macro as well as the micro picture, taking a more holistic, ecological perspective that brings the human and natural worlds together in a symbiotic relationship where each depends on the other for its sustenance.

CASE STUDY: a guerrilla park in Athens

Guerrilla gardening is a countercultural movement that has been steadily spreading across Europe. With its roots in environmentalism, the movement has an explicitly political aim to bring about a re-evaluation of land ownership in the city. Rather like street art, its followers reclaim and beautify derelict or drab spaces within cities. Guerrilla gardeners plant profusions of vegetables, fruit, herbs, trees and flowers in grey corners to bring nature and colour back into city life. They do so in night raids on traffic islands and abandoned yards or buildings, working under the cover of darkness to avoid apprehension by the police or local authorities.

An extreme instance of a guerrilla park is the 'Parko Navarinou' in Exarcheia (a radical neighbourhood of Athens), created by local residents in March 2009 following riots in Athens the previous year. On hearing the news that a vacant parking lot was to be developed commercially, residents rebelled and took collective action to turn the space into a public park. Overnight they mobilised many supporters who dug up the asphalt, replacing it with soil, trees and other vegetation. Suddenly a grey, bleak space was transformed into a tranquil garden for all to enjoy. Some people donated benches and tables, others laboured to create beautiful mosaic walls and paths (Figure 7.1), whilst still others developed flowerbeds and vegetable patches (Figure 7.2). Volunteers also constructed a playground area with climbing frames and other attractions for children.

Six years later, the park is a profusion of green foliage, colourful flowers and people who come to socialise, engage in intellectual debates, play with their children or repose alone. From young to old, there are many different groups that use the park; it now evokes a public square of bygone times that invites participation and interaction. Events are held regularly and span a huge range of activities: talks (often with an anti-consumerist theme), films,

Figure 7.1 A fruit garden in Exarcheia Park
Source: photo by Andreas Chatzidakis

Figure 7.2 Mosaic floor in Exarcheia Park
Source: photo by Andreas Chatzidakis

poetry nights, theatrical performances, concerts and gifting bazaars. Many local organisations, artists and movements otherwise disconnected from each other use the park for special events. No commercial ventures are permitted and events should not be explicitly linked to any political parties – the idea is that different ideologies should mix and share the space without domination by any one ideology (except perhaps capitalism!). In this way the park also encourages new forums for dialogue, emphasising intellectual rather than monetary exchange.

Maintained through volunteer work and donations, the park is run by regular open meetings and special commissions that are set up to look after particular aspects of its maintenance. Anyone can join in and help to govern the park. The authorities have left it alone, scared to intervene in such an anarchical place for fear of inflaming further riots. A city space has been successfully reclaimed from being 'economised', instead becoming part of the commons once again, a resource for all Exarcheians and a major contributor to public life in the area (Figure 7.3).

The Exarcheian guerrilla park reflects a growing dissatisfaction with the spread of global capitalism to all areas of our lives, a capitalism that is perceived to frequently act in unethical ways, particularly through marketing and consumerist activities. As such guerrilla gardening links to other social movements, like *Reclaim the Streets*, that seek to prevent the encroachment of corporate forces into community life and public spaces.

Figure 7.3 Exarcheia Park, 2016
Source: photo by Andreas Chatzidakis

Seminar exercises

Discussion topics

1 Following on from Table 7.1, select two advertisements that you think illustrate the difference between marketing and sustainability thinking (one for each) and discuss why you have made these choices.

2 Discuss the reasons why consumers may not behave as ethically as they say they will – i.e. the 'attitude–behaviour gap' – and relate each of your reasons to specific product categories if you can. (Reading Salzer-Mörling and Strannegård (2007) will help you with this task.)

3 Identify an ethical brand (not one already named in this chapter) and discuss the particular values it espouses.

4 How do organisations benefit from implementing Corporate Social Responsibility policies and what problems might they experience? Give examples where you can.

Group exercises

1 Read the article by Chatzidakis et al. (2012) and analyse the case study of the Guerrilla Park in Athens:

- In what ways is the Guerrilla Park a heterotopia? Justify your answer with a detailed analysis of the various heterotopian characteristics.
- Find an example of another guerrilla park on the internet and study the similarities and differences to the one in Athens.
- Consider other social movements that try to reclaim public space and, taking a specific example, explore their key motivations and structures.

2 Choose a brand that you believe is part of the 'moralised brandscape' and analyse how it positions itself using ethical values:

- Compare and contrast two key competitors' strategies.
- Study what consumers are saying about the brand on the web, i.e. using product reviews or web forums, and analyse their main perceptions of the brand.
- What makes the brand's claims authentic and are there any dangers of 'green-washing' accusations?

Note

1 http://research.yougov.com/news/2014/04/08/truth-advertising-50-dont-trust-what-they-see-read/

Internet resources

Adbusters: www.adbusters.org/

Ethical Consumer: www.ethicalconsumer.org/boycotts
Global 100 Sustainable Companies: www.global100.org
Greenpeace: www.greenpeace.org.uk

Key readings

Arvidsson, A. (2011). Ethics and value in customer co-production. *Marketing Theory*, 11(3): 261–278.
Gordon, R., Carrigan, M. and Hastings, G. (2011). A framework for sustainable marketing. *Marketing Theory*, 11(2): 143–163.
Kilbourne, W.E. (2004). Sustainable communication and the dominant social paradigm: Can they be integrated? *Marketing Theory*, 4(3): 187–208.
Peattie, K. (2006). Sustainable marketing: Marketing re-thought, re-mixed and re-tooled. In M. Saren, P. Maclaran, C. Goulding, R. Elliot, A. Shankar and M. Catteral (eds), *Critical marketing defining the field*. Oxford: Butterworth-Heinemann, 192–210.

References

Chatzidakis, A., Maclaran, P. and Bradshaw, A. (2012). Heterotopian space and the politics of ethical and green consumption. *Journal of Marketing Management*, 3(4): 494–515.
Crane, A. and Matten, D. (2004). *Business ethics, a European perspective: Managing corporate citizenship and sustainability in the age of globalization*. Oxford: Oxford University Press.
Devinney, T.M., Auger, P. and Eckhardt, G.M. (2010). *The myth of the ethical consumer*. Cambridge: Cambridge University Press.
Dobscha, S. (1993). Women and the environment: Applying ecofeminism to environmentally-related consumption. *Advances in Consumer Research*, 20(1): 36–40.
Dolan, C.S. (2007). Market affections: Moral encounters with Kenyan Fairtrade flowers. *Ethnos*, 72(2): 239–261.
Dolan, C.S. (2011). Branding morality. In M. Warrier (ed.), *The politics of fairtrade*. London: Routledge, pp. 37–52.
Holt, D.B. (2004). *How brands become icons: The principles of cultural branding*. Boston, MA: Harvard Business Press.
Klein, N. (1999). *No logo: Taking aim at the brand bullies*. London: Picador.
Koku, P.S., Akhigbe, A. and Springer, T.M. (1997). The financial impact of boycotts and threats of boycott. *Journal of Business Research*, 40: 15–20.
Mohr, L.A., Webb, D.J. and Harris, K.E. (2001). Do consumers expect companies to be socially responsible? The impact of corporate social responsibility on buying behavior. *Journal of Consumer Affairs*, 35(1): 45–72.
Packard, V. (1957). *The hidden persuaders*. London: Longman, Green.
Prahalad, C.K. and Ramaswamy, V. (2004). Co-creation experiences: The next practice in value creation. *Journal of Interactive Marketing*, 18(3): 5–14.
Salzer-Mörling, M. and Strannegård, L. (2007). Ain't misbehavin' – consumption in a moralized brandscape. *Marketing Theory*, 7(4): 407–425.
Sherry, J.F., Jr. (1986). Cereal monogamy: Brand loyalty as a secular ritual in consumer culture. Paper presented at the Seventh Annual Conference of the Association for Consumer Research, Toronto.

Stevens, L., Maclaran, P. and Kearney, M. (2014). Boudoirs, cowdillacs and rotolactors: A salutary tale of Elsie the brand mascot. In S. Brown and S. Ponsaby (eds), *Brand mascots*. London: Routledge.

Tissiers-Desbordes, E. and Maclaran, P. (2013). Ritualisation des espaces des consommation. *La Nouvell Revue de Psychosociologie*, 16 (Autumn): 171–86.

Tomlinson, J. (2007). *The culture of speed: The coming of immediacy*. London: SAGE.

Visconti, L., Minowa, Y. and Maclaran, P. (2014). Public markets: An ecological perspective on sustainability as a megatrend. *Journal of Macromarketing*, 34(3): 349–368.

8 Politicising consumption
Consumerising politics

Introduction

Everyday consumption is commonly viewed as largely disconnected from the more consequential realm of politics. Ethical and green variants aside (Chapter 7), mass consumerism remains rampantly individualistic, hedonistic and self-serving, contrasting sharply with the more altruistic and civic virtues assumed in liberal democratic notions of 'citizenship'. As we will see in this chapter, the binary between consumption and citizenship is problematic, not least because more sophisticated accounts on the history and politics of consumption suggest otherwise. Consumer movements, for instance, have been largely responsible for the abolition of the slavery movement, gender equality and, more recently, the advancement of social and environmental justice across commodity supply chains (e.g. Newholm et al., 2015). Everyday consumers, both through their purchasing choices and non-choices, and through more organised forms of political participation (e.g. Micheletti and Stolle, 2004), are fundamental yet often neglected actors in the institutional nexus of corporations, national and transnational institutions, markets, third-sector organisations and social movements.

Thinking about consumption politically (as well as about politics through the lens of consumption) is further complicated by the fact that what is meant by politics is inherently contentious and multidimensional. For some, the intersection of consumption with politics is encapsulated in – and reduced down to – notions of 'political consumerism' and 'consumption as voting'. Within this paradigm, consumption can be viewed as a new form of political participation whereby everyday consumers, through their purchases and non-purchases, vote in favour of and against particular social, environmental and national issues. For many neo-Marxist and critical scholars, however, the point of departure in thinking about consumption and politics is Marx's account of commodity fetishism. As David Harvey (1990), one of the foremost social theorists, puts it, the grapes we find on our supermarket shelves (and indeed any commodity) are very silent about the social conditions of their production. Accordingly, politics at that level would require – among other things – cognitive maps that educate consumers about the inner workings of capitalist markets and decommodification attempts through alternative and solidarity-based economies. Finally, at least one more avenue for looking at consumption politically is by questioning the very role that consumers and consumerism play in contemporary societies. Here the vocabulary of consumerism, the very essence of consumers' fantasies and subjectivities, is put to question with a view to uncover why being a 'consumer' (as opposed to e.g. citizen) in neoliberal societies is the preferred mode of social action and mental organisation. In this chapter, we look at these different ways of understanding the politics of consumption, whilst also taking account of their respective contradictions and interconnections.

Voting in the marketplace

To be sure, thinking about the consequences of everyday consumption, and its political implications, is not the prerogative of contemporary civilisations. According to some accounts, questions around the politics of consumption can even be found in the dialogues of Socrates and Plato, whereby the preconditions (that is, acceptance of slavery) for the luxurious lifestyles of wealthy Athenians were explicitly contemplated (Bradshaw et al., 2013). More commonly, however, the predecessors to what is now understood as political consumerism are viewed to be the anti-slavery boycotts of the 18th and 19th centuries. Within the UK, for instance, the first 'consumers' league' was established in 1897 by Clementina Black to address existing labour concerns (Hilton, 2007). Members of the league were encouraged to boycott the goods of employers who paid unjustifiably low wages and/or allowed intolerable working conditions in their factories. Accordingly, a list of 'fair' employers was created to allow shoppers within the vicinity of Bond Street, Oxford Street and Regent Street to choose more wisely. Eventually, however, the league failed because, as Clementina Black explained, it proved impossible to produce a full and accurate guide for politically minded consumers at a larger level and it could by no means replace the effectiveness of more direct workers' struggles (Hilton, 2007).

Nowadays, of course, it is far less difficult to be informed about the working conditions in the offices and factories of big multinational corporations, not least because of the numerous media exposés but also due to the emergence of very sophisticated shopper guides by the likes of the UK's *Ethical Consumer* magazine (www.ethicalconsumer.org) and even smartphone applications that provide live information for consumers on the go such as the Buycott (www.buycott.com). Meanwhile, a variety of labels, from Fair Trade and organic certifications to the recent Edge certification guaranteeing equal gender pay, make civic-minded consumers' shopping trips a far easier task than Clementina Black's supporters' back in the late 19th century. For political science scholars, this is indicative of our era of 'individualised collective action', that is 'the practice of responsibility-taking... on the part of citizens alone or together with others to deal with problems that they believe are affecting what they identify as the good life' (Micheletti, 2003: 26). Contrasting with the previous era of 'collectivist collective action', contemporary Western societies are witnessing a decrease in traditional forms of political participation, such as campaigning, voting in elections, protesting and joining political parties and an increase in more personal political actions and emotions that are disconnected from consolidated political structures and organisations.

It is worth clarifying here that ethical consumerism (see Chapter 7) as a form of individualised collective action overlaps with political consumerism but there are also key differences. First, political consumerism may not necessarily be viewed as 'ethical'. Beyond trading relationships with the developing world and environmental issues, it can be used as an expression of identity politics (as in the case of staging a same-sex kiss-in in anti-LGBT restaurant chains; Severson, 2012), international politics (e. g. boycotting Israeli products; www.waronwant.org/) and as a means to support rather less morally worthy aims, for example in the case of supporting extreme right corporations (Chatzidakis, 2013) and even the pro-colonial regime of the 19th century (Newholm and Newholm, 2016). In addition, political consumerism is more than just boycotting or 'buycotting' particular services and products on the basis of their social and environmental credentials (Copeland and Atkinson, 2016). It is also about campaigning through discursive and non-discursive means (e.g. writing letters to corporations, taking companies to court) and about endorsing lifestyle politics, in the sense of making 'the personal political' and trying to live one's life in line with their political ideals.

A common line of criticism against political consumerism, as a new individualised form of political participation, is that it substitutes for more traditional forms of political activism, that is it 'crowds in' rather than 'crowds out' the political energies and impulses of everyday consumer-citizens. Various empirical studies, however, have consistently shown that political consumers are more likely than non-political consumers to be engaged in a broader sense. For instance, they exhibit much higher participation rates in behaviours such as voting in elections, contacting politicians and working for political parties and organisations (see Copeland and Atkinson, 2016). This contradicts commonplace critiques of political consumerism on the basis that it impedes people from engaging in more traditional forms of political action. Instead, it can be seen as an evolution of the ways in which contemporary consumer-citizens choose to exercise their political impulses and express their values.

Notwithstanding, political consumerism is still very much about individualised solutions to collective problems. For many critics, as we discuss later in the chapter, it serves to remove responsibility from traditional top-down actors, such as the state and transnational institutions. The consequences are often less obvious at the micro level of individual consumer choice and yet deeply profound. For instance, consumers are called to bear the burden of equitable and environmentally sustainable trading with developing world producers, leaving little space for political action against the very institutions (e.g. the World Trade Organization or International Monetary Fund) that are responsible for uneven geographical development and unfair trading arrangements in the first place. Furthermore, the implicit emphasis on 'individualised' collective action tends to ignore the numerous modern-day examples of 'collectivised' collective action across spaces and places whereby alternative imaginaries of politicised consumption exist. For instance, Chatzidakis et al. (2012; see Chapter 7) talk about Exarcheia, as an urban neighbourhood where new ways of doing consumer activism are constantly tried out. These bear little resemblance to the model of 'individualised' collective action documented (mainly) in Northern European and American cities. More broadly, there is a wealth of anthropological and geographical research pointing to how politically motivated consumption takes different forms and meanings outside the 'global North' (e.g. Ariztia et al., 2016). Even within the global North, there is a vast array of alternative economic activities and practices of political consumption that lie outside the conventional, if not restrictive, realm of marketplace exchange (Gibson-Graham, 2006).

Beyond voting in the marketplace? The politics of degrowth

An interrelated critique of political consumerism – including its ethical and green variants – is that it is based less on challenging the dominant consumerist culture and more on maintaining it by casting votes firmly within (rather than outside) the conventional marketplace. In other words, it is a form of self-enlightened behaviour focused mostly on moderating some of the unintended consequences of consumer choice(s) as opposed to radically challenging Western consumer culture altogether. For proponents of 'degrowth', an increasingly influential tradition that places the insistence on economic 'growth' at the centre of contemporary social and environmental problems, this is a very limited model of civic-minded consumption. Degrowth

> does not only challenge the centrality of GDP as an overarching policy objective but proposes a framework for transformation to a lower and sustainable level of production and consumption, a shrinking of the economic system to leave more space for human cooperation and ecosystems.
> (www.degrowth.org/definition-2)

Interestingly, for degrowth activists and scholars, the somewhat religious preoccupation with economic expansion through the use of more natural resources, technological advances and the stimulation of consumption is not a characteristic of advanced capitalist markets only. It concerns all modern societies, including the planned economies of the Soviet Union. Contrasting the productivist orientation of these regimes, degrowth scholars advocate that societies of the global North enter a 'virtuous circle of cultivated contraction' (Latouche, 2009). This would include reassessment of societal values, redistributing wealth between the North and the South and reassessing the meaning of life altogether.

Everyday consumption plays a key role within the degrowth agenda, not least because it is at this level where everyday needs will have to be re-evaluated, relocalised and underpinned by an ethos of communality, care and sharing (e.g. Latouche, 2009). Unlike political consumerism, which is about boycotting and buycotting individual products in the way of expressing one's political values, the model of civic-minded consumption that is advocated by degrowth advocates and scholars is closer to what has been described in the consumer literature as voluntary simplicity or downshifting; that is, the forgoing of Western-style (over)consumption habits (e.g. Shaw and Newholm, 2002). It is also in line with what the political philosopher Kate Soper (2008, 2016) defines as 'alternative hedonism', urging us to reconsider materialism and indeed the extent to which the 'good life' is or should be associated with shopping an ever-expanding list of items. Interestingly, Soper emphatically argues that even if current Western consumer lifestyles were indefinitely sustainable and socially desirable, they would still be incapable of enhancing happiness and well-being, or not beyond a point that has already passed. Numerous studies have documented the lack of correlation between material wealth and happiness after a certain level.

Chatzidakis et al. (2014) have recently contrasted more explicitly the model of consumption underpinned by the imperative for radical degrowth as opposed to more conventional campaigns in favour of social and environmental sustainability. As these authors explain, when business and other institutional actors urge us to consume more ethically or politically what they in effect espouse is a model of economic organisation that is still underpinned by an (over)productivist ethos, albeit of a more sustainable nature through the use of technological advancements and through minimising harm wherever possible. According to many authors, the limits of this model have already become apparent given the inability of current societies to meet even modest sustainability targets as evident in the famous 1992 Kyoto Protocol and/or the more recent 2015 Paris Agreement. Accordingly, the associated model of consumption in societies of degrowth can be characterised as post- or de-consumerism in the sense that it rejects the idea of consumption as a central and meaningful act in and of itself. The primary focus is instead on collectivised forms of consumption, based around community participation, sharing and the reimagining of local communities. The differences are summarised by the authors in Table 8.1.

Getting behind (and working against) the veil of commodity fetishism

Whereas political consumerism is about managing and engaging with the consequences of particular consumption choices and 'deconsumerism' (and related notions of alternative hedonism and voluntary simplicity) about the consequences of Western consumption levels altogether, neo-Marxist and

Table 8.1 Logics of growth in consumption (Chatzidakis et al., 2014: 753)

Countervailing logic	Underpinning assumptions	Actors	Implications for consumption	Identity of the consumer
Cultivated growth	Economic rationality, Adam Smith's invisible hand, neoclassical theories of economics	Multinational, world-wide market elites. Concerned primarily with maximising economic growth and profitability, and with social order only in relationship to market threats	Use up, use more (when possible) and throw away	'Sovereign consumer'. Self-interested, position in society is defined by conspicuous consumption
Sustainable growth	Market and society interact and impact upon one another	Governments and middle class – those concerned with maintaining social order within existing nation-states	Buy ethical and green; reduce, reuse, recycle	'Ethical consumer'. Socially aware, role and identity in society defined by consumption of ethical goods
Degrowth	Society resists the domination of market logics	Consumer-citizens Activists	Don't buy any-thing, produce what is needed within small communities; alternative hedonism	'Post- and de-consumerist'. Role in society defined by social participation rather than consumption

various related critical perspectives take a different point of departure. Here the emphasis is on consumption objects themselves and the way in which affluent consumers of capitalist societies are entirely oblivious of their social nature. The notion of commodity fetishism is first presented in Karl Marx's first chapter of *Capital: Critique of Political Concept* (1867) as a means of explaining how in capitalist societies social relations between people are instead presented as 'an immense accumulation of commodities'. For Marx, this is because of the enigmatic or mystical nature of commodities: 'A commodity appears at first sight an extremely obvious, trivial thing. But its analysis brings out that it is a very strange thing, abounding in metaphysical subtleties and theological nic-eties' (1976: 163). Marx clarifies that in pre-capitalist societies there was nothing mystical about objects in so far as these were judged by their use-value. For instance, a table was the product of human labour (cutting and carving wood) aimed to provide some kind of utility (somewhere to dine, write and so on). Instead, the mysterious character of the table (and any other object) arises once it becomes a commodity because it is at this point – when the object acquires monetary value and is exchanged in the marketplace – that the social characteristics of human labour are presented as objective characteristics of the products themselves. What is a social relation between people now becomes 'the fantastic form of a relation between things' (p. 165).

Put differently, in capitalist societies we perceive commodities as having some kind of autonomous value, expressed in monetary terms and understood solely in comparison to all other commodities. We tend to be entirely oblivious to their social nature, as we hardly ever wonder who makes them, under which conditions, how long it takes for them to be produced and so on. From this perspective, then, understanding and engaging with the politics of consumption involves, first and foremost, understanding the politics of concealment: why and how capitalist markets silence social information and relations and how, in turn, we can begin to imagine alternatives to current modes of production and consumption. As David Harvey (1990: 423) puts it, 'the grapes that sit upon the supermarket shelves are mute; we cannot see the fingers of exploitation upon them or tell immediately what part of the world they are from'. Accordingly, a substantial amount of academic and grassroots activism has been devoted to the development of cognitive maps that reconnect consumers with the producers and distributors of their commodities, aiming ultimately, 'to get behind the veil, the fetishism of the market and the commodity, in order to tell the full story of social reproduction' (Harvey 1990: 423).

Exemplary of this approach to consumption politics is Ian Cook's project titled 'follow-the-thing' (see e.g. Cook et al., 2004). Among others, Cook has been the main figure behind followthethings.com, a spoof website that looks like amazon.com but aims instead to tell the stories of the various commodities that we buy, using a variety of available resources – from news reports and documentaries to undergraduate student dissertation projects. Clicking on the grocery section, for instance, one comes across the story of avocados produced in Israel: Freddie Abrahams, an undergraduate student,

> is shocked to discover that the Israeli avocados he eats may be grown on illegally seized Palestinian land. There's a campaign going on in the UK to boycott these fruits. So he contacts the company that imports them into the UK and travels to Israel to find out more.
> (www.followthethings.com/grocery.shtml; accessed 17 October 2016)

This approach to linking consumers with producers and reimagining the relations between them (also discussed in the case study section) has in turn inspired a variety of other resources that inform consumers on the go through online tracking and barcode scanning such as http://wiki.p2pfoundation.net/Fair_Tracing and www.buycott.com.

Another approach to redressing the 'veil of the markets' is through so-called 'decommodification' projects that directly link consumers and producers and alter the ways in which commodities are traded. The decommodification perspective (e.g. Lekakis, 2012) has inspired a vast array of alternative markets and economic practices. Examples include trading directly with Zapatistas, the revolutionary leftist group based in Chiapas, Mexico (Chatzidakis, 2013), community-supported agriculture and various eco-villages (e.g. Thompson and Coskuner-Balli, 2007) as well as more mainstream alternatives such as

Fair Trade consumerism. Such economic arrangements clearly vary in the extent to which they pose a real challenge to capitalist markets. For instance, although perhaps the most widespread example of decommodification, Fair Trade networks are typically viewed as very limited in terms of their ability to establish radical economic relationships. They only pose (at best) a symbolic challenge to commodity fetishism, in so far as they employ practices that are largely mediated by conventional markets (e.g. supermarket chains; multinational retailers) and are fully confined by capitalist imperatives (Fridell, 2006). For harsher critics, Fair Trade products, like any other ethical product and/or examples of cause-related marketing, are in effect reflective of 'guilt fetishism' (Cremin, 2012). That is, they address a tendency by Western affluent consumers to look for ecological and ethical signifiers, ultimately assuaging themselves from the guilt they would otherwise experience knowing the real politics behind the commodities they buy.

More generally, an often cited approach to explaining what happens to countercultural and alternative consumer movements is co-optation theory (e.g. Holt, 2002). According to this perspective, in so far as consumer resistance functions from within the dominant symbolic order it remains open to adaptation and commercialisation by powerful marketplace actors. Somewhat ironically, through their everyday practices and resistance tactics, consumers provide creative resources that are ultimately converted into new commodities. For example, past the 1960s many successful multinational brands, such as Volkswagen and Levi's, embraced the anti-authoritarian ethos of youth movements, adding to their brand image countercultural sensibilities that allowed them to attract what would otherwise remain an elusive market segment. Altogether then, co-optation theory suggests that rebelling against the (perceived as) conformist mainstream is impossible, and somewhat ironically it only serves to reinforce the dominant symbolic order that seamlessly absorbs countercultural tastes and converts them into marketplace commodities. Although this may seem a likely outcome for a variety of market-mediated ethical and political projects, Thompson and Coskuner-Balli (2007) suggest that more intimate and human-scale initiatives, such as local food networks and solidarity trading arrangements, sufficiently diverge from the modalities of mainstream markets. Despite remaining a by-product of the global economic system, they allow their members to participate in infrastructures that are less alienating and further removed from unintended ecological and socioeconomic outcomes. In addition, they provide space for experimenting with doing things differently and for creating 'cracks' in current capitalist logics and practices (Holloway, 2010); a precondition for the formation of subjectivities other than that of the highly individualised and apolitical mainstream consumer (Chatzidakis et al., 2012).

However, what if removing the fetish character of commodities proves all the more impossible? What if peeling off one mystical layer was to reveal another mystical layer leaving nothing but layer upon layer upon layer? At least this seems to have been the case with Fair Trade (and other ethical) products, whereby otherwise genuine attempts to demystify forms of commodity production have led, as noted above, to the creation of yet another kind of fetishism, described as 'guilt fetishism' (Cremin, 2012). Correspondingly, many authors now speak about the 'ethical spectacle' (akin to the moralised brandscape; Chapter 7), which has come to replace, or at least co-habit, the symbolic realm of many everyday commodities. Contemplating this state of affairs, Stevphen Shukaitis (2013) argues that rather than trying to escape the mystical realm of commodities, a more politically progressive approach may be to dispel it. In fact, that was exactly the logic of 1920s Russian constructivists who had to contemplate the role of objects in the building of a communist society. Their purpose, in many ways, became 'confronting the phantasmic power of the community object and reclaiming it for socialism' (Kiaer, 2005 in Shukaitis, 2013: 440). Accordingly, some of the products of the Constructivist era were designed not only with utility in mind but also the more sociopolitical role they could play in harnessing collective living. A prime example here has been Soviet clothing with two famous designers, Varvara Stepanova and Liubov' Popova, taking somewhat different approaches (Kravets, 2013). Stepanova designed patterns such that their dynamism came from the chromatic vibrating effect in the fabric design, an effect that multiplied when seen on many dresses at once, hence enhancing the dress's sociality. Popova, on the other hand, focused on constructing versatile designs that could be transformed through use rather than tailoring. In both cases the dresses were meant to be more 'honest' and social. Although such logics seem miles apart from the highly individualised, fast-fashioned and sweatshop-fuelled garments of our day, Chatzidakis (2013) reminds us that there are still many commodities that are politically invested in a decidedly phantasmic manner: such as 'fascist rice', a rice that was removed from Athenian solidarity trading networks due to its producers' affiliation with neo-Nazi parties, and 'anarchist drinks' consumed in various squats and social centres in support of political causes. The question whether and how such objects can be effectively implicated in political struggles remains open.

Being a consumer in a neoliberal world

A different entrée to understanding the intersection of politics with consumption is through questioning the very role that consumption and consumerism play in our everyday lives, as a discourse and as an identity that we are increasingly asked to adopt in spheres other than our traditional seller–customer encounters. For instance, in spaces such as hospitals and universities we are increasingly treated as 'consumers' or 'customers' rather than patients or students. Importantly, we are often complicit in this, foregrounding the language of consumer rights and demanding procedures and services that up until recently would have been viewed as incompatible with the provision of public goods. For many philosophers and social thinkers of our time, this is exemplary of the particular era of late capitalism, aka neoliberalism, that we live in. According to Zygmunt Bauman (2009), for instance, consumerism as we understand it is the product of 'liquid modernity', a distinct period that started in the latter part of the 20th century. Under liquid modernity we transitioned from a society of producers to a society of consumers; and grew accustomed to be recognised mostly and primarily on the basis of our buying power. This has very profound implications in terms of how we understand the world and engage with it. Our contemporary vocabulary is one that favours words such as customer and consumer over citizen, choice and markets over community ties, self-interest over solidarity, individual over collective. More than just describing a reality, these words directly feed into our everyday dreams and fantasies, constructing and reinforcing our subjectivities (Massey, 2013).

But what is neoliberalism and how is consumption so heavily implicated in it? Neoliberalism, as David Harvey (2007) explains, is in the first instance, 'a theory of political economic practices that proposes that human well-being can best be advanced by promoting individual entrepreneurial freedoms and skills within an institutional framework characterised by strong private property rights, free markets, and free trade'. To do so, the role of the state must be restricted. Firstly, it has to guarantee that this framework is effectively implemented, for example by ensuring the integrity of the financial system and by providing services such as policing and enforcing the implementation of laws and regulations. Other than that, state interventions must be kept to a minimum and called to task only if there are opportunities for creating markets that do not yet exist, such as those around the use of land, water, healthcare, education and environmental protection. The underlying assumption is that compared to the private sector, state investments provide a far less efficient means to dynamic entrepreneurship and innovation (despite compelling evidence suggesting the contrary, e.g. Mazzucato, 2013).

Neoliberalism is distinct from classical or traditional liberalism. To begin with, critics highlight that the former serves more particular class interests in so far as, at least in practice, financial capital is protected at any cost. Many liberal economists, for instance, would advocate letting a big bank pay for the risks it has undertaken, even if that translates into bankruptcy or institutional collapse. Instead, as the 2008 crisis has rather vividly illustrated, neoliberalism supports the privatisation of financial risk-related profits and the collectivisation of risk-related losses (in the form of governmental bail-outs that use taxpayer money). Perhaps more importantly and certainly more profoundly, classical liberalism and neoliberalism differ in their implicit assumptions about human nature. Whereas the former has traditionally assumed that humans are innately individualistic, competitive and acquisitive, neoliberalism assumes that these values cannot be taken for granted and thus need to be cultivated by the state and other institutional actors (Gilbert, 2013). Accordingly, neo-liberalism is invested in promoting particular modes of thinking and being, ones that celebrate entrepreneurial virtues, marketplace freedoms, personal accountability for successes and failures (as opposed to any structural constraints or systemic injustices such as class exclusions) and at best forms of 'individualistic' as opposed to collectivist egalitarianism (e.g. via widening access to private property ownership).

It is the convergence of neoliberal values with the rationalities and the promises of Western-style consumerism that have foregrounded the latter as the key arena of everyday action. As Noam Chomsky, the famous public intellectual puts it, neoliberalism is invested in the production of consumers instead of citizens, of shopping malls instead of communities. Accordingly, the emphasis on consumer choice as basic to individual freedom and personal well-being – as opposed to any form of collective investment in and/or dependency upon common or social goods – is paramount to neoliberal forms of governance. To be sure, this is not to say that prior to neoliberalism people did not enjoy shopping or that they did not develop passionate attachments to things. There is a vast amount of anthropological and historical research on 'consumer cultures' that vividly illustrates the contrary (e.g. Trentmann, 2016). Likewise, various studies have heavily criticised traditional critiques of consumers as passive and easily manipulated, portraying instead a far more active and subversive role of consumers and consumer subcultures. However, such counter-criticisms are often based on oversimplifying traditional Marxist critiques of consumerism and/or ignoring their more recent reformulations and adaptations (Schor, 2007). In the era of full-fledged privatisation and marketisation of pretty much everything (from public transport to social housing and hospitals), it is hard to argue there is a lack of connection between neoliberalism and the focus on consumer choice and entrepreneurial individualism.

Furthermore, as the feminist scholar Lynne Segal (2017) puts it, nowadays Marx's notion of commodity fetishism has been given a rather more dystopian twist, with not only products obscuring the social relations behind their production but also with consumers becoming commodities, competing to improve their 'brand value' and impact on social media (see Facebook) and beyond. Wendy Brown, another famous social theorist, acknowledges that such new technologies of consumption can be indeed much fun and seductive, rendering them all the more dangerous:

> It's exciting and delicious in many ways to think about how to enhance the value of various bits of your self, how to brand yourself, how to attract investors, how to get more likes on Facebook, how to get re-tweeted, how to self-invest and get others to invest in you.
>
> (Cruz and Brown, 2016: 84)

For critics such as Segal and Brown, what is problematic with these otherwise pleasurable and seemingly benign activities is the intensification of particular modes of thinking about one's selfhood, our lives and our way of relating to our surrounding world. That is, we normalise a certain kind of atomised individualism and forms of self-branding and 'human capital' that are akin to the neoliberalisation of all spheres of social life. Rather inevitably, any form of dependency or insistence on more collectivised forms of consumption and alternative socialisation are viewed as lefty side projects that are irrelevant to the population at large. The perils of such new technologies of consumption and (ultimately) selfhood, however, are increasingly felt across the world, with many individuals deciding to break away from social media – even if only temporarily (e.g. whilst on holidays). Popular TV series such as Black Mirror portray zombie-like people that are too busy looking at their smart phones and trying to improve their personal ratings; and political parties such as Podemos publish their political programmes in the form of IKEA-like catalogues – even if only to subvert their brand-savvy electorate.

What is to be done? More than three decades ago, before new technologies of consumption and self-branding were conceived, Michel Foucault put it rather eloquently:

> The political, ethical, social, philosophical problem of our day is not to try to liberate the individual from the economy... but to liberate us both from the economy and from the type of individualization that is linked to the economy. We have to promote new forms of subjectivity through the refusal of this kind of individuality which has been imposed on us.
>
> (Foucault, 1983 in Gibson-Graham, 2006: xvi–xvii)

For many political activists and scholars, new politics of collective action (and anti-consumption) are urgently needed, not only ones that address people's everyday needs – from solidarity economies to gifting bazaars and community gardens – but also ones that help them cultivate new ways of thinking about themselves, their desires and their social relations; ones that are devoid of (socially and environmentally) damaging market logics and neoliberal vocabularies.

Summary

There are multiple ways of understanding the intersection of politics with everyday consumerism. This chapter has outlined three key perspectives. The first focuses on the consequences of everyday consumption and the extent to which more politicised consumer choices can achieve desirable outcomes such as the promotion of certain environmental and labour standards. A related stream of research focuses on the need to reduce consumption levels altogether rather than carrying on consuming, albeit more conscientiously. A second perspective to understanding the politics of consumption centres on Marx's notion of commodity fetishism and the extent to which people are oblivious of the social nature of the goods (and services) they consume. Accordingly, what becomes imperative is the advancement of new politics of 'decommodification' that inform consumers of the actors and politics involved in commodity supply chains, as well as attempts to narrow the distance between consumers and producers through alternative and solidarity-based economies. Finally, a different stream of scholarly thought has focused on the role of consumption within neoliberal regimes. At stake here are the ways through which we as 'consumers' unknowingly reproduce modes of thinking and feeling that are aligned with the increased commodification of everyday life, ultimately leading to the normalisation of a socially and environmentally unjust economic system.

CASE STUDY: decommodifying Jamaican papayas

Attempts to reconnect consumers with the producers and distributors of their commodities often draw on Professor Ian Cook's follow-the-thing approach. Cook (2004) provides an example of this approach by identifying seven key 'stakeholders' in the production–consumption nexus of Jamaican papayas (imported to the UK): that is the papaya fruit, the papaya farmer, the farm workers, the Jamaican economy, the UK buyer, the UK importer and the UK consumer. Each of these stakeholders is implicated in the fetishisation of papayas, albeit in different ways.

The UK buyer

Mina has been a speciality fruit and vegetable buyer for major UK super-market chains for over eight years. Her main role involves assessing the demand and supply for speciality fruits and vegetables, a task that is far more complex and challenging than it may seem. It involves, among other things, monitoring the quality and quantity of their production across an international range of suppliers whilst also assessing consumer trends and attitudes. In the case of papayas, for instance, the two main supply routes are from Brazil and Jamaica. Either way, papayas have to be the right look and size, the right taste and sold under the psychological £1 barrier (per item) whilst also allowing for a profit margin of at least 16 percent. Mina once visited one of the production sites of pineapple in Ivory Coast and got rather depressed with the amount of poverty she witnessed. Yet, such memories have little space in her everyday work rhythm of constantly checking spreadsheets and computer screens, writing reports and making phone calls.

The political economy of Jamaica

Jamaica remains a relatively impoverished economy with a big national debt. It has long moved away from relying on sugar production, not least because of the colonial references, the tough working conditions and more importantly, the various 'free trade' agreements imposed by organisations such as the European Union and World Trade Organization and which have made Jamaican sugar uncompetitive. Jamaica's economy is now far more diversified and focused on niche, higher-value tropical fruits such as papayas.

The UK importer

Tony is a supplier of fruits based in a small suite of offices in central London. He is in effect a broker between international suppliers and (UK-based) buyers and has known Jim, the Jamaican papaya farm owner, for quite some time. In general, much of Tony's work involves visiting suppliers with a view to establishing trust and confidence in their business. Such visits often prove rather unpleasant as they involve direct exposure to the exploitation entailed in the production of global commodities. However, at the end of the day Tony cares more about feeding his own family back in London – his focus is on getting the supplier to sell at the right price (usually lower rather than higher) and to exploit circumstantial factors such as currency fluctuations.

The papaya plant

Papayas come in different shapes and they are susceptible to various climatic changes and plant viruses. Among other things, their size fluctuates depending on tree height and gender, with the hermaphrodite variety being the one that is actually sold on supermarket shelves. Yet according to the FAO/WHO/WTO (1993) Codex Alimentarius volume 5B, there is only one shape, colour and look for papayas, not least for the sake of 'consumer safety'.

The papaya farmer

Jim is a second-generation white Jamaican who back in 1990 took the risk of setting up one of the first papaya farms and now enjoys considerable demand and reputation for his products. However, he still has to be on top of things, including protecting the farm from the very real risk of viral diseases, weather fluctuations and a constant expectation to meet the quality and quantity standards set in each order.

The workers

Phillips is the *farm foreman*, dealing with day-to-day decisions such as illness, time off, discipline and so on. His main task is to be authoritative without ever losing his temper. Pru is one of the papaya *packers*. Like the rest of her colleagues she has to work really hard, often staying at work until the late evening hours. Her standards of living deteriorated massively due to the Jamaican currency devaluation, making most of the commodities that she buys significantly more expensive. Papaya packers such as Pru would often get blistered fingertips and thumbs from the latex-like skin of unripe papayas. Other workers include packing house *supervisor(s)*, papaya *pickers, weighters, washers* and *wrappers*.

The UK consumer

Emma is a 25-year-old, AB young professional who enjoys cooking and travelling in exotic destinations. She likes experimenting with various ingredients in her cooking although she does not buy papayas… Why is she here? Because she still consumes, rather unknowingly, the white latex found in unripe papaya peduncle, aka 'papain'. Because of its unique protein-digesting enzymes, papain is found in a remarkably diverse range of products, from chewing gum and toothpaste to canned meats, leather goods and vegetarian cheese. The politics of papaya consumption are therefore rather trickier to untangle. And so are the politics of decommodification more broadly.

Seminar exercises

Discussion topics

1   Discuss critiques of political consumerism. What are the key arguments in favour of and against the idea of casting our votes in the marketplace? What is your opinion?
2   Following Donald Trump's win in the 2016 US election, there have been various calls for boycotting retailers that have been in support of his campaign (www.businessinsider.com/trump-related-businesses-boycotted-2016-11/#belk-3). Is this an effective form of political activism? Discuss by presenting arguments and counter-arguments.
3   Go to www.theguardian.com/world/2016/jun/09/podemos-manifesto-ikea-catalogue-flat-pack-policies. How can you explain this advert from a 'politics of consumption' perspective? Or is this more about the 'consumption of politics'?
4   What is wrong with the idea of 'branding' ourselves through social media such as Instagram and Facebook? Discuss with reference to neoliberalism and neoliberal subjectivities.

Group exercises

1   Read the article by Cook (2004) in the Key readings section.

   • Assume your group represents one of these stakeholders. From your perspective, can you make a case for buying or not buying papayas?
   • Compose the whole supply chain and identify the ethical dilemmas involved in each stage.
   • Would you, as an individual consumer, cast your consumption vote in favour for or against papayas?

2   Go to www.youtube.com/watch?v=z8fAmi0mHgA and watch the film 'Skoros: Anti-consumption in Crisis'.

   • How is this form of collective anti-consumption different from casting our votes in the marketplace?
   • How and why did the economic crisis challenge the original ideas of the collective?

- In the last part of the film it becomes clear that the members of the collective disagree about the extent to which Skoros still represents an anti-consumerist initiative. What is your view?

Key readings

Bradshaw, A., Campbell, N. and Dunne, S. (2013). The politics of consumption. *Ephemera*, 13(2): 203–216.

Chatzidakis, A., Larsen, G. and Bishop, S. (2014). Farewell to consumerism: Countervailing logics of growth in consumption. *Ephemera*, 14(4): 753.

Cook, I. (2004). Follow the thing: Papaya. *Antipode*, 36(4): 642–664.

Cremin, C. (2012). The social logic of late capitalism: Guilt fetishism and the culture of crisis industry. *Cultural Sociology*, 6(1): 45–60.

Gilbert, J. (2013). What kind of thing is 'neoliberalism'? *New Formations*, 80(1): 7–22.

References

Ariztia, T., Kleine, D., Bartholo, R., Brightwell, G., Agloni, N. and Afonso, R. (2016). Beyond the 'deficit discourse': Mapping ethical consumption discourses in Chile and Brazil. *Environment and Planning A*, 0308518X16632757.

Bauman, Z. (2009). *Does ethics have a chance in a world of consumers?* Cambridge, MA: Harvard University Press.

Chatzidakis, A. (2013). Commodity fights in post-2008 Athens: Zapatistas coffee, Kropotkinian drinks and fascist rice. *Ephemera*, 13(2): 459.

Chatzidakis, A., Maclaran, P. and Bradshaw, A. (2012). Heterotopian space and the utopics of ethical and green consumption. *Journal of Marketing Management*, 28 (3–4): 494–515.

Copeland, L. and Atkinson, L. (2016). Political consumption: Ethics, participation and civic engagement. In D. Shaw, M. Carrington and A. Chatzidakis (eds), *Ethics and morality in consumption: Interdisciplinary perspectives*. Abingdon: Routledge, pp. 171–188.

Cruz, K. and Brown, W. (2016). Feminism, law, and neoliberalism: An interview and discussion with Wendy Brown. *Feminist Legal Studies*, 24(1): 69–89.

Fridell, G. (2006). Fair trade and neoliberalism assessing emerging perspectives. *Latin American Perspectives*, 33(6): 8–28.

Gibson-Graham, G.J. (2006). *The end of capitalism (as we knew it): A feminist critique of political economy*. Minneapolis: University of Minnesota Press.

Harvey, D. (1990). Between space and time: Reflections on the geographical imagination. *Annals of the Association of American Geographers*, 80(3): 418–434.

Harvey, D. (2007). *A brief history of neoliberalism*. Oxford: Oxford University Press.

Hilton, M. (2007). Consumers and the state since the Second World War. *Annals of the American Academy of Political and Social Science*, 611(1): 66–81.

Holloway, J. (2010). *Crack capitalism*. London: Pluto Press.

Holt, D.B. (2002). Why do brands cause trouble? A dialectical theory of consumer culture and branding. *Journal of Consumer Research*, 29(1): 70–90.

Kravets, O. (2013). On things and comrades. *Ephemera: Theory and Politics in Organization*, 12(2): 421–436.

Latouche, S. (2009). *Farewell to growth*. Cambridge: Polity.

Lekakis, E.J. (2012). Will the fair trade revolution be marketised? Commodification, decommodification and the political intensity of consumer politics. *Culture and Organization*, 18(5): 345–358.

Marx, K. (1976). *Capital*, Volume 1, trans. Ben Fowkes. London: Penguin.

Massey, D. (2013). Vocabularies of the economy. *Soundings*, 54: 9–22.

Mazzucato, M. (2013). *The entrepreneurial state: Debunking private vs. public sector myths*. London: Anthem.

Micheletti, M. (2003). *Political virtue and shopping: Individuals, consumerism, and collective action*. New York: Palgrave.

Micheletti, M. and Stolle, D. (eds) (2004). *Politics, products, and markets: Exploring political consumerism past and present*. Piscataway, NJ: Transaction Publishers.

Newholm, T. and Newholm, S. (2016). Consumer ethics in history. In D. Shaw, M. Carrington and A. Chatzidakis (eds), *Ethics and morality in consumption: Interdisciplinary perspectives*. London: Routledge, pp. 97–115.

Newholm, T., Newholm, S. and Shaw, D. (2015). A history for consumption ethics. *Business History*, 57(2): 290–310.

Schor, J.B. (2007). In defense of consumer critique: Revisiting the consumption debates of the twentieth century. *Annals of the American Academy of Political and Social Science*, 611(1): 16–30.

Segal, L. (2017). *Radical happiness*. London: Verso.

Severson, K. (2012). Chick-fil: A thrust back into spotlight on gay rights. *New York Times*, 25 July. www.nytimes.com/2012/07/26/us/gay-rights-uproar-over-chick-fil-a-widens.html

Shaw, D. and Newholm, T. (2002). Voluntary simplicity and the ethics of consumption. *Psychology and Marketing*, 19(2): 167–185.

Shukaitis, S. (2013). Can the object be a comrade? *Ephemera*, 13(2): 437.

Soper, K. (2008). Alternative hedonism, cultural theory and the role of aesthetic revisioning. *Cultural Studies*, 22(5): 567–587.

Soper, K. (2016). Towards a sustainable flourishing: Ethical consumption and the politics of prosperity. In D. Shaw, M. Carrington and A. Chatzidakis (eds), *Ethics and morality in consumption: Interdisciplinary perspectives*. Abingdon: Routledge, pp. 11–27.

Thompson, C.J. and Coskuner-Balli, G. (2007). Countervailing market responses to corporate co-optation and the ideological recruitment of consumption communities. *Journal of Consumer Research*, 34(2): 135–152.

Trentmann, F. (2016). *Empire of things: How we became a world of consumers, from the fifteenth century to the twenty-first*. London: Penguin.

9   Marketing spaces and places

Space is normally taken for granted, treated as the static physical container where marketing and consumption activities take place. Marketing management approaches most often treat space as a logistical challenge, covered by the typical distribution concerns incorporated into the 'p' of place in the marketing mix. Hence, when the importance of space and place is acknowledged, the focus tends to be limited to store atmospherics and servicescape design. With an emphasis on sensory stimulation and store layout, such perspectives usually adopt information-processing models to look at stimuli input and their resultant consumer outputs in terms of emotional and behavioural responses. Importantly, however, the cultural significance of space and place tend to be overlooked by these models. Disciplines across the social sciences and humanities recognise that space and place are not static entities, but are instead dynamic and constantly evolving. Spaces become 'places' when they hold meanings for the people who use or inhabit them.

The rise in destination marketing in recent years attempts to maximise and, indeed, influence the shared meanings about specific countries, regions or cities in order to create place-based identities that appeal to tourists. Often the meanings of places like these are contested by various stakeholders (urban planners, residents, tourists, politicians, commerce and so forth) as different interests clash and sometimes try to suppress other voices. Nor is this type of contestation solely in relation to destination marketing. We already noted in Chapter 2 how a botched refurbishment by the management of a shopping centre alienated many local consumers who perceived it to have lost its special ambience and associated symbolic meanings.

This chapter focuses on the many dynamics of turning marketing spaces into places, and how we can analyse and understand these dynamics holistically. First, we begin by taking a closer look at how we form attachments with places we know and how they can become an important part of our identity. Then we go on to discuss how marketers encourage place attachment through particular branding strategies. We consider the spectacular nature of much contemporary retail and set this in its historical context, showing how specific forms of retail have evolved in terms of creating a sense of place. After highlighting the significance of theming, especially in relation to newer forms of retail, such as flagship brandstores, we continue with a discussion of the social role commercial locations may perform. Finally we look in more detail at the different kinds of spaces within which consumption takes place and introduce key theorists and concepts on consumption *in* space.

Place attachment and identity

We build attachments to places throughout our lives, usually starting with our home environment (house or neighbourhood) and radiating outwards from that as we grow up, move away and get to know other places, whether for temporary or more permanent stays. These places – be they workplaces or holiday resorts, countries or local villages, churches or pubs – can become highly significant to us and contribute strongly to our sense of who we are. The term 'place attachment' encapsulates such feelings of familiarity and belonging that we develop around the meaningful places in our lives. How we experience the places in our lives varies greatly depending on a host of factors.

In his seminal work 'Place and Placelessness', the geographer Edward Relph (1976) identifies a continuum of experiential place intensity that ranges from direct experience at one end to abstract thought at the other. Some spatial experiences will be instinctive and bodily, whereas others will be cerebral and intangible. The former are more likely to be taken-for-granted under-standings of place, and the latter more analytical and reflective. Thus, we may move around the rooms in our home in habitual ways that elicit little reflec-tion, taking for granted the contours and contents. In contrast we may be awestruck by the magnificence of a Gothic cathedral and self-consciously reflect on the beauty of its lofty spires. Many other spatial experiences will be nuanced mixtures of these two extremes. The point is that understanding the subjective lived experiences that people have in particular places is essential to appreciate the dynamics inherent in place.

Many heterogeneous spatial encounters in everyday life have the power to order our actions and intentions. Our actions and thoughts in the sacred space of a church are likely to be very different from those we have on enter-ing a pub. Whereas the former may awaken feelings of reverence that encou-rage us to bow our heads and retreat into silent prayer, the latter may provoke feelings of conviviality that encourage us to seek connections to others around us, rather than to a transcendental entity. Of course, how we react in and to a space will also depend on our own sociocultural background that heavily influences how we interpret the space. In the examples just given, we will only bow our heads if religiously inclined, and the pub experience may be very different depending, for example, on whether we are male or female. As a woman walking alone into a traditional English bar, where men often con-gregate on stools at the counter, we may feel alienated by the gendered nature of the space and disinclined to approach the bar to order a drink.

Thus, we can see how place influences identity, not only in relation to material factors such as the built, physical environment or natural landscape it contains, but also on account of social interactions that occur there. The relationship between people and their environment is always a dynamic and interactive one which encompasses a myriad of social, cultural, psychological, environmental, economic and political factors that are in continual interplay. As a consequence, our relationships with places can take many diverse forms, depending on the positive or negative associations that they engender in us and whether we experience affection, alienation or simply indifference to a place. As we have just seen in the example of the pub, the same space may provoke very different reactions in people depending on their own socio-cultural backgrounds, as well as how they interpret their ongoing experiences there. Relph (1976) uses the term 'insideness' to denote the degree of attachment that a person or group has with a place. So in the instance of the pub, the men at the bar feel safe and secure because they are regulars, insiders who know the place well, whereas we as outsiders (and women) feel vulnerable and threatened. The term 'outsideness' encapsulates these feelings of alienation, a sense of being separate and apart.

At its simplest 'outsideness' can be the homesickness we feel when we move to a new location. In practice these two poles – insideness and outsideness – represent a dialectical process through which we experience differing spatial intensities. It plays a significant role in our self-concept and, like other aspects of identity, it helps us differentiate ourselves from others ('I'm a Londoner' and so forth). Place identity also gives us an anchoring point, lending a sense of rootedness that makes us feel more secure. It is not only our sense of individual self to which place contributes, but also our social identity. Social identity is also usually tied to specific places that make us feel connected to certain reference groups (nation, neighbourhood, family, ethnic or religious group).

Apart from influencing our identity, places also establish their own identity, a special sense of place (genius loci) that allows somewhere to be differentiated from other places. Place identity is a complex mixture of memories, perceptions, interpretations and feelings. As we will see below, there are three key components that various theorists on space (e.g. Relph, 1976; Lefebvre, 1991; Soja, 1996; Agnew, 2005) identify and, although they all use different terms for these, they commonly include: 1) the physical setting with its material contents; 2) the activities and events that take place within the space; and 3) the meanings created (both individual and group) through people's experiences and intentions in relation to the space. Whereas the first has to do with physical structures and objects, the second concerns people's phenomenological (lived) experiences. The third is more abstract and covers the ideologies embedded in a space (e.g. the masculine culture of the bar counter). Relph (1976: 64) also usefully distinguishes between authentic and inauthentic senses of place, seeing the former as 'a direct and genuine experience of the entire complex of the identity of places – not mediated and distorted through a series of quite arbitrary social and intellectual fashions about how that experience should be, nor following stereotyped conventions'. We will see as we continue in the next section that there is often a danger of marketers creating inauthentic places and contributing to what Relph describes as *placelessness*, the eradication of what is distinct about a place through standardisation of its elements.

Destination marketing and branding

Destination marketing – promoting a town, city, region or country – is probably the first thing that springs to mind when we think of the intersection of place and marketing. Destination marketing has grown enormously over the last two decades, fuelled by the huge growth in the tourism and services industry sectors. A major aspect of destination marketing is developing a place identity and communicating this to potential visitors, investors or residents to influence their decisions about where to travel, invest in or live. At the heart of destination marketing lies the concept of place branding, i.e. encoding a place with a particular image, associations and values that differentiate it from other places and give it a unique identity. In such ways, marketing communications attempt to encourage a sense of place attachment in various audiences being targeted.

Often place branding efforts can go awry, however, reflecting only one constituency's perceptions of a place and failing to engage other stakeholders. To explain this type of failure in terms of Relph's (1976) terminology: by trying to create feelings of insideness for visitors, you may alienate the original inhabitants (insiders), bringing them a sense of outsideness and a place with which they can no longer identify. Unless they appreciate such dynamics, marketers risk creating an image that fails to resonate with anyone who has a vested interest in the place. Traditional marketing approaches overlook the many complexities inherent in the concept of place, treating place instead as if it were a product whose essence can be distilled into a single meaning and communicated to a target market. In so doing, marketers ignore a key distinction between places such as cities or regions and conventional products: rather than being owned by one individual or organisation, they are composed of different public and private ownerships (Warnaby and Medway, 2013). In addition, traditional approaches see identity as static, something that can be manipulated at will through a new logo and a catchy promotional message. They are usually the output of top-down decision-making processes (usually at local council/government level in conjunction with a consultant) that decide what positive aspects to emphasise about a place and what negative ones to mask. Place branding's role in this process is to encapsulate this identity and communicate its relevance effectively to various audiences.

Locals widely derided a city branding exercise for Belfast, Northern Ireland, even going so far as to describe it as 'putting lipstick on a gorilla' (Brown et al., 2013: 1251). Admittedly, Belfast City Council and their consultants did not have an easy mission to rebrand Belfast, a city long tainted by 'the troubles', years of religious conflict and terrorist slaughters. However, many commentators accused the resultant heart-shaped B logo – duly accompanied by 'Be' messages such as 'Be vibrant' and 'Be inspired' – of whitewashing the town's history and producing a copycat city stereotyping. They noted its remarkable similarity to promotional logos used for two English towns, Barrow-in-Furness and Blackburn, who also tilted the B in a similar heart-shaped fashion, as well as its likeness to Milton Glaser's iconic 'I Love New York' logo from 1977. Yet, somewhat surprisingly, despite its many vociferous critics, the rebranding of Belfast has been a success, precisely, Brown et al. (2013) conclude, because it was an innocuous, middle-of-the-road choice that offended no one, a significant advantage in a city whose fighting spirit is legendary.

So although marketers often ignore the complexities underpinning place relationships, sometimes this may be deliberate, as in the case of Belfast, where they sought a blander alternative that papers over the cracks, so to speak, and masks differences. Despite the seemingly positive outcome against all the odds – no doubt on account of Belfast's uniquely troubled history – this case is a good illustration of what Relph (1976) refers to as 'mass identities of places', identities designated by opinion makers rather than by the communities that live there. This leads to an inauthentic sense of place in Relph's view, one mediated and even distorted by marketers as they apply textbook principles in creating a cultural transformation package to differentiate the city and increase visitor numbers. As Patterson and Hodgson (2011: 297) so succinctly put it in their study of the city branding of Liverpool:

> The tried and tested format of such a makeover, to a cynic at least, involves: scouring the history books for points of hometown distinction; celebrating a sense of place by making local landmarks more tourist friendly, perhaps by installing a touch-screen kiosk or two, erecting plinths in honour of famous locals from the past and present, renovating and renewing public architecture, shopping precincts and generally polishing the town's jewels, whatever they might be, for the purposes of public display. Ultimately, the goal is to create a more palatable and exciting place tale.

Pursuing a makeover formula like this becomes a zero-sum game if every city does it as, ultimately, a formulaic approach that erodes any real cultural differentiation. The commodification of the city to such an extent can destroy its soul, with its 'form and spirit remade to conform to market demand, not residents' dreams' (Holcolm, 1999: 69). In celebrating difference, marketers may in fact be imposing uniformity. For example, Manchester's Canal Street celebrates gay culture, Birmingham's Jewellery Quarter testifies to its English heritage, while Dublin's Temple Bar signals Irish artistic endeavours. Despite their cultural distinctiveness, each area is crammed with bars, restaurants and retail that erode difference and give them more in common, all ultimately facilitating a hedonistic consumerist experience that carries little differentiation.

It is in this sense that Warnaby and Medway (2013: 358) highlight how 'the very act of place marketing can dilute and weaken the unique appeal of the place product', overlooking deeper, more engrained symbolic significances that inhabitants hold dear in the search for touristic thrills.

To retain a more authentic sense of place, one that reflects the genuine experiences of its inhabitants, Kavaratzis and Hatch (2013) propose an identity-focused place-branding framework. Moving away from a top-down perspective, the authors acknowledge place as dynamic and polyphonic with many different stakeholders. Theirs is a participatory model that encourages ongoing dialogue between all stakeholders but especially local communities. Three key pivotal points are in continuous interplay – culture, identity and image – to co-create the brand identity among all interested parties. This process-based model recognises that as people interact with their surroundings their understandings of place are constantly produced and reproduced. Consequently, place identity never remains static, and should involve ongoing negotiation between all stakeholders. The place-branding exercise becomes part of this process. By allowing local cultural meanings to surface, the process ensures inhabitants' feelings are respected and participants gain confidence over time as they see their own experiences reflected back to them.

Spectacular retail environments

Cities are often marketed as sites of spectacular consumption that include the city's architectural heritage (museums, cathedrals, castles, etc.) intermingled with more contemporary consumptionscapes such as shopping malls that also make a visual statement. Spectacular consumptionscapes such as these are a crucial part of city branding, providing key visitor attractions. Think of the world's largest shopping and entertainment complex, the Dubai Mall with 1,200+ retail outlets, which makes Dubai one of the world's top destinations. Each consumptionscape creates its own sense of place as well as contributing to the overall 'place of the city'. Shopping malls, festival marketplaces like Covent Garden, London and flagship brand stores like Prada and Louis Vuitton are designed to inspire a sense of awe, as well as acting as cultural resources for individualised identity projects. Although we tend to regard the intertwining of commerce and culture as a relatively new phenomenon, this is not strictly accurate. City planning has a long history of fantasy-inspiring retailscapes. Nineteenth-century shopping arcades and department stores were the precursors of the modern shopping mall.

Shopping arcades

Glazed shopping arcades were the first major retailing innovation to take place with the onset of industrialisation. Creating a public space that was sheltered from both weather and traffic, lavishly designed galleria brought new ways to sell the burgeoning number of luxury products flooding the market. Major European cities each developed their own spectacular arcades. Paris, in particular, was famed for the creative elegance of its many arcades such as the *Galeries de Bois*, one of the earliest arcades constructed in the 1780s. Architecturally, arcades made much use of atriums, marble panelling, highly ornate fixtures and fittings that, together with an abundance of greenery, conveyed opulence and awoke desire. In its conception, the arcade was very much a fantasy-provoking realm, a space designed to offer shoppers undisturbed browsing of extravagant displays of merchandise. Today in Paris, one can still admire the faded grandeur of a few surviving arcades (at their height they totalled 150+ in the city). Now mainly devoted to bric-a-brac shops, they draw tourists who seek immersion in their nostalgic ambience.

The department store

The advent of the department store in the mid-1800s heralded the demise of the arcades and its arrival was certainly one of the defining moments in the development of consumer culture. The department store introduced many innovations to the retail trade: a status-free environment where all shoppers were treated as equal; pricing of merchandise to replace individual bargaining; free entrance without the moral obligation to buy which dominated the atmosphere of other shops; and the right to exchange goods or obtain refunds. Perhaps the most significant innovation for modern retailing was the encouragement to browse around the shop, to wander and enjoy the experience without feeling committed to a purchase. Reekie (1993: 4) describes the lavish settings of early department stores such as *Bon Marché, Galeries Lafayette, Printemps, Bloomingdale's, Selfridges* and *Harrods*, as 'palaces of consumption' because of the irresistible temptations that they offered to strolling shoppers. Stores such as these also prided themselves on a continual supply of novelty merchandise, sending buyers around the world in search of remarkable items. While the department store has largely become a redundant form of retail, famous stores like the aforementioned still thrive today, a crucial part of the cityscapes to which they belong, with their illustrious histories acting as major tourist draws.

Significantly, department stores were the forerunner for what Ritzer (1999: 42) terms 'the new means of consumption' whereby social relations have become profoundly altered, now more often expressed through interactions with objects rather than with people. The department store brought about a cultural change, unveiling a world where commodities began to symbolise the search for experience, rather than possession representing an end in itself. The emphasis on the spectacular features of consumerism was all part of this experiential development, creating illusionary 'dreamworlds' (Williams, 1985), places that transported their visitors away from everyday reality and into a fantasy realm.

The idea of 'shopertainment' (Hannigan, 1998) – the convergence of retail and entertainment that is so prevalent today – also found its origins in the department store tradition. Many department stores in the late 1800s provided free entertainment to lure shoppers into their midst. Sometimes they would have orchestra music, art shows or other cultural diversions. Siegel-Cooper, famous for having the largest store in the world when it opened its New York branch in 1896, ran a six-week-long 'Carnival of Nations' (Hannigan, 1998). In a flamboyant attempt to outdo its rivals, the highlight of the carnival was an exotic Turkish harem and parade of Turkish dancing girls. Tearooms – a slightly more mundane way to encourage clients to linger – were also common in department stores, encouraging shoppers to socialise and relax over assorted teas and cakes. This tearoom tradition is still celebrated in London department stores such as Fortnum & Mason's and Harrods', although now largely catering for tourists to the city.

The shopping mall

Drawing on design features from both these predecessors – arcades and department stores – shopping malls play a pivotal role in contemporary consumptionscapes. Shopping is the foremost leisure activity (after television) and families go for a day out to the mall in the same way that they might have gone to the seaside fifty years ago. As our previous example of the Dubai Mall evidenced, malls have developed on ever grander scales since first introduced to retailing in the 1950s. Now they regularly mix a variety of leisure activities within one complex to keep customers entertained there as long as possible. The challenge for marketers is to give each mall its unique sense of place. Often this is done through theming the environment in some way, a topic that we will discuss more in the sections that follow.

Shopping mall design borrowed heavily from the fantastic aspects of department stores and their theatrical nature. Victor Gruen designed the first enclosed mall in 1956 in Southdale, Minnesota, to protect shoppers from harsh weather. He introduced the notion of the shopping complex as a world unto itself, where there could be a respite from the cares and toils of everyday life. Southdale's impressive atrium was filled with a fabulous profusion of flowers (including orchids, magnolias and azaleas) which bloomed all year round in what was called the 'Garden Court of Perpetual Spring'. Envisioning the mall as a new type of urban public space, Gruen encouraged the creation of a controlled environment that emulated the buzz and excitement of the city but without its attendant nuisances. The principles that guided the Southdale Mall design quickly became the blueprint for shopping centres across America and beyond.

As regards a sense of place, a major difference between mall developments and earlier marketplace types such as bazaars, Parisian arcades and department stores, is that the latter thrived in the heart of the city. In contrast, malls are often located in city suburbs and have to work much harder to create their own sense of place. Gigantic malls like the West Edmonton Mall, Canada and the Metro Centre, Gateshead, England reflect less their local surroundings in terms of demography and geography, instead drawing on a cultural legacy of centuries of recreational and theatrical entertainment (Davis, 1991). This new form of mall combines two sets of spatial practices and understandings: those that characterise the performance of leisure spaces and those that characterise the performance of commercial sites. On the one hand the mall epitomises the retailer's intention to sell goods and is designed to promote purchasing; on the other hand the mall is also a physical space where individuals seek a certain urban ambience (Gottdiener, 1997). In other words, the mall is both an economic space organised as an exchange-nexus and a social arena that possesses characteristics of both leisure sites and public spaces.

Major mall developments like the West Edmonton Mall and the Mall of America have maximised this new cultural form. For example, the West Edmonton Mall, completed in 1986, is one of the world's largest shopping and indoor leisure complexes and Alberta's top tourist attraction with more than 800 stores and an estimated 30 million+ visitors a year. Claiming to be inspired by the traditional urban bazaars of Persia where 'shopping and entertainment were plentiful and operated in tandem', the mall covers 5.3 million square feet, making it the size of a small city. Size matters when it comes to shopping malls with each making its own unique claims in this respect – check out the SM Mall of Asia's website that claims its construction used 2 million bags of cement – as well as 44,000 gallons of paint – and included installing 1.9 million floor tiles!

As already noted, separation from the city makes it essential for a mall to develop its own unique place-based identity. This separation, as well as the implied journey, become part of the fantasy aspects, giving the illusion of a voyage to another world. Creating a sense of displacement is therefore a key spatial practice that also conveys the feeling of being between two contrasting worlds. A theatrical approach to mall management heightens this effect. In his detailed study of the *Malling of America*, Kowinski (1985) describes the principles of retail drama where a fantasy world is managed and orchestrated to persuade customers to buy. The tenant mix is a fundamental part of the show and is selected carefully to reinforce the overall image of the mall. The drama analogy is carried through to merchandising and displays as crucial parts of the acts. Customers are not only the audience, but also the actors, playing key roles in the action.

Themed shopping environments

As we can see from the above, contemporary retail is more about telling stories. Shopping structures such as department stores, malls, shopping centres and so forth become discursive statements that invite interpretation. Postmodern retail design (see Chapter 2's case study) acknowledges this and often makes use of open-ended narrative structures that are deliberately ambiguous, allowing multiple interpretations. This process encourages consumers to engage in their own subjective fantasising and meaning creation. Perhaps the best examples of postmodern retail are the plethora of themed environments to be found in the contemporary marketplace: flagship brand stores such as ESPN zone (Kozinets et al., 2002); brand museums (Sherry, 1998); Irish pubs (Patterson and Brown, 2002); festival marketplaces (Maclaran and Brown, 2005); and many shopping malls, restaurants, hotels and other leisure venues. These elaborately designed locations create spectacular environments that appeal to consumers' imaginations and emphasise the experiential elements of the product or service they are offering. Making a crucial contribution to Hannigan's (1998) concept of the 'fantasy city' or the 'postmodern metropolis', they enchant and entice visitors to linger and immerse themselves in their surreal ambience.

Over the last decade, there has been a major growth in the development of themed stores that encourage consumers to engage in a relationship with their brands. The spiritual aspects of such stores can even be likened to the emotions inspired by cathedrals, with their dazzling displays being like shrines where consumers can come to worship the brand. Similarly, highlighting a form of shopping motivation that is ideological, as opposed to simply utilitarian or hedonistic, Borghini et al. (2009) identify how *American Girl Place*'s brand ideology is manifested in focal areas of the store. Themed stores can thus evoke much more than basic sensory responses to their richly imaginative surroundings. These quasi-spiritual or moral elements accord with Pine and Gilmore's (1999) notion of transformational experiences whereby a customer is changed in some way as a result of her store visit. Whereas the memory of sensory stimuli fades in time, these authors argue, transformations are more permanent and inspirational. 'Mindscapes' like these are at the forefront of themed environments, according to Kozinets et al. (2002), because they combine entertainment, therapeutics and spiritual growth.

Part of a themed environment's ability to transcend everyday reality and, indeed, to have a longer-lasting transformational effect, is how it conveys a sense of elsewhereness, a sense of liminality (being between two worlds) that has long been associated with the marketplace more generally. Likewise it has been noted that the illusionary elements of shopping mall design often make more pronounced these inherent liminoid characteristics. Such references draw on the works of two famous anthropologists, Arnold van Gennep (1960) and Victor Turner (1969). The former introduced the concept of liminality in his study of rites of passage, rites that mark societal transitions from one life stage to another (puberty, marriage, death, etc.), transitions composed of three separate stages: separation – liminal period – reassimilation. At the first stage, the person undertaking the ritual leaves behind their current social status before entering into a liminal phase where they are 'betwixt and between' identities. Finally the initiate emerges with a new social status to be reassimilated into society. Victor Turner further developed this work (1969,

1974), particularly in relation to understanding the liminal period of transition and its relevance to industrialised society. He distinguished between liminal activity as practised through rituals in pre-industrialised societies and liminoid activity that has developed in contemporary society to differentiate work from play and from which, Turner believes, transformations can grow. Noting that individuals are socially and structurally ambiguous during the liminal (or liminoid) phase, Turner developed his idea of anti-structure, whereby liminal individuals, on account of their betwixt and between status, develop a sense of communitas through their shared experiences.

Turner's ideas have been very influential within marketing and consumer research, with regard to both understanding essentially anti-structural, extraordinary consumption experiences (e.g. Kozinets, 2002) and more mundane, structural ones that are performed within scripted and ritualised settings such as brand stores (e.g. Kozinets et al., 2002; Borghini et al., 2009) and retail environments (Maclaran and Brown, 2005). More recently, however, Lanier and Rader (2015) have noted that current research has almost entirely focused on the structural/anti-structural dimension of consumer experiences, ignoring another key dimension, that is function and anti-function (Merton, 1957). The former refers to the manifest, intended consequences of a certain consumption activity whereas the latter refers to the more latent and unintended ones. Lanier and Rader (2015) observe that less attention has been paid to anti-functional consumer experiences, which they further distinguish between stochastic and adventurous ones. Stochastic experiences are those that are still highly structured and scripted but can have unintended consequences, such as gambling in a casino. A key difference from Turner's anti-structural experiences is that they tend to be highly individualistic. Adventurous experiences are also individualistic but they tend to refuse both any kind of structure and a pre-determined consequence. Although they are often as extraordinary as anti-structure experiences (e.g. visiting the Burning Man festival), they differ in their insistence on not having a functional outcome. A perfect example would be backpacking in a less known and unsafe tourist destination with a view to experience excitement and danger. From Lanier and Rader's (2015) analysis it is clear that stochastic and adventure experiences remain less explored and understood by place marketers.

The social role of place

In contrast to spectacular retail, there are also many more mundane places that are meaningful to consumers and that facilitate social interaction and a sense of community. Often we form emotional attachments to everyday commercial locations such as coffee shops, bars and even grocery stores. We may rely on such places to help us establish routines (morning coffee, nightly pints, weekly shop) and make us feel more rooted in place. They can enhance our social life, providing gathering points where we spend time with others. Sometimes referred to as 'third places' (Rosenbaum, 2006), pubs, coffee shops and other leisure spaces such as gyms provide a place between home (first place) and work (second place). An important defining characteristic of third places is that they are somewhere we can take time out, relax and interact with others. Fast food restaurants are, therefore, unlikely to meet this requirement as they encourage customers to move quickly through their establishments, rather than lingering to socialise, with layout designed to be functional as opposed to atmospheric. The coffee shop where everyone meets in the famous US sitcom *Friends* or the pub in *Cheers* are perfect examples of third places.

Traditionally, social scientists assumed that retail environments are too uniform and regularly remodelled to allow any meaningful form of social and symbolic interaction. However, through retailers' ongoing attempts to enhance liminality, authenticity and creativity in their environments (as illustrated above), consumers have begun to develop significant emotional bonds to commercialised third places. There is now growing consensus that place attachment to commercial locations is entirely possible and it occurs particularly when they provide experiences that go beyond what consumers believe the market usually offers (Debenedetti et al., 2013). More specifically, Debenedetti et al. illustrate that attachment to bars and restaurants often emerges from a blend of familiarity, authenticity and security, which is altogether akin to a sense of 'homeyness'. Importantly, homeyness not only arises from the various spatial features of the commercial space but also from the way in which pro-prietors and employees interact with customers, allowing them to feel unique and appreciated; for example, through engaging in genuine conversations, allowing back-stage access and offering unexpected gifts. In turn, consumers often 'give back' to their treasured commercial spaces, through practices such as volunteering, tipping and acting as their informal brand ambassadors.

A sense of homeyness, therefore, is a key state or liminal feeling that can bridge the divide between private and public spaces but also commercial and non-commercial ones. Accordingly, consumers often invest in product con-stellations that reproduce a sense of personalisation and domesticity not only in their homes and second spaces such as their workspaces (e.g. Tian and Belk, 2005) but also public and commercialised spaces such as sports events and music festivals (e.g. Bradford and Sherry, 2015). For philosopher Edward Casey (1993), this is because of two fundamental modes of 'dwelling-in-place' that date back to antiquity: that is hestial and hermetic. Whereas the hestial mode of dwelling is private, self-enclosed and inward-looking, the hermetic mode remains public, open and outward-directed. Importantly, Casey sees them as complementary modes of dwelling, that is we enjoy residing in a particular place (the exemplar hestial place being the home) but we also appreciate travelling and wandering (exemplar hermetic places being airports, restaurants, hotels and other consumptionscapes). As noted above, however, consumers often attempt to reassert the hestial in otherwise hermetic places and with that, a sense of familiarity and domesticity; for instance, by having a favourite spot in one's local pub or by personalising and decorating one's tent whilst attending sports and music festivals. It is often through hestialising practices that more specific forms of place attachment and place identity can develop.

Rather than reasserting the private into the public, some consumer activists attempt to do the opposite; that is embrace the 'public' or a more collectivised and political ethos in what otherwise may be deemed as individualised place making. For instance, the radical and anti-structural nature of some public spaces (from Kozinet's Burning Man festival to Chatzidakis et al.'s guerrilla park in Exarcheia) often allows consumers to challenge taken-for-granted assumptions and to develop alternative forms of community and sociality that are devoid of market logics. At stake is the development of new subjectivities that challenge possessive individualism and atomised logics and practices (this is explained in more detail in Chapter 8).

Towards a typology of spaces

Arguably because of a deeper appreciation of the social role of place, more recent research highlights the numerous ways through which consumption is implicated in the production and social construction of any kind of space, from shopping malls and flagship stores to urban bars and restaurants, residential neighbourhoods and national parks. Drawing on this observation, Castilhos and Dolbec (forthcoming) have attempted to provide a more systematic typology of spaces and how certain logics and practices of consumption are excluded/included within them, identifying four main types: that is, public spaces, market spaces, emancipating spaces and segregating spaces. These are in turn largely constituted by two underlying dynamics, first being a contradiction between negotiation and consensus and second, a contradiction between participation and subjugation (see Figure 9.1). *Public spaces* include streets, squares, urban and national parks, mountains, beaches and waterfronts, among other things. They are, by their very inception, public goods or 'commons' that are participatory and inclusive of different social groupings. However, they are also continuously contested by the variety of stakeholders that inhabit them or represent them, from local and national authorities to various commercial actors, citizen groups and, not least, consumers. For example, Visconti et al. (2010) identify different ideologies of public space consumption, e.g. individualistic versus collectivist, and how these in turn affect the kind of street art found in different urban neighbourhoods. Likewise, public spaces are increasingly designed or revamped with specific (consumer) groups in mind and not others. As evident in this chapter, *market spaces* are those that are most examined by consumer researchers. Unlike public spaces, they are owned and/or governed by commercial actors only (or mostly) and they are exclusionary, in the sense that only consumers of particular socio-economic and cultural groupings are allowed. However, as we have seen above, commercial actors often attempt to 'democratise' their market spaces with a view to enhance their authenticity and, ultimately, consumer satisfaction and place attachment.

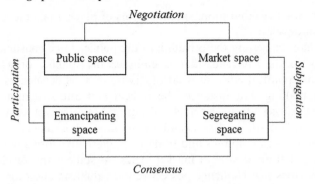

Figure 9.1 Castilhos and Dolbec's (forthcoming) typology of spaces

Castilhos and Dolbec (forthcoming) also identify *segregating spaces* such as houses, gated communities, private clubs, ghettos and favelas. They differ from market spaces in the sense that they may be owned and/or governed not by commercial interests alone but by social actors who are actively invested in consensual spaces that fit their private interests. Like market spaces, they are exclusionary but on the basis of class, race, age and gender (to name a few variables) rather than market logics alone. However, consumption is also central in segregating spaces, in so far as particular practices and rituals foster a sense of community and homogeneity, both enabling and hindering certain commercial opportunities. Finally, *emancipating spaces* are spaces of subversion and resistance to hegemonic ideas of public space consumption. Similar to segregating spaces they are produced upon consensus but unlike them, they are participatory and open to everyone who is actively engaged in overturning the status quo, either temporarily, as in the case of the Burning Man festival (Kozinets, 2002) or permanently, as in the case of the urban neighbourhood of Exarcheia (Chatzidakis et al., 2012).

Theorising consumption *in* space

Castilhos and Dolbec's typology exemplifies a move away from treating space (solely) as the object of consumption (e.g. consuming or not consuming themed stores, shopping malls, tourist destinations, etc.) to understanding space as the context of any consumption activity. That is, all consumption is *in* space and consumers, both knowingly and unknowingly, are implicated in the construction of space. Perhaps more profoundly, consumer logics and practices are also somewhat 'produced' or at least depend upon the kind of space(s) they inhabit. This highlights the need to develop more nuanced and multidimensional understandings of how consumers experience space. In line with the so called 'spatial turn' in social sciences various anthropologists and sociologists have attempted to develop more sophisticated frameworks, drawing on seminal spatial theorists such as Henri Lefebvre (1991), Ed Soja (1996) and David Harvey (2004). Common in such approaches is the conceptualisation of different variants of space, for instance the descriptive, the phenomenological and the social constructivist (Chatzidakis et al., forthcoming); and the embodied, affective, discursive and relational (e.g. Low, 2016), to name a few.

Chatzidakis (2017) has recently attempted to apply a triadic understanding to the Exarcheian space – the urban neighbourhood discussed in Chapter 7 – drawing on three key dimensions: material, symbolic and sociospatial. Focusing on the *material* space, he mentions how even factors such as the size of the building blocks and road intersections affect the kind of social interaction and mobilisation that a particular area allows. Frequent road intersections, for instance, allow for the quick spread of communication and activity such as rioting, which would be impossible in areas with higher exposure and visibility. Importantly, Chatzidakis (2017) discusses how the Exarcheian marketplace is also specific to the particular material and aesthetic features of the area. All shops are small, independent and somewhat rustic, whereas there is a disproportionate amount of bookstores, print shops and record shops, catering to the area's countercultural sensibilities. Bar and restaurant names include 'Molotov', 'Kalashnikov Garden' and 'Necropolis', contrasting with a generation of new 'happy' cafes and restaurants that opened after the early 2000s. Focusing on *symbolic* space, Chatzidakis mentions how the neighbourhood is legendary for its range of affective and embodied experiences. For instance, people often talk about the particular 'air that one breathes when entering Exarcheia', a sense of 'tension' and 'urgency' that contrasts with the significantly calmer and less politicised surrounding neighbourhoods. This is because, in many ways, the area is explicitly positioned against the production of individualised and apolitical 'consumers' that frequent highly commoditised spaces such as retail parks, shopping districts and malls. At stake is the production of new subjectivities and ways of thinking that are devoid of the consumption-centric social order. Accordingly, the area is fertile ground for the production of alternative consumption logics and practices, centred on voluntary simplicity, solidarity and alternative trading economics, time banks, gifting bazaars, numerous DIY projects, collective cooking events and no-ticket cinema screenings, among other things. Ultimately, as Chatzidakis puts it, consumption *in* the Exarcheian space reflects and reproduces logics of normative and 'aesthetic revisioning' (Soper, 2008) that stand in opposition to those of mainstream consumer society and are felt alike by both fans and despisers of the area.

Finally, akin to Castilhos and Dolbec's (forthcoming) understanding of public and emancipatory space, Exarcheia can be viewed as the *sociospatial* product of competing stakeholders, including residents, street artists, marketplace actors, city and state planners. For instance, multinational retail chains such as Starbucks are anything but welcome in the area, and the real threat of being firebombed keeps them well outside the neighbourhood's borders. Likewise, symbols of conspicuous consumption such as expensive cars often get vandalised. Perhaps more strikingly and certainly more illustrative of the area's countervailing logics to public space consumption is Exarcheia's 'park' or 'Navarinou park' (discussed in Chapter 7), which operates on the principles of mutuality, solidarity, anti-commercialisation and gift economy. Altogether then, what Chatzidakis' (2017) study highlights is the multiple ways in which space frames (if not produces) any kind of consumption activity and is in turn framed by it. What may seem as natural and desirable in some spaces (e.g. carrying a Gucci bag) may be frowned upon in others and may even prove dangerous. Likewise, the way in which we think and fantasise about consumption is dependent upon the options we have in our everyday whereabouts and the various material, symbolic and social cues we get from our environment. Put differently, our consumption logics and practices both constitute and are constituted by our marketplaces and public spaces.

Furthermore, recent research on the intersection of space and consumption has attempted to move beyond the 'visual', with a view to explore the different ways in which senses such as smell and sound interpenetrate our consumption in space. For instance, Canniford et al. (forthcoming) counter-propose smell as a key gateway to feeling, practising and producing space. Specifically, the function of smell is three-fold. First, smell encodes space in so far as particular spaces are associated with specific odours and not others. For instance, the deodorised ambience of a department store, the lack of lingering smell in a professional trading floor and the sweaty smell of a gym floor. Second, smell identifies bodies with spaces; for example, when specific 'country smells' are associated with people that carry them around, literally or metaphorically. Finally, smell 'moves spaces'. That is it helps punctuate movements and changes in spaces; for instance, various professional districts are associated with the smell of junk or take away food after dark whereas rural spaces are characterised by winter and summer smells as well as Saturday and weekday smells. As Henshaw et al. (2016) note, similar observations about the olfactory identity of different times and places have long been exploited by place marketers, if only intuitively. More generally, Canniford et al.'s (forthcoming) and Henshaw et al.'s (2016) studies are part of recent ethnographic attempts to advance more 'multisensorial' understandings of consumption in and of space; and to treat time and space as inextricably linked (Chatzidakis et al., forthcoming).

Summary

Moving beyond a simplistic understanding of place as one of marketing's 4ps, this chapter explores the various dynamics of turning spaces into places. First, we took a closer look at how place attachments and place-related identities develop, before considering how marketers attempt to influence such processes through place branding and marketing efforts. Subsequently, we considered the spectacular nature of much contemporary retail and set this in its historical context, showing how specific forms of retail have evolved in terms of creating a sense of place. We then moved on to consider the social role of places and a typology of spaces that accounts for the different ways in which everyday consumption is implicated in these. Finally, we concluded with an attempt to develop a more multidimensional understanding of consumption *in* (rather than of) place.

CASE STUDY: eating Dans le Noir?

Dans le Noir? is a themed restaurant franchise where you eat in the dark.[1] It has locations in London, Paris, Barcelona and St Petersburg. Its name – Dans le Noir? – deliberately provokes the question of who is in the dark. Customers are looked after by blind serving staff who move dextrously in the darkened surrounds where sighted consumers find themselves completely disorientated and immobilised. A visit to the restaurant is highly organised, orchestrating a ritualistic process to take the patron through the eating-in-the-dark experience as efficiently and safely as possible. This experience can be broken down into a four-stage structure that is inherent in rites of passage (see van Gennep, 1960).

Preparation

On arrival at the restaurant, guests enter the fully lit bar area where they wait in anticipation of their eating experience. Staff offer them colour-coded menus: green (vegetarian), red (meat), blue (fish) or white (surprise). Then they ask customers to leave their bags, watches and phones in lockers. This simulates the preparation of initiates for a rite of passage. As customers leave the customary trappings of the civilised world behind, they are being metaphorically stripped of their social status. In final preparation they also visit the bathroom, a type of purification ritual before immersion in the dark. This stage creates feelings of excitement, anticipation and unease among visitors as they assemble for their departure into the dark.

Separation

Customers form a line behind the blind staff member who leads them into the eating area. They must pass along a darkened corridor that acts as a threshold between the two worlds (light/dark; abled/disabled). To undertake this journey they each place their left hand on the shoulder of the person in front. At the head of this human chain, the blind server assumes authority (like a ritual elder: Turner, 1969), leading his customers slowly into the dark. The touching required at this stage begins to prepare diners for the process of physical disabling that is to follow and many experience symptoms of physical anxiety such as racing hearts or butterflies in the stomach.

The liminoid phase

As they are led to their table in complete darkness, diners suddenly find themselves quite helpless, trying to ascertain where their eating utensils are and who is next to them. The blind servers become the able-bodied people in this environment, moving with an air of confidence and calm that is in sharp contrast to the disorientated fumbling of their customers. This is the topsy-turvy world associated with liminal spaces where role reversals are typical (Bakhtin, 1968). Touch becomes the most important sense and patrons touch everything around them to establish the parameters of the new world in which they find themselves. Often this is messy as they spill drink or food over themselves and others. Much eating takes place with hands and there is an overall sense of regression to childhood, a feeling that also heightens the loss of status in this liminal stage and of being transformed.

Reassimilation

Finally the eating experience is over and customers are led back into the light. Now the light blinds them as they blink and try to readjust to their return. For many it has been a challenge that they are proud to have survived, while, for others, it has been a more empathetic experience and they return full of admiration for the blind serving staff. Consistent with having completed a ritual process, everyone feels a little different, even transformed in some way, as they reflect on their eating-in-the-dark and how much they have taken their own sighted world for granted.

Seminar exercises

Discussion topics

1   Think of a place to which you are attached and discuss the ways in which this place makes you feel an insider. Who could be termed the outsiders?

2   Go to www.youtube.com/watch?v=Xu4szbNFPwM&spfreload=10. Following Turner, would you describe this as a structure or anti-structure consumption experience? Subsequently, think of the different senses involved in this consumption experience. How would you analyse this from a multisensorial perspective?

3   Identify a commercial location that you frequent and that could be described as a 'third place', elaborating on the social role it plays in your life and in the life of others who go there. How is place attachment achieved within that place?

4   Place marketers are quickly catching up with place-making research, as evident in http://lifeathome.ikea.com/home/. Go to the website and have a look at the section titled 'place'. How is this linked to ideas of 'homeyness' and hestialising third place? Can you think of any counter-arguments to the idea of extending the home 'beyond the four walls of a residence'?

Group exercises

1   Identify (from the internet, papers or your own local knowledge) and detail a recent case of city branding. How authentic or inauthentic do you think the result of this branding exercise has been? Justify your answer by making reference to Relph's (1976) theories on this.

2   Think of the neighbourhood in which you live.

   - How does it affect your consumption logics and practices and how is it in turn affected by them?
   - Try to analyse this in relation to Chatzidakis' (2017) three dimensions, that is material, symbolic and sociospatial.
   - Can you apply a more multisensorial perspective?

Note

1   This section is from an ongoing research project with Elisabeth Tissiers-Desbordes, ESCP Europe, Paris and Andrea Davies, University of Leicester.

Internet resources

IKEA: http://lifeathome.ikea.com/home/
Dans le Noir? https://london.danslenoir.com/en/home/
SM Mall of Asia: http://smmallofasia.com/moa/?p=1097

Key readings

Castilhos, R.B. and Dolbec, P.-Y. (forthcoming). Conceptualizing spatial types: Characteristics, transitions, and research avenues. *Marketing Theory*.
Chatzidakis, A. (2017). Consumption in and of crisis-hit Athens. In D. Dalakoglou and G. Aggelopoulos (eds), *Critical ethnographic approaches and engaged anthropological perspectives*. London: Routledge.
Kavaratzis, M. and Hatch, M.J. (2013). The dynamics of place brands: An identity based approach to place brand theory. *Marketing Theory*, 13(1): 69–86.
Warnaby, G. and Medway, D. (2013). What about the 'place' in place marketing? *Marketing Theory*, 13(3): 345–363.

References

Agnew, J. (2005). Space: Place. In P. Cloke and R. Johnston (eds), *Spaces of geographical thought: Deconstructing human geography's binaries*. London: Sage, pp. 81–96.
Bakhtin, M. (1968). *Rabelais and his world*. Cambridge, MA: MIT Press.
Borghini, S., Diamond, N., Kozinets, R.V., McGrath, M.A., Muniz, A., Jr. and Sherry, J.F., Jr. (2009). Why are themed brandstores so powerful? Retail brand ideology at American Girl Place. *Journal of Retailing*, 85(3): 363–375.
Bradford, T.W. and Sherry, J.F., Jr. (2015). Domesticating public space through ritual: Tailgating as vestaval. *Journal of Consumer Research*, 42: 130–151.

Brown, S., McDonagh, P. and Shultz II, C.J. (2013). A brand so bad it's good: The paradoxical place marketing of Belfast. *Journal of Marketing Management*, 29(11–12): 1251–1276.

Canniford, R., Riach, K. and Hill, T. (forthcoming). Nosenography: How smell constitutes meaning, identity and temporal experience in spatial assemblages. *Marketing Theory*.

Casey, E.S. (1993). *Getting back into place*. Bloomington: Indiana University Press.

Chatzidakis, A., Maclaran, P. and Bradshaw, A. (2012). Heterotopian space and the politics of ethical and green consumption. *Journal of Marketing Management*, 3(4): 494–515.

Chatzidakis, A., Morven, M. and Warnaby, G. (forthcoming). Consumption in and of space and place: Introduction to the special issue. *Marketing Theory*.

Davis, T.C. (1991). Theatrical antecedents of the mall that ate downtown. *Journal of Popular Culture*, 24(4): 1–15.

Debenedetti, A., Oppewel, H. and Arsel, Z. (2013). Place attachment in commercial settings: A gift economy perspective. *Journal of Consumer Research*, 40(5): 904–923.

Gottdiener, M. (1997). *The theming of America: Dreams, visions, and commercial spaces*. Boulder, CO: Worldview Press.

Hannigan, J. (1998). *Fantasy city: Pleasure and profit in the postmodern metropolis*. London: Routledge.

Harvey, D. (2004). Space as a keyword. Marx and Philosophy Conference, May, Institute of Education, London. http://frontdeskapparatus.com/files/harvey2004.pdf

Henshaw, V., Medway, D., Warnaby, G. and Perkins, C. (2016). Marketing the 'city of smells'. *Marketing Theory*, 16(2): 153–170.

Holcolm, B. (1999). Marketing cities for tourism. In D.R. Judd and S.S. Fainstein (eds), *The tourist city*. New Haven, CT: Yale University Press, pp. 54–70.

Kowinski, W.S. (1985). *The malling of America*. New York: William Morrow & Co.

Kozinets, R.V., Sherry, J.F., Jr, DeBerry-Spence, B., Duhachek, A., Nuttavuthisit, K. and Storm, D. (2002). Themed flagship brand stores in the new millennium: Theory, practice, prospects. *Journal of Retailing*, 78: 17–19.

Lanier, C.D. and Rader, C.S. (2015). Consumption experience: An expanded view. *Marketing Theory*, 15(4): 487–508.

Lefebvre, H. (1991). *The production of space*. Oxford: Blackwell.

Low, S.M. (2016). *Spatializing culture: The ethnography of space and place*. Abingdon: Routledge.

Maclaran, P. and Brown, S. (2005). The center cannot hold: Consuming the utopian marketplace. *Journal of Consumer Research*, 32: 311–323.

Merton, R.K. (1957). *Social theory and social structure*. Glencoe: Free Press.

Patterson, A. and Brown, S. (2002). Reading writer, quaffing quiddity and rejoicing Joyceans: Unpicking the packaging of an Irish icon. In S.M. Broniarczyk and K. Nakamoto (eds), *Advances in consumer research*. Valdosta, GA: Association for Consumer Research, pp. 504–509.

Patterson, A. and Hodgson, J. (2011). Re-imagining the city of Liverpool as a capital of consumption. In A. Bradshaw, P. Maclaran, and C. Hackley (eds), *European advances in consumer research*. Duluth, MN: Association for Consumer Research, pp. 298–303.

Pine, B.J. and Gilmore, J.H. (1999). *The experience economy: Work is theatre and every business a stage*. Boston, MA: Harvard Business Press.

Reekie, G. (1993). *Temptations: Sex and selling in the department store.* Sydney: Allen and Unwin.

Relph, E. (1976). *Place and placelessness.* London: Pion.

Ritzer, G. (1999). *Enchanting a disenchanted world: Revolutionizing the means of consumption.* Thousand Oaks, CA: Pine Forge Press.

Rosenbaum, M.S. (2006). Exploring the social supportive role of third places in consumers' lives. *Journal of Service Research*, 9(1): 59–72.

Sherry, J.F., Jr. (1998). The soul of the company store: Nike town Chicago and the emplaced brandscape. In J.F. Sherry, Jr. (ed.), *Servicescapes: The concept of place in contemporary markets.* Lincolnwood, IL: NTC Business Books, pp. 109–146.

Soja, E.W. (1996). *Thirdspace: Journeys to Los Angeles and other real-and-imagined places.* Cambridge, MA: Blackwell.

Soper, K. (2008). Alternative hedonism, cultural theory and the role of aesthetic revisioning. *Cultural Studies*, 22(5): 567–587.

Tian, K. and Belk, R.W. (2005). Extended self and possessions in the workplace. *Journal of Consumer Research*, 32 (September): 297–310.

Turner, V.W. (1969). *The ritual process: Structure and antistructure.* Ithaca, NY: Cornell University Press.

Turner, V.W. (1974). *Dramas, fields, and metaphors: Symbolic action in human society.* Ithaca, NY: Cornell University Press.

Van Gennep, A. (1960). *The rites of passage.* Chicago: University of Chicago Press.

Visconti, L.M., Sherry, J.F., Borghini, S. and Anderson, L. (2010). Street art, sweet art? Reclaiming the 'public' in public place. *Journal of Consumer Research*, 37(3): 511–529.

Williams, R.H. (1985). *Dream worlds: Mass consumption in late nineteenth-century France.* Berkeley, CA: University of California Press.

10 The globalised marketplace

Introduction

Our lives are now extraordinarily intertwined with those of people living in distant lands. We are influenced by an increasingly globalised spread of information, goods and ideas. The food we eat, the clothes we wear, the music we listen to and the books we read are infused with the views and experiences of distant others; so too are the ideas we are exposed to about culture, politics and religion. These processes of globalisation have been advanced by developments in transportation and electronic communications, in particular the advent of the internet. The world is now seemingly smaller than ever and we are all citizens of a global society.

While globalisation has had a whole host of effects on economies, politics and cultures, of particular interest to marketers and consumer researchers is the way in which this increasingly globalised marketplace impacts on our everyday experiences of consumption. The chapter uses two contrasting stories of globalisation to explore its impact on consumers and consumer culture. These stories are one of grobalisation and one of glocalisation (Ritzer, 2004: xiii). Grobalisation describes the process whereby the drive towards constant growth (i.e. to keep on increasing sales and profits) pushes organisations to expand into more and more areas of the globe and impose themselves on localities. Whereas in processes of glocalisation, rather than the global *imposing* on the local, the two interact to produce something new – the glocal. The final section discusses alternatives to these stories exploring how individuals and communities are organising themselves in the face of globalisation. First, however, it is important to examine what we mean by globalisation and its accompanying processes as there is significant disagreement and debate surrounding these terms and their effects. This discussion is followed by a brief consideration of the rise of global brands as central to processes of globalisation.

What is globalisation?

While globalisation can be seen as an economic, political and cultural process it is generally agreed that economics tends to be the driving force behind it.

Recent times have seen the opening up of world markets to allow increased flow of capital, goods and technologies across national borders; this has resulted in the interdependence of markets across the globe. The emergence of institutions such as the World Bank, International Monetary Fund and the World Trade Organization are clear evidence of a global economy. To encourage international trade governments have set up preferable trading arrangements which have bolstered the rise of multinational corporations (MNCs) such as McDonald's, Nike, Samsung and Sony. Closer to home the global reach of these companies means that we now eat American fast food, wear Chinese clothes, talk on Korean mobile phones and drive Japanese cars. These companies also source their head office and technical staff from the global marketplace producing a group of relatively placeless transnational workers. Politically governments have increasingly begun to work together to manage trade and the economy. For example, institutions such as the European Union bind together European countries and the North American Free Trade Agreement, which joins Canada, North America and Mexico together. Global political pressure groups have also emerged to deal with issues affecting the environment and human rights such as Amnesty International, Greenpeace and the World Wildlife Fund. However, in developed countries it is perhaps culturally that we experience the most obvious impacts of globalisation in our everyday lives (Lash and Lury, 2007). Our cultures are becoming more mixed through migration and infused with values and ideas from other cultures. We are also seeing the emergence of global standards in fashion, food, films and sport. The dominance of a shared global football culture is a good example of this (Tiesler and Coelho, 2013), with teams such as Manchester United having more fans outside than within the UK, and players such as David Beckham becoming global celebrities in their own right. Brands themselves also embody values which travel globally; Coca-Cola is probably the most obvious example of this – the company even promotes a global universalism and harmony as their key brand value (Ger and Belk, 1996).

However, the above discussion suggests that globalisation is a relatively uncontested process and this is far from the case. Debates on globalisation have raged long and hard over the past few decades. Broadly speaking there are proponents and opponents of the phenomenon, with each side identifying different accompanying dynamics and sets of processes to support their case. One of the more positive proponents of globalisation is the journalist and political economist Philippe Legrain. In his 2002 book *Open World: The Truth about Globalization*, he argues that globalisation is a positive, liberating force that results in an open world where goods, services and information are exchanged freely, and where people can move freely across borders. Similarly, Thomas Friedman, in his 2005 book *The World Is Flat*, argues that globalisation is an inevitability that societies should not resist and one that is creating an increasingly level playing field. Drawing on the free market economics of Hayek, Adrián Ravier views globalisation as: 'the process that arises spontaneously in the market and acts by developing a progressive international division of labour, eliminating restrictions on individual liberties, reducing transportation and communication costs, and increasingly integrating the individuals that compose the 'great society' (Ravier, 2009: 2). This concept of the 'great society' that Ravier is referring to originates from Lyndon B. Johnson's radical reforms in 1960s America to improve education and medical care and reduce widespread poverty. In this sense Ravier sees globalisation as a positive force improving quality of life and bringing benefits to all.

Critics of globalisation point to a series of unwanted effects of the process including the increased power of MNCs putting democracies at risk, the cost to the environment of privileging corporate imperatives over any others and the dilution and gradual dissolution of local cultures across the globe. More generally critics argue that the process of globalisation is trenchantly unequal in its effects, as Held and McGrew observe:

> Since a significant segment of the world's population is either untouched by globalization or remains largely excluded from its benefits, it is a deeply divisive and, consequently, vigorously contested process. The unevenness of globalization ensures it is far from a universal process experienced uniformly across the planet.
>
> (Held and McGrew, 2000: 4)

The rise of global brands

The process of branding is at the heart of MNCs' attempts to globalise their operations. Brands are important here in two senses: as facilitating globalisation from a production point of view and also from a consumption point of view in providing a shared global language for consumers around the globe.

In terms of *production* brands act as vehicles for the spread of globalisation; functioning as mediators of the supply and demand of products and services, they frame the activities of the market and they organise the very logics of global flows of products, people, images and events (Lury, 2004). So central are brands to processes of globalisation that Celia Lury sees brands as the 'logos of the global economy'. Brands have immense value for companies in their own right, which is typically termed brand equity and is based on the fact that well-known brand names can significantly increase the sales of products and services. For example, the Apple brand was identified as the number 1 global brand in 2015 valued at $170,276 million, followed by Google at $120,314 million and Coca-Cola at $78,423 million (Interbrand, 2015).

Perhaps because brands are the most visible element of MNCs they have been at the heart of critiques of globalisation. Naomi Klein's book 'No Logo: Taking Aim at the Brand Bullies' is probably the most well known of these critiques. Klein ties the huge expansion of MNCs closely to the invention of the brand:

> The astronomical growth in the wealth and cultural influence of multi-national corporations over the last fifteen years can arguably be traced

back to a single, seemingly innocuous idea developed by management theorists in the mid-1980s: that successful corporations must primarily produce brands, as opposed to products.

(Klein, 1999: 3)

Klein charts the impact of the rise of global brands (and by association MNCs) on experiences of work in both developed and developing countries and on local cultures and public space. She describes the 'race to the bottom' where MNCs contract out production to the lowest bidder resulting in extreme inequalities as factory workers in developing countries are forced to work faster for longer hours in poor and often dangerous sweatshop conditions to meet the terms of these contracts. While Klein reported on these issues back in 1999 death and injury are still common resulting from illegal working practices and poorly maintained factories. In November 2012, a fire broke out at the Tazreen Fashions garment factory in the Ashulia industrial area 24km north of the Bangladeshi capital of Dhaka. The factory manufactured clothes for global brands such as Walmart, C&A, Sears and Kik. More than 1,150 people were inside the factory at the time, 117 employees died and more than 200 were injured in the fire. The blaze broke out in the open-air ground floor, where large mounds of fabric and yarn were illegally stored. Managers and security guards on some floors reportedly ordered employees to ignore the fire alarm and continue to work. In addition, windows were secured with iron grilles making it impossible for some employees to escape. In the years following the fire one of the key issues highlighted by worker and human rights organisations was the convoluted and opaque supply chain which makes it difficult to police compliance with international labour standards. Suppliers often use multiple subcontractors to meet orders. This means that when an accident occurs buyers can easily wash their hands of it. After the Tazreen blaze retailers denied all responsibility, saying they had not authorised production at the factory and that suppliers had subcontracted production without informing them.

One of the attractions of global brands to *consumers* is undoubtedly that they make them feel like global citizens. Consumers view these brands as symbols of cultural ideals and use them to create an imagined global identity (Holt et al., 2004: 3). 'Like entertainment stars, sports celebrities and politicians, global brands have become a lingua franca for consumers all over the world' (p. 2). Brands like Nike, Coca-Cola, Apple and BMW speak a global language that can be understood by all. Brands like these are symbolically very powerful, for example in a survey of 7,000 people in six different countries (Germany, Australia, India, Japan, the UK and the US), 88 percent identified the brand logos of McDonald's and Shell whereas only 54 percent recognised the Christian cross (Sponsorship Research International, 1995).

One of the reasons brands can impact so powerfully on individuals is their ability to create reassurance and familiarity. Authors have developed the concept of the brandscape to describe the interplay between brands and the sites and spaces they inhabit (Klingman, 2007; Salzer-Mörling and Strannegård,

2007; Wood and Ball, 2013). As Wood and Ball suggest: 'brandscapes can be viewed as more or less successful organisational attempts to inscribe spaces and their inhabitants in their own terms' (2013: 59). Thus 'control' here is not only about encouraging shoppers to visit several stores as they pass through the mall, or to linger longer through the manipulation of the environment. Brands act at a significantly deeper level, as Askegaard (2006: 98) observes: 'Branding as a (global) ideoscape... provides the ideological basis for the establishment of new meaning systems, new practices and new identity forms for the members of the consumer culture'. As such Thompson and Arsel (2004) develop the construct of the 'hegemonic brandscape'. Using the case of Starbucks they argue that it is through the development of oppositional meanings (i.e. the anti-Starbucks discourse) that local coffee shops are constituted, as such these local cafés depend on these hegemonic meanings for their identity as 'other'. In other words these global brands significantly influence the smaller local operations because they set the terms of the game, i.e. they set the norms regarding what a coffee shop or food retailer should look like, norms against which all coffee shops or supermarkets, etc. are measured.

Grobalisation: the death of the local and the scripting of consumption

The American sociologist George Ritzer coined the term 'grobalisation' to capture the way in which corporations' drive to grow and expand at all costs results in imperialistic ambitions which stifle and colonise other parts of the globe (Ritzer, 2003, 2004). Ritzer (1993) argues that this has been made possible through the process of McDonaldisation. He uses the fast food chain McDonald's as the ultimate example of what he sees as a new period in the organisation of production. Essentially this new period began in the 1920s when Henry Ford produced standardised cars on a mass scale using assembly line machinery and semi-skilled labour. McDonaldisation represents the final globalised expression of this process of *rationalisation*, one which involves *efficiency, predictability, calculability* and *control*. These processes result in a drive towards time saving at all costs, the reproducibility and standardisation of goods and production processes (labour) through increased control of smaller and smaller aspects of production. Taking McDonald's as an example:

- *Efficiency* is equated with time saving – finding ways to take orders, cook and serve the food as quickly as possible. This is achieved, for example, through tightly timed interactions with customers and the breaking down of food preparation into small, discrete tasks, avoiding duplication and leading to operational efficiency.
- *Predictability* is equated with the standardisation of the product and service so that wherever a customer enters a McDonald's they will receive the same product and have the same experience. This is achieved for example through the scripting of staff–customer interactions and the

uniform design of restaurant interiors. Standardisation is also applied to the workforce so workers' tasks are highly routine and repetitive.

- *Calculability* is equated with the ability to use objective measures wherever possible in the business so, for example, sales quantity and service speed are prioritised over food taste and quality.
- *Control* is achieved through the above processes but also the replacement of human labour with technology. McDonald's kitchens are highly automated, for example, with conveyer ovens and toasters. In some restaurants McDonald's is replacing sales assistants altogether with touch screen kiosks for ordering food.

Ritzer argues that these principles have spread beyond McDonald's to other corporations (such as Benetton, the Body Shop and Starbucks) but also that they have begun to dominate more and more sectors of American society (i.e. education, healthcare and the media). But perhaps most crucially these principles have spread through processes of globalisation to other country contexts. While these principles have spread *through* globalisation it is also important to note that these principles have *enabled* corporations to globalise their operations.

Through these processes of McDonaldisation and grobalisation Ritzer argues that we are increasingly moving from 'something to nothing'. In his book *The Globalization of Nothing*, Ritzer defines 'nothing' as 'generally centrally conceived and controlled forms that are completely devoid of distinctive and substantive content' (2004: xi). He argues that it is much easier to globalise that which is centrally conceived and controlled and also that it is much easier to globalise largely empty forms than those that are loaded with distinctive local content. He discusses four types of 'nothing' which are non-places, non-things, non-people and non-services. He argues that these forms have proliferated precisely because they involve certain conveniences and efficiencies. Non-places are characterised by sameness and homogeneity which are easy to control, reproduce and market. The mega mall might be thought of as a non-place because it is centrally owned and managed and the environment is highly controlled – from the lighting and air conditioning to the behaviours allowed within it (malls are heavily policed largely through the use of surveillance cameras). The environment of shopping malls is deliberately designed to manipulate shoppers' behaviour by provoking specific moods and dispositions (Goss, 1993). The spaces themselves are also structured to facilitate a flow of people which provides optimal exposure to the goods on offer. The range of shops you might find in the mega mall would probably include a series of global brands and associated mass-produced goods which you might find in any mall in any country context. This uniformity and lack of distinctive content means that if dropped into a mall at random you may have little idea which country you are in. In many cases local sites and spaces have become replaced by non-places. In the UK context this can be seen in the closure of independent high street shops and cafés as shoppers gravitate to Aldi, Primark and Starbucks.

Perhaps these non-places are popular as they place few expectations on the consumer and they require very little of the self as individual. In these highly controlled and controlling spaces the consumer knows exactly what they are expected to do, there is little room for uncertainty or surprise, in fact any ambiguity is eliminated because it has the potential to produce inefficiencies. In particular the spaces embody the *predictability* principle of Ritzer's McDonaldisation thesis. Auge (1995) identifies non-places as including supermarkets, train stations, airports and hotels, arguing that in non-places individuals are connected in a uniform manner and creative social life is very limited if not non-existent.

> a person entering the space of non-place is relieved of his usual determinants. He becomes no more than what he does or experiences in the role of passenger, customer or driver. Perhaps he is still weighed down by the previous day's worries, the next day's concerns; but he is distanced from them temporarily by the environment of the moment. Subjected to a gentle form of possession, to which he surrenders himself with more or less talent or conviction, he tastes for a while – like anyone who is possessed – the passive joys of identity loss, and the more active pleasure of role-playing.
>
> (Auge, 1995: 103)

Here consumers are reduced to automatons mindlessly reproducing the imperatives of MNCs through their daily work tasks and consumption choices. Lifestyles are sold pre-packaged, safe and devoid of any real distinctive local content. The scripting of consumption by corporations effectively stamps out any creativity and individuality.

Glocalisation: a return to local, creative consumption

Ritzer's second story of globalisation he terms 'glocalisation'. To better understand this as a process he observes that it is synonymous with heterogenisation and hybridity. While grobalisation leads to a world that is becoming more and more similar or homogeneous, for example through the spread and dominance of global brands, glocalisation suggests that when these global brands meet the local culture something new and hybrid is formed. So glocalisation suggests that rather than the world becoming more homogeneous, local differences are still important and they perpetuate heterogeneity. So, for example, the language of global brands is not absorbed uniformly by consumers; it is read and understood by them in relation to their own localised culture and circumstances. Research also shows that global brands have different meanings for the same consumers in different local contexts, i.e. when consumers travel abroad the meanings of global brands change for them (Bengtsson et al., 2010).

All of the above suggests that brands are co-created as much by consumers at the local level as by marketers working in the head offices of MNCs

(Pongsakornrungsilp and Schroeder, 2011). There is evidence to suggest that consumers value personalised and authentic retail spaces rather than bland dehumanised environments (as per the 'non-places' discussed above). In response to this many MNCs are attempting to rehumanise their products at the shop-floor level by using ethical and fairly traded products (Body Shop) and insisting that products are sourced locally (Tesco's regional buying offices, which reduce food miles and encourage local producers). While the retail landscape has seen the rise of standardised and discount stores (such as Aldi, Lidl, Greggs and Primark in the UK), it has also seen an increase in speciality and niche chains, for example family-run service stations stocking locally produced and artisan products (see the case study of Westmorland Services at the end of this chapter), independent micro breweries and pubs and farmers' markets to name but a few. Many of these operations have sprung up in response to the overhomogenisation of the retail landscape and a frustration at the uniformity of what is on offer, combined with a reflexive approach to retailing that attempts to think through the impact of the business on workers, customers and the local population alike. Indeed, Ger (1999: 65) argues that local corporations can 'out-localise' global firms by mobilising local cultural capital in international marketing contexts.

It can be argued that grobalisation narratives overemphasise the processes of production; suggesting that corporations merely deliver a pre-packaged consumer experience that misses out on the productive behaviours of consumers at the local level. Consumer researchers have long been mindful of the whole range of practices consumers engage in to personalise and transform goods and services at the point of consumption. This work recognises that consumers are creative and playful in their translation of goods and services from the shop floor into their own homes and lives. Researchers have emphasised that the work of consumption often occurs in partnership with organisations – as a form of 'co-creation' of meanings (Prahalad and Ramaswamy, 2004). If this is indeed the case it contradicts the idea that consumers are mindlessly absorbing the meanings that MNCs are folding into their goods and services during production. Consumers have significant agency and are not merely pawns of MNCs (Eckhardt and Mahi, 2004). Work on co-creation suggests that the relationship is two-way with consumers both receiving and creatively interpreting brand meanings, but also having input into the various stages of the production process including product and packaging design, advertising and store interiors. This trend again contradicts the idea that MNCs can grow and expand globally merely by imposing their values on local populations. Numerous examples abound of instances where local populations knowingly and deliberately reappropriate the meanings of global brands. For example Caldwell's (2004) study of McDonald's in Russia explores the way in which Russian consumers domesticate the meanings of McDonald's foods and restaurants to create new nationalistic identities. Yazıcıoğlu (2010) finds that in the reterritorialisation of rock in Turkey global symbols are reinterpreted by individuals to establish local meanings. Likewise, Takhar et al. (2012) highlight how a global imaginary of 'Indian-ness' is consumed at the local level through the film genre Bollywood to produce a range of new hybrid identifications.

Eckhardt and Mahi's (2012) work on consumption in India finds that in negotiating tensions between local cultural traditions and globalised consumption meanings consumers create their own discourses which in turn shape the marketplace. As such flows of meanings are certainly not one way and top down. Askegaard and Eckhardt's (2012) study of 'glocal yoga' similarly reveals the multidirectional flows of culture in globalisation. They find that yoga practices are reappropriated in the Indian context 'after a process of sanctioning in (most often) the western hotbed of consumer culture production' (p. 46). Here discourses of yoga and yoga practice in the West are reappropriated to form new South Asian discourses on yoga. In these examples we see global flows of culture which involve a two-way interaction of the global and the local where 'local consumptionscapes become a nexus of numerous, often contradictory, old, new and modified forces' (Ger and Belk, 1996: 271). Wilk (1995) similarly highlights the paradox of globalisation in his study of beauty pageants in Belize. This format is embedded locally, invested by specific local meanings by unique local groups in the community while at the same time winners still conform to a more 'New York standard of beauty than that of Belize City', being tall and fair-skinned. Kjeldgaard and Nielsen (2010) similarly find that global gender identity narratives interact with locally saturated cultural categories of gender in the Mexican telenovela *Rebelde*.

In a study of McDonald's in Israel, Ram (2004) usefully identifies a split between structural–institutional and symbolic-expressive levels of globalisation. He argues that homogenisation occurs at the structural-institutional level but that the symbolic–expressive level still allows for heterogeneity, diversity and local difference. In his example of the Golani Junction McDonald's in Israel falafel is included on the menu, the hamburgers are larger than usual and the local air force brigade banner is used rather than the McDonald's golden arches. As Ram observes, therefore,

> On the symbolic level, the 'difference' that renders the local distinctive has managed to linger on. At the same time, on the structural level, that great leveller of 'sameness' at all locales prevails: the falafel has become McDonaldized; the military has privatized food provisioning; and Air Force 'Ms' can hardly be told apart from McDonald's' 'M'.
>
> (2004: 24)

Thus, while symbolically the local still has a voice, structurally it remains that the global tends to subsume the local and mobilise it for its own ends (Belk, 2000).

In summary, the either/or argument of the consumer as a creative agent as in the story of glocalisation or as mindless automaton as in the story of grobalisation, is oversimplified, as Sassatelli observes (2010: 177):

Thus we do not find ourselves facing a split between a free and active consumer and a McDonaldized one: for example, in response to global commodities, consumers can either negotiate standardization through propping up local cultural repertoires and traditional hierarchies, or they can embrace the elements of universalism which mass culture always contains to unhinge the inequalities embedded in their traditions.

However, while recognising that globalisation can prompt creative responses, we should bear in mind that it remains a process that people of the world certainly do not participate in on equal terms. For the privileged minority it certainly delivers but for a subaltern majority its outcomes are at best distant and at worst pernicious in effect. Rather than delivering a democracy of consumption opportunity global consumption influences tend to produce social inequality, class polarisations, stress, materialism and threats to health and the environment (Ger and Belk, 1996). For a majority that live on the margins of global flows of capital, the consumption dream passes them by. They are more likely to participate on the global stage as sellers of labour than consumers of a cornucopia of globalised goods (Belk, 2006; Varman and Vikas, 2007).

Emerging alternatives

In closing it is useful to consider some of the alternative narratives of globalisation that have begun to emerge. Recent work within critical marketing recognises the ways in which marketing ideology and practice shapes global markets (Bjerrisgaard and Kjeldgaard, 2013). Commentators have argued that the global spread of 'marketing think and marketing speak', in fact 'the globalization of the very idea of marketing', acts as a vehicle for the spread of neoliberalism. As we have seen above in relation to the brand, marketing ideology also shapes our view of the consumer by subjectifying consumers in particular ways (Fougère and Skålén, 2013). Marketing communications and brand values are increasingly designed to address consumers as global citizens. Taken as a whole this work argues that painting the consumer as sovereign, promoting market choice as a form of liberation and markets themselves as democracies within which the consumer-citizen freely operates is problematic. Sassatelli argues that it is possible to see consumer sovereignty in an alternative light:

> as something other than consumer choice as predicated on the variables singled out by neoclassical economics and free market ideologies alike (i.e. price and quantity). The value-for-money logic does not hold when the target is not only individual satisfaction, but (also) a set of public goods.
>
> (Sassatelli, 2010: 187)

The question remains as to how in practice we might achieve this focus on public as opposed to private goods. Chatzidakis and colleagues put forward a politics of degrowth as one answer:

> It is about simple living and localisation of production and consumption, as opposed to a globalised economy. In a de-growth society small, self-organised communities would produce and consume what is needed, and the wealth that is produced would not be defined in economic terms, but through quality of life, social relations, equality and justice.
>
> (Chatzidakis et al., 2014: 760)

On the ground a whole host of initiatives have sprung up which contrast starkly with the globalised world of the MNC. The Slow Food Movement is one good example which was set up in response to the dominating influence of supermarkets, fast food chains and agribusiness. Originating in Italy in 1986 the movement initially focused on regional traditions, good food and a slow pace of life. Since its inception the movement has grown significantly and now has over 100,000 members in more than 130 countries (Andrews, 2008). It has evolved to develop a comprehensive politics of food to include a celebration of the local and local food systems; education of the dangers and risks of fast food, factory farms and monoculture; lobbying for organic farming and lobbying against the use of pesticides and genetic engineering. The Fair Trade movement has similarly targeted global systems of food provision offering minimum prices to small producers and ensuring the protection of workers' rights and the environment. These are just two examples of a whole raft of initiatives which essentially go against the grain of grobalisation and all that it stands for. Other examples include farmers' markets, co-operatives and ethical finance initiatives. These initiatives frame the consumer as a political actor within the wider net of production recognising that they can be key to effecting wider social change.

Summary

This chapter has explored two sides to the story of globalisation. In the story of grobalisation, processes of globalisation have the ability to stifle local consumer culture replacing local difference with a bland sameness. Here global brands have the power to manipulate the consumer into mindlessly responding to their call to consume. On the other hand, in the story of glocalisation processes of globalisation produce something new and innovative where the global meets the local. Here the consumer is seen as an active agent creatively translating global brand meanings into something new in his or her own local context. The reality is that neither of these narratives tells the whole story. Focusing solely on grobalisation and the sameness it delivers confers too much power on the MNC and too little on the individual consumer by emphasising production over consumption. This story also misses out on the importance of local specificity and difference. However, focusing solely on glocalisation means that we overcelebrate the agency of the consumer and fail to recognise the very real power wielded by MNCs. One potential solution to this problem (as suggested by Ram, 2004) is to recognise that globalisation operates at different levels: the structural–institutional and the symbolic–expressive; while homogenisation occurs at the structural–institutional level the symbolic–expressive level still allows for heterogeneity, diversity and local difference. A second solution, one which has been promoted by consumer researchers, is rather than sticking to either/or binaries we should recognise the multidirectional flows of culture and the co-creative capacities of consumers and producers.

CASE STUDY: Westmorland Services – re-placing motorway service stations

British motorway service stations are a good example of the non-places (Auge, 1995; Ritzer, 2004) discussed earlier in this chapter. High barriers to entry mean that 90 percent of UK services are owned by just four companies; this means that there is little difference between them. They are designed to funnel visitors through as efficiently as possible with very little thought to environment. Sanitised environments typically populated with fast food outlets such as McDonald's, KFC and Starbucks, they are soulless places with very little distinctive local content. One media commentator described service stations recently as 'A forecourt smelling of cooking fat, someone mugging you to join the AA, weak coffee and the gentle trill of arcade machines' (Henry, 2015).

The Westmorland family decided to go against the grain of the average motorway service station with a deliberate attempt to return to the local. In 1972 local farmers Barbara and John Dunning opened Tebay Services in Cumbria in partnership with local bakers when the M6 cut through the Lune Gorge. It included a small café serving locally sourced, home-cooked food. It was the first and still is the only family-run motorway service station in the UK. In 2004 they opened two farm shops at Tebay Services selling high-quality locally produced products. The butcher counters in the shops sell beef and lamb produced on the family farm butchered in the family's butchery units with a whole-animal approach to ensure sustainability and account-ability in the food production chain. The meat is also served in the service station cafe.

The family opened a second services area in 2014 in Gloucester run on the same principle of championing the locality by working with regional food producers (Figure 10.1). The service station itself has been built using natural materials and designed to blend in with the natural environment (see Figures 10.2 and 10.3). The Gloucester Services has a charity arm which works with Gloucester Gateway Trust, a charity which funds community projects and training courses for local people. A third of the employees at Gloucester Services have come from these training courses. Small producers

Figure 10.1 The food team at Gloucester Services Northbound

Figure 10.2 Inside Gloucester Services café

are also benefitting – several have expanded into new premises and taken on extra staff to meet demand.

The family base their service station business on a series of values which they describe on their website using the statements: 'Rooted in this Place', 'As Farmers We Understand Our Connection with the Land', 'We Believe in

Figure 10.3 External Gloucester Services

What We Sell', 'We Run Our Business Like a Family', 'We Are Better for Being Part of Our Community' and 'Small Is Beautiful'. It is not difficult to see how these values are in direct contrast to those of grobalisation, which promotes principles such as uniformity, efficiency and control. For the consumer the experience of visiting these service stations is a world away from the sanitised, soulless environments of the big chains. While the quality of food is definitely a big bonus, its regional distinctiveness offers an opportunity to get a sense of the local food culture and it is also an antidote to the 'sameness' that pervades every other service station experience.

Seminar exercises

Discussion topics

1 Identify the key features of grobalisation and glocalisation and discuss how each perspective sees the consumer. Reflecting on your own experiences, which view of the consumer do you identify with most strongly?
2 Discuss the problems with focusing either on grobalisation or glocalisation.
3 Thinking about a global brand of your choice discuss why global brands might impact so powerfully on consumers.
4 With reference to the case study on Westmorland Services, identify the ways in which the policies of these service stations go against the ethos of grobalisation. Think in particular about how they contrast with the 'non-places' of grobalisation.

Group exercises

1   Identify a global fast food restaurant or coffee shop (e.g. McDonald's, KFC, Starbucks, Caffè Nero, etc.) and compare it with a local independently run coffee shop you are familiar with.

  • Discuss the extent to which each operation might be seen as global or as local (think about brand values, product range and quality, store environment (i.e. music, lighting, interior design) and staffing/service).
  • Consider which one would you rather visit and why.
  • Discuss why you think people are sometimes drawn to global brands as opposed to local ones.

2   Read the paper by Thompson and Arsel (2004) listed in the Key readings section.

  • What criticisms have been made of Starbucks' business in the past? Why do you think Starbucks has been such a target for protest and criticism?
  • What is 'glocalisation'? What evidence of this process can you find in the paper?
  • How do the authors describe a 'hegemonic brandscape'?
  • What are 'experiential brands', and why do you think they are particularly powerful in influencing consumers?
  • What are the two types of consumer described in the paper? And how do they each describe Starbucks? Create a list for each group (think also about the use of the language of aesthetics/style for one group and the use of the language of politics for the other group). How might their descriptions relate to their identity (i.e. who they want others to see them as)?
  • Referring to the discussion section of the paper, what 'desires' are the two groups acting on?

Internet resources

Global Policy Forum: <www.globalpolicy.org/globalization.html

International Monetary Fund – key issues: globalisation: www.imf.org/external/np/exr/key/global.htm

Interbrands – Best Global Brands Survey: http://interbrand.com/best-brands/best-global-brands/2015/

Global Transformations: www.polity.co.uk/global/default.asp

Globalist – an online magazine on the global economy, politics and culture: www.theglobalist.com/

Westmorland Services: www.westmorlandfamily.com/

Key readings

Klein, N. (1999). *No logo: Taking aim at the brand bullies.* Toronto: Knopf.

Ritzer, G. (2004). *The globalization of nothing.* London: SAGE.
Sassatelli, R. (2010). Contexts of consumption. In *Consumer culture: History, theory, politics.* London: SAGE, pp. 174–192.
Thompson, C. and Arsel, Z. (2004). The Starbucks brandscape and consumers' (anticorporate) experiences of glocalization'. *Journal of Consumer Research*, 31 (December): 631–642.

References

Andrews, G. (2008). *The slow food story: Politics and pleasure.* London: McGill–Queens University Press.
Askegaard, S. (2006). Brands as a global ideoscape. In J.E. Schroeder and M. Salzer-Mörling (eds), *Brand Culture.* London: Routledge, pp. 91–102.
Askegaard, S. and Eckhardt, G.M. (2012). Glocal yoga: Re-appropriation in the Indian consumptionscape. *Marketing Theory*, 12(1): 45–60.
Auge, M. (1995). *Non-places: An introduction to supermodernity.* London: Verso.
Belk, R.W. (2000). Wolf brands in sheep's clothing: Global appropriation of the local. In J. Pavitt (ed.), *Brand New.* London: Victoria and Albert Museum, pp. 68–69.
Belk, R.W. (2006). Out of our sight and out of our minds: What of those left behind by globalism? In J.N. Sheth and R. Sisodia (eds), *Does marketing need reform?* Armonk, NY: M.E. Sharpe, pp. 209–216.
Bengtsson, A., Bardhi, F. and Venkatraman, M. (2010). How global brands travel with consumers: An examination of the relationship between brand consistency and meaning across national boundaries. *International Marketing Review*, 27(5): 519–540.
Bjerrisgaard, S.M. and Kjeldgaard, D. (2013). How market research shapes market spatiality: A global governmentality perspective. *Journal of Macromarketing*, 33(1): 29–40.
Caldwell, M.L. (2004). Domesticating the french fry McDonald's and consumerism in Moscow. *Journal of Consumer Culture*, 4(1): 5–26.
Chatzidakis, A., Larsen, G. and Bishop, S. (2014). Farewell to consumerism: Countervailing logics of growth in consumption. *Ephemera*, 14(4): 753–764.
Eckhardt, G.M. and Mahi, H. (2004). The role of consumer agency in the globalization process in emerging markets. *Journal of Macromarketing*, 24(2): 136–146.
Eckhardt, G.M. and Mahi, H. (2012). Globalization, consumer tensions, and the shaping of consumer culture in India. *Journal of Macromarketing*, 32(3): 280–294.
Fougère, M. and Skålén, P. (2013). Extension in the subjectifying power of marketing ideology in organizations: A Foucauldian analysis of academic marketing. *Journal of Macromarketing*, 33(1): 13–28.
Friedman, T. (2005). *The world is flat: The globalised world in the twenty first century.* London: Penguin.
Ger, G. (1999). Localizing in the global village: Local firms competing in global markets. *California Management Review*, 41(4): 64–83.
Ger, G. and Belk, R.W. (1996). I'd like to buy the world a Coke: Consumptionscapes of the less affluent world. *Journal of Consumer Policy*, 19(3): 271–304.
Goss, J. (1993). The 'magic of the mall': An analysis of form, function, and meaning in the contemporary retail built environment. *Annals of the Association of American Geographers*, 83(1): 18–47.

Held, D. and McGrew, A. (2000). *The global transformations reader.* Chichester: Wiley.

Henry, D. (2015). Is this the best motorway service station in the UK? *Telegraph,* 1 May.

Holt, D.B., Quelch, J.A. and Taylor, E.L. (2004). How global brands compete. *Harvard Business Review,* 82(9): 68–75.

Interbrand (2015). Best global brands ranking. http://interbrand.com/best-brands/ best-global-brands/2015/ranking/

Kjeldgaard, D. and Nielsen, K.S. (2010). Glocal gender identities in market places of transition: MARIANISMO and the consumption of the telenovela *Rebelde. Marketing Theory,* 10(1): 21–44.

Klingman, A. (2007). *Brandscapes: Architecture in the experience economy.* Cambridge, MA: MIT Press.

Lash, S. and Lury, C. (2007). *Global culture industry: The mediation of things.* Malden, MA: Polity.

Legrain, P. (2002). *Open world: The truth about globalization.* London: Abacus.

Lury, C. (2004). *Brands: The logos of the global economy.* London: Routledge.

Pongsakornrungsilp, S. and Schroeder, J.E. (2011). Understanding value co-creation in a co-consuming brand community. *Marketing Theory,* 11(3): 303–324.

Prahalad, C.K. and Ramaswamy, V. (2004). Co-creating unique value with customers. *Strategy and Leadership,* 32(3): 4–9.

Ram, U. (2004). Glocommodification: How the global consumes the local McDonald's in Israel. *Current Sociology,* 52(1): 11–31.

Ravier, A.O. (2009). Globalization and peace: A Hayekian perspective. *Libertarian Papers,* 1(10): 1–18.

Ritzer, G. (1993). *The McDonaldization of society.* Thousand Oaks, CA: SAGE.

Ritzer, G. (2003). Rethinking globalization. *Sociological Theory,* 21(3): 193–209.

Ritzer, G. (2004). *The Globalization of nothing.* London: SAGE.

Salzer-Mörling, M. and Strannegård, L. (2007). 'Ain't misbehavin': Consumption in a moralized brandscape. *Marketing Theory,* 7(4): 407–425.

Sponsorship Research International (1995). *More widely recognised than the Christian cross.* London: SRI.

Takhar, A., Maclaran, P. and Stevens, L. (2012). Bollywood cinema's global reach: Consuming the 'diasporic consciousness'. *Journal of Macromarketing,* 32(3): 266–279.

Tiesler, N.C. and Coelho, J.N. (2013). *Globalised football: Nations and migration, the city and the dream.* London: Routledge.

Varman, R. and Vikas, R.M. (2007). Freedom and consumption: Toward conceptualizing systemic constraints for subaltern consumers. *Consumption, Markets and Culture,* 10(2): 117–131.

Wilk, R. (1995). Learning to be local in Belize: Global systems of common difference. In D. Miller (ed.), *Worlds apart: Modernity through the prism of the local.* London: Routledge, pp. 110–131.

Wood, D.M. and Ball, K. (2013). Brandscapes of control? Surveillance, marketing and the co-construction of subjectivity and space in neo-liberal capitalism. *Marketing Theory,* 13(1): 47–67.

Yazıcıoğlu, E.T. (2010). Contesting the global consumption ethos: Reterritorialization of rock in Turkey. *Journal of Macromarketing,* 30(3): 238–253.

Index

Note: Information in figures and tables is indicated by *f* and *t*.